Innovation and Inequality

# Innovation and Inequality

## How Does Technical Progress Affect Workers?

**Gilles Saint-Paul**

**Princeton University Press**
**Princeton and Oxford**

Published by Princeton University Press,
41 William Street, Princeton, New Jersey 08540

In the United Kingdom: Princeton University Press,
6 Oxford Street, Woodstock, Oxfordshire OX20 1TW



ISBN: 978-0-691-12830-6 (alk. paper)

Library of Congress Control Number: 2008921816

British Library Cataloging-in-Publication Data is available

This book has been composed in LucidaBright
Typeset by T&T Productions Ltd, London

Printed on acid-free paper ∞

press.princeton.edu

Printed in the United States of America

10 9 8 7 6 5 4 3 2 1

# Contents

# Introduction

The effect of technical progress on the welfare of workers has long been a matter of controversy. Historically, one can document famous episodes of violent protests against productivity improvements that workers felt threatened their jobs. In *Das Kapital*, Marx (1867) documents an episode of revolt against the introduction of machinery, which actually led to innovation being stalled:[1]

> In the 17th century nearly all Europe experienced revolts of the workpeople against the ribbon-loom, a machine for weaving ribbons and trimmings, called in Germany Bandmühle, Schnurmühle, and Mühlenstuhl. These machines were invented in Germany. Abbé Lancellotti, in a work that appeared in Venice in 1636, but which was written in 1579, says as follows: "Anthony Müller of Danzig saw about 50 years ago in that town, a very ingenious machine, which weaves 4 to 6 pieces at once. But the Mayor being apprehensive that this invention might throw a large number of workmen on the streets, caused the inventor to be secretly strangled or drowned."
>
> In Leyden, this machine was not used till 1629; there the riots of the ribbon-weavers at length compelled the Town Council to prohibit it.

In 1768, a group of spinners broke into the home of James Hargreaves, the inventor of the "Spinning Jenny," a machine which was capable of doing the work of eight workers, and destroyed his machines.

In the early nineteenth century, textile workers—the Luddites—organized against the introduction of advanced machinery that made their skills redundant. This movement is described as follows on the Web page[2] of Dr. Steve Anderson from Utah University:

> For at least three hundred years the weavers from in and around the central English town of Nottingham, though commoners, enjoyed the status and rewards accorded to fine craftsmen. The weavers of Nottinghamshire produced lace and stockings that dominated the English markets and were prominent items in export trade. These products were hand made, often in the weaver's home.... In the first years of the 19th century stocking frames and the early automation of the power loom threatened this long-standing way of life.... The weavers complained bitterly that the machines made mass produced products of shamefully inferior quality. Naturally, the weavers saw the new technology

[1] See www.marxists.org/archive/marx/works/1867-c1/ch15.htm#S5.

[2] See www.usu.edu/sanderso/multinet/lud1.html.

> as the most powerful tool of their new oppressor, the factory owner.... During a short period climaxing in the spring of 1812, inspired perhaps by the French Revolution and the writings of Thomas Paine, the weavers formed into something akin to a guerrilla army and took substantial control over the territory near Nottingham and several neighboring districts.... The Luddites often appeared at a factory in disguise and stated that they had come upon the orders of General Ned Ludd. These demands included restoration of reasonable rates of compensation, acceptable work conditions, and probably quality control. Faced by the intimidating numbers and the surprisingly disciplined actions of the Luddites, most factory owners complied, at least temporarily. Those that refused found their expensive machines wrecked.... The nonviolent period of Luddism ended at Burton's power loom mill in Lancashire on April 20, 1812. A large body of Luddites, perhaps numbering over a thousand attacked the mill, mostly with stick and rocks.... A government crackdown ensued, and many suspected Luddites were convicted, imprisoned, or hanged.

Such incidents have led to the famous controversy between Marx and Ricardo over the role of machinery. Marx forecast a world where innovation made workers ever more useless, leading to their impoverishment, along with a secular increase in the share of capital in national income. On the other hand, Ricardo and the neoclassical economists who followed him thought that innovation allowed a single worker to produce more output per unit of time, which led to an increase in wages and living standards.[3]

The explosion in living standards over the last two centuries has proved that the neoclassicists were right, while Marx was wrong. This is why the most influential growth model used by economists is the Solow (1956) one, where the economy converges to a balanced growth path in which wages grow in line with productivity. In recent years, however, economists have documented a worrying trend toward greater wage inequality in the United States and other countries. Not only has the distribution of wages widened, but real wages have fallen for the lowest paid workers (the bottom 20%, say), despite continuing growth in GDP per capita.

A large empirical literature has studied this phenomenon[4] and has found that the returns have increased for all the dimensions of skill:

[3] The neoclassicists in fact admitted a negative impact of technical progress on wages in the short run, but not in the long run. They had in mind the short-run complementarities between labor and capital that are analyzed in chapter 2 of this book (see Beach 1971).

[4] See in particular Juhn et al. (1993), Levy and Murnane (1992), and Katz and Murphy (1992). An important survey, which in many ways complements this book, can be found in Acemoglu (2002b).

education, experience, and unobserved ability. A number of explanations have been proposed and they are detailed in the following paragraphs.

A first explanation, put forward by, for example, DiNardo et al. (1996) and Blau and Kahn (1996), ascribes the rise in inequality to an increased role for market forces, relative to institutional forces, in the determination of wages. As conservative governments came into power in the United Kingdom and the United States in 1979 and 1981, respectively, wages became more closely aligned with individual productivity, and were less determined by union contracts. This situation creates a move toward greater wage inequality because unions tend to compress wages between skill levels. On the other hand, unions tend to increase income inequality by putting some workers out of jobs, but that is not reflected in measures of wage inequality since these measures take into account only the employed. The merit of this explanation is that it accounts for the fact that inequality has not increased in countries such as France and Germany where labor-market institutions have not evolved. On the other hand, it fails to explain the fact that inequality started increasing around 1975, long before the reforms of Margaret Thatcher and Ronald Reagan were implemented.

A second explanation is that because of immigration by unskilled workers, skilled workers have become relatively scarcer in the labor market. This explanation has been discarded on the grounds that whereas immigrants tend to be less skilled than natives in the destination country, this trend is more than offset by the increase in secondary and tertiary education enrollment rates, which tends to raise the relative supply of skilled workers.[5] Thus, it appears that the rise in wage inequality must be explained by shifts in relative demand, rather than shifts in relative supply.

A third explanation is international trade. This says that developed countries are now immersed in a world economy in which factor-price equalization prevails. The relative wages of unskilled workers are now determined by their relative scarcity worldwide, rather than within a given country. As a result, integration in the world economy should be associated with widening wage inequality in developed countries, and shrinking inequalities in developing countries. This is essentially the famous Stolper–Samuelson theorem (see Stolper and Samuelson 1941): any factor that is scarce in a given country, relative to the rest of the world, sees its return fall when the country opens up to trade. While the debate on this hypothesis is not totally settled, Lawrence and Slaughter

[5] Note that a similar point can be made with respect to the increase in female labor-market participation. On the effect on labor-market outcomes, see Borjas et al. (1997).

(1993) have shown that it is inconsistent with a number of basic facts. Most notably, if international trade were the driving force for the rise in inequality, we should observe that within each firm in the West the ratio of unskilled workers to skilled workers increases. The argument is that if technology has not changed, firms are faced with a lower relative wage of the unskilled, which induces them to increase their relative input of that factor. Of course, at the aggregate level, activity is relocated away from unskilled-intensive industries toward the skilled intensive ones; the unskilled-intensive industries are faced with a fall in their prices, because of competition from less developed countries, and therefore reduce their activity. However, it remains true that within any *existing* firm, one should observe a greater use of unskilled workers. Indeed, the reallocation of activity toward skilled-intensive industries is the countervailing force necessary to keep the skill ratio unchanged at the aggregate level. Lawrence and Slaughter have shown that the skill ratio did not evolve in favor of unskilled workers at the firm level; on the contrary, firms increased their demand for skilled workers.

This suggests that there has been technological change that has altered the relative factor demand in favor of skilled workers—the fourth explanation.[6] A key potential driving force has been the sharp progress in information technology, which picked up in the mid 1970s. Research has documented how computers and a number of other information and communication technologies (ICTs) are complementary with skilled labor and substitute for unskilled labor.[7]

While the empirical research has been quite extensive, this book's ambition is to provide an analytical perspective on the effects of technical progress on the distribution of income. I hope to show that these effects are pervasive, and that one cannot simply think of "information technology" as a black box that just shifts the relative demand of one category of workers.

---

[6] The theoretical literature has also investigated the interactions between various explanations. For example, Acemoglu et al. (2001) study a model in which skill-biased technical progress induces a fall in the power of unions, because skilled workers opt out from them as their outside option in bargaining has gone up. There also exists a burgeoning literature on the interactions between trade and technology. For example, Grossman and Maggi (2000) use the class of models described in chapter 8 of this book to derive novel predictions about how differences in the *distribution* of skills between countries with identical aggregate factor endowments and identical technologies lead to gains from trade. Manasse and Turrini (2001) use the superstars models analyzed in our chapter 7 to argue that globalization leads to an increase in market size for the most talented workers, which tends to widen the distribution of income. Thoenig and Verdier (2003) argue that skill-biased technical change may arise as protection against imperfect enforcement of intellectual property abroad.

[7] See in particular Autor et al. (1998, 2003).

This book studies how different categories of workers gain or lose from innovation, and it shows that this crucially depends on the nature of innovation. In particular, one must consider the following questions:

- Does innovation increase the efficiency of physical capital, human capital, or labor?
- Does innovation affect the way workers interact with each other, for example by making it easier to communicate and to access knowledge, or by changing the number of people affected by a given worker's activity?
- Does innovation affect the way the economy is organized? For example, how is the hierarchical structure of the workplace changed? Is the allocation of resources to different stages of production affected?
- Is innovation "vertical" (increasing productivity in existing goods) or "horizontal" (increasing the range of available goods)?

Another important methodological aspect is how we think of the labor market. In macroeconomics, one typically assumes that labor can be reduced to a vector of homogeneous inputs in the production function. Thus, production depends on the aggregate input of raw labor, human capital, and perhaps more detailed things such as beauty, strength, health, etc. This means that an individual endowed with, say, 0.6 units of strength and 0.4 units of intelligence would earn $0.6w_{\mathrm{S}} + 0.4w_{\mathrm{I}}$, where $w_{\mathrm{S}}$ is the market price of strength and $w_{\mathrm{I}}$ is the market price of intelligence. Another individual endowed with 1 unit of strength and 0.7 units of intelligence would earn $w_{\mathrm{S}} + 0.7w_{\mathrm{I}}$. Furthermore, the first individual might just decide to save on his or her strength and intelligence and just supply half of them, then earning $0.3w_{\mathrm{S}} + 0.2w_{\mathrm{I}}$. This is what we can call the "homogeneous-input" view of the labor market. Many labor markets do not work in this way, in that individuals are actually unique and not reducible to a fungible vector of characteristics. One cannot be a part-time professional footballer, for example. Nor can one replace a good professional footballer with two bad ones. And an intelligent footballer cannot supply his football skills to Manchester United and his intelligence to MacKinsey at the same time. This can be referred to as the "quality-input" view of the labor market.

This book shows that the effect of technology on the distribution of income differs greatly according to which of these two views of the labor market one takes.

Under the homogeneous-input view, what is important is the degree of substitutability and complementarity between technology and the different inputs in the production function. Technology harms substitute factors and benefits complementary factors. In the long run, additional effects arise from the fact that some factors (such as physical and human capital) can be accumulated. For example, technology may be detrimental to labor and beneficial to capital if it is substitutable with labor, i.e., if it is equivalent to an increase in the labor input. But this increases the return to capital, which induces people to accumulate more capital, which in turn boosts wages. One can show that under standard (but not necessarily correct) assumptions, wages cannot then fall in the long run.

Under the quality-input view, a key aspect is the extent to which high-quality individuals can spread their talent over a larger market. For a footballer, this might mean having more viewers thanks to satellite television. For a manager, it might mean supervising more people by means of e-mail and video conferencing. For an accounting consultant, it might mean embodying his knowledge in a piece of software that can be distributed to millions of clients. A recurring theme is that technical progress does not then harm the poorest, because they are not substitutes for quality workers. Rather, they can watch better football, are supervised by better managers, and are more productive because their firm, thanks to the new software, accesses better accounting services at a lower cost. Those who suffer are those who are at the bottom of the ability distribution of quality workers, say the average accountant who cannot compete with the new software and is displaced to another occupation—presumably one where individual quality is less important and where the labor input is more homogeneous.

Chapters 2–5 discuss the impact of technology on wages if labor inputs are homogeneous. I start with simple neoclassical growth models, comparing the short-run effects with the long-run effects, and then move to more complex models with three factors of production: labor, human capital, and physical capital. I also distinguish between technical change as a shift to a single production function for the economy and technical change as the introduction of a new technology, summarized by an alternative production function, which may be used along with the old technology. I discuss the possibility of counterintuitive *supply effects*: for instance, the fact that an increase in the supply of human capital may trigger a rise, rather than a fall, in its return, because more use is made of technologies intensive in that factor.

Chapters 6–8 analyze the impact of technical change when labor is a quality input. I focus on two key phenomena. First, more talented individuals can spread their talent over a larger market—"The Economics of

Superstars." Technical change then affects the relative "market size" for two individuals with different skills, which in turn has an effect on the distribution of income. Second, a worker's quality affects the productivity of his or her coworkers. These interactions within the firm determine its willingness to pay for workers of different quality. It also affects the way workers of different quality are matched together. Depending on the technology, workers of similar qualities are matched in the same firms—a segregated outcome—or firms hire workers with heterogeneous skills—a "unitary" outcome. Technical change has an effect on both the nature and the size of the interactions between the workers, and then again on both the pattern of segregation and the distribution of income.

In all of these examples, technical change has a nonproportional impact on the marginal product of different factors of production. It may come as a surprise that the distribution of income may also be changed when technical progress has a proportional effect on marginal products. Yet this is possible, through general equilibrium demand linkages, if there are nonproportionalities in demand. Chapters 9 and 10 study these nonproportionalities. One can show that growth can affect the distribution of income through its effect on monopoly markups if the utility of consumers is nonhomothetic. This evolution of markups may be immiserizing for workers if utility is such that the price elasticity of demand for a good falls when consumers become richer. This will be the case, in particular, if the level of utility that can be obtained from consuming a good is bounded (an assumption weaker than, but similar to, that of satiation). Roughly speaking, the rich become "careless" consumers as they near satiation, which triggers a rise in monopoly markups and harms workers.

Another interesting consequence of nonhomothetic utilities is that conflicts of interest between the rich and the poor arise with respect to the level of innovation: under plausible conditions, the rich value the introduction of new goods more than the poor do.

We also study, building on work by Matsuyama (2002), how technical change affects the distribution of welfare through its effect on the range of goods consumed by different people. It is shown that, under a utility function with a hierarchy of needs, technical change may trigger a virtuous circle: the economy converges to a "mass consumption society." As new consumers of industrial goods start buying them, those goods can be produced more efficiently, because of learning by doing. This reduces the cost of these goods, inducing more people to buy them. These new consumers in turn lead to further advances in productivity, and so on.

This book is based on lectures that I have given to Ph.D. students in Toulouse, at MIT, and in Paris, as well as to students in summer schools in

Barcelona, Kiel, Rotterdam, Steyr, Ammersee, and Gerzensee.[8] It requires technical knowledge of economics at M.Sc. level, and the reader with such knowledge can start the book from chapter 2. On the other hand, the book should be accessible to readers with less knowledge of economics but basic proficiency in calculus and analysis, provided they read the introductory material presented in chapter 1.

[8] It has benefited from their comments, as well as comments by David Autor, Richard Baggaley, and two anonymous reviewers.

# Innovation and Inequality

# 1
# Which Tools Do We Need?

This book is about the effect of technical change on the distribution of income. Most results build on a standard set of tools and models, which are briefly introduced here. The reader familiar with these tools can skip this chapter at no cost; the reader unfamiliar with this material may want to complement it with more detailed treatments in the textbooks by Romer (2000), Blanchard and Fischer (1989), Barro and Sala-i-Martin (2003), Aghion and Howitt (1997), and Bertola et al. (2005).

At any point in time, people earn part of their income as the return to the factors of production that they bring to the market. Some of these factors, such as machinery and equipment, are simply goods that they own; in particular, they can buy more of them if they save enough, or get rid of them by selling them. Therefore, one usually aggregates this source of income with the financial claims they may have on firms, governments, or individuals, i.e., capital income. Other factors of production are embodied in themselves, such as skills and personal characteristics. To earn the returns to these characteristics, the individual must participate in the labor market. To summarize, an individual $i$'s income is given by

$$z_i = z_{\mathrm{L}i} + z_{\mathrm{K}i},$$

where $z_{\mathrm{L}i}$ is labor income and $z_{\mathrm{K}i}$ capital income. Labor income is the sum of the returns to all the characteristics brought by the individual to the labor market. Denote this vector of characteristics by $(h_{i1}, \dots, h_{iJ})$. In the usual case (the "homogeneous-input view"), which applies in chapters 2–5, 9, and 10, competition between firms and equilibrium in the labor market yield a single homogeneous price $\omega_j$ for characteristic $j$. Therefore,

$$z_{\mathrm{L}i} = \sum_{j=1}^{J} \omega_j h_{ij}. \tag{1.1}$$

The distribution of individual wages derives from the vector of factor prices and from the distribution of these factors among individuals. A theory of the distribution of income is a theory of how these two things are determined.

## 1.1 Production and Factor Prices

A first step is therefore understanding the determinants of factor prices.

Assume that there is a single, homogenous final good, whose production uses $M \geqslant J$ factors of production. The factors indexed by $j > J$ are thought of as capital goods, i.e., those not embodied in people. The factors indexed by $j \leqslant J$ are the human-capital goods, i.e., those that are embodied in people. Using the preceding notation, if there are $P$ people in the economy, then the aggregate input in factor $j$ is the sum, across all individuals, of their supply of that factor:

$$H_j = \sum_{i=1}^{P} h_{ij}.$$

The final good is produced with a constant-returns-to-scale, concave production function:

$$Y = F(H_1, \dots, H_M).$$

We will typically assume that this production function has standard properties. It is increasing in all its arguments, concave, and has constant returns to scale, i.e., $F(\theta H_1, \dots, \theta H_M) = \theta F(H_1, \dots, H_M)$ for $\theta \geqslant 0$, which is equivalent to the "Euler condition":

$$\sum_{j=1}^{M} F'_j H_j = F. \tag{1.2}$$

A key phenomenon of interest is technical progress. In general, we can represent this by adding a shift parameter $A$ to the production function. We would then have $Y = F(H_1, \dots, H_M; A)$. Technological improvements are then represented by an increase in $A$, which allows greater production with the same factor use, i.e., $\partial F / \partial A > 0$. More generally, technical progress could be multidimensional, in which case one would add several such parameters to the production function, each of which would shift the function in a different way.

The final good is produced by perfectly competitive firms. They take factor prices as given. Normalizing the price of $Y$ to 1, they therefore maximize

$$\max_{\{H_j\}} Y - \sum_{j=1}^{M} \omega_j H_j.$$

The first-order condition tells us that the price of factor $j$ must be equal to its marginal product:[1]

$$F_j'(H_1,\dots,H_M) = \omega_j. \tag{1.3}$$

Thus, if we know the stock of all factors $H_i$ employed, we know the vector of factor prices. Furthermore, by concavity of the production function, the increase in the supply of one factor always reduces its price:

$$F_{jj}'' = \frac{\partial \omega_j}{\partial H_j} \leqslant 0.$$

On the other hand, an increase in the supply of factor $j$ reduces the price of $i$ if they are substitutes, i.e., $F_{ij}'' < 0$, and increases it if they are complements, i.e., $F_{ij}'' > 0$.

Because of (1.2), if all the marginal product conditions hold, the total cost must be equal to

$$\sum_{j=1}^{M} \omega_j H_j = \sum_{j=1}^{M} F_j' H_j = Y,$$

which is equal to total revenues given that the price of output is normalized to 1. Thus, profits must be equal to 0. If profits were positive, firms could—by virtue of constant returns—replicate their operations on an arbitrarily large scale and make arbitrarily large profits. The firm's maximization problem is only meaningful if profits are zero. That can only be true for some values of factor prices. If, for example, starting from a zero-profit input mix, I reduce the price of one factor, holding the others constant, then profits clearly become positive. Of course, in general equilibrium, the zero-profit condition must be met, since infinite production is not feasible. The set of factor prices defined by (1.3) as a function of the vector of factor inputs always satisfy the zero-profit condition, but an arbitrary vector of factor prices in general does not.

If factor prices do not lead to zero profits, the firm's optimization problem has no interior solution. However, the firm may still minimize costs given output (this is usually referred to as the dual problem). The

[1] Throughout the book, the partial derivative of a function $\varphi$ will be denoted either with a prime and a relevant subscript (which may, depending on convenience, be either the label of the variable or its order in the sequence of arguments of $\varphi$), or with the traditional $\partial\varphi/\partial x$ notation. Hence, the partial derivative of $\varphi(x,y)$ with respect to $x$ may be denoted by $\partial\varphi/\partial x$, $\varphi_x'$, or $\varphi_1'$. Similarly, its cross-second derivative can be written $\partial\varphi/\partial x\partial y$, $\varphi_{xy}''$, or $\varphi_{12}''$, and so on.

corresponding optimization problem is

$$\min_{\{H_j\}} \sum_{j=1}^{M} \omega_j H_j,$$
$$\text{s.t. } Y = F(H_1, \dots, H_M).$$

The first-order condition is

$$\lambda F'_j = \omega_j,$$

where $\lambda$ is the Lagrange multiplier. The value that this minimization problem yields is the *cost function* $\Gamma(\omega_1, \dots, \omega_M; Y)$, which tells us, given factor prices, the minimum cost at which a quantity of output equal to $Y$ can be produced. Denoting by

$$\mathcal{L} = \sum_j \omega_j H_j + \lambda(Y - F(H_1, \dots, H_M))$$

the Lagrangian of that minimization problem, the envelope theorem implies that

$$\frac{\partial \Gamma}{\partial Y} = \lambda$$

and that

$$\frac{\partial \Gamma}{\partial \omega_j} = H_j. \tag{1.4}$$

Thus, $\lambda$ is the marginal cost of output, and, if I know both the cost function and $Y$, I can compute the optimal factor input $H_j$ as the derivative of the cost function with respect to $H_j$—a result referred to as Shepard's lemma (Shepard 1953). Note that the profit-maximization case analyzed above is a special case with $\lambda = 1$, i.e., the marginal cost of output is equal to its price. Also, constant returns to scale imply that $\Gamma$ must be proportional to $Y$; if a vector $(H_1, \dots, H_M)$ satisfies the first-order conditions for $Y$, then $(\theta H_1, \dots, \theta H_M)$ satisfies them for $\theta Y$. The cost function can then be rewritten as

$$\Gamma(\omega_1, \dots, \omega_M; Y) = Yc(\omega_1, \dots, \omega_M),$$

where $c(\cdot)$ is the *unit cost function*, also equal to the Lagrange multiplier $\lambda$. Furthermore, (1.4) is equivalent to

$$\frac{\partial c}{\partial \omega_j} = \frac{H_j}{Y},$$

i.e., the derivative of the *unit* cost function with respect to factor price $i$ is the *unit* input of that factor at the given prices. Finally, it is easy

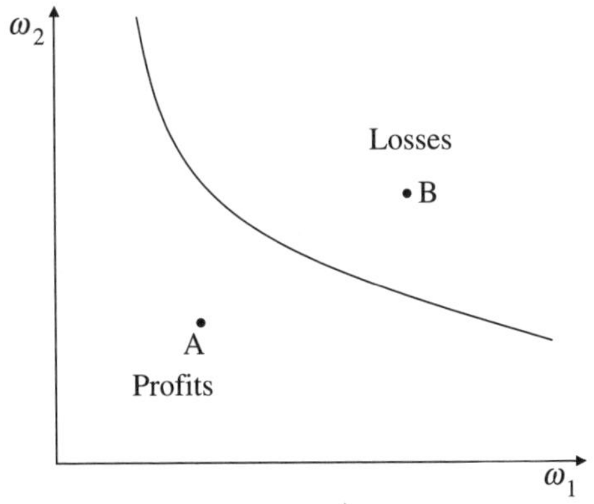


**Figure 1.1.** The factor-price frontier.

to show that both $\Gamma$ and $c$ are concave in the vector of factor prices $(\omega_1, \dots, \omega_M)$.[2]

One can also compute the firm's profit, which must then be equal to

$$\Pi(\omega_1, \dots, \omega_M; Y) = (1 - c(\omega_1, \dots, \omega_M))Y.$$

There are then three possibilities:

- If $c(\omega_1, \dots, \omega_M) > 1$, then there is no way the firm may get nonnegative profits; it will just shut down.
- If $c(\omega_1, \dots, \omega_M) < 1$, then profits are positive, and the firm could make them infinite by picking $Y = \infty$. This cannot be an equilibrium outcome.
- If $c(\omega_1, \dots, \omega_M) = 1$, then profits are zero, and the profit-maximization analysis applies. Unsurprisingly, one then has $\lambda = 1$.

  Thus, equilibrium prices must necessarily satisfy the following restriction:

$$c(\omega_1, \dots, \omega_M) = 1.$$

This defines a surface of dimension $M - 1$ in the $M$-dimensional space, which is called the *factor-price frontier* (FPF). Figure 1.1 depicts it in the two-dimensional case. Its shape reflects the concavity of the cost function. Its slope at each point is equal to the opposite of the ratio of the two factors' input requirements, $H_1/H_2$. This ratio falls as $\omega_1$ goes up: the cost-minimizing input vector is less intensive in a factor, relative

[2] Call this price vector $\boldsymbol{\omega}$, and call the corresponding cost-minimizing vector of unit input requirements $\boldsymbol{h}^*(\boldsymbol{\omega})$. Then $c(\boldsymbol{\omega}) = \boldsymbol{\omega}\boldsymbol{h}^*(\boldsymbol{\omega}) \leqslant \boldsymbol{\omega}\boldsymbol{h}$ for any vector $\boldsymbol{h}$ such that $F(\boldsymbol{h}) = 1$. Then, $\theta c(\boldsymbol{\omega}_0) + (1-\theta)c(\boldsymbol{\omega}_1) \leqslant \theta\boldsymbol{\omega}_0\boldsymbol{h}^*(\theta\boldsymbol{\omega}_0 + (1-\theta)\boldsymbol{\omega}_1) + (1-\theta)\boldsymbol{\omega}_1\boldsymbol{x}^*(\theta\boldsymbol{\omega}_0 + (1-\theta)\boldsymbol{\omega}_1) = c(\theta\boldsymbol{\omega}_0 + (1-\theta)\boldsymbol{\omega}_1)$.

to the other factor, when the relative price of this factor goes up. If one knows the economy's aggregate inputs, $\bar{H}_1$ and $\bar{H}_2$, then factor prices are determined by the fact that the economy must lie on the FPF, at a point where its slope is precisely equal to $-\bar{H}_1/\bar{H}_2$. The FPF can also be understood as a zero-profit locus. At point A, factor prices are "lower" than on the FPF, and firms make positive profits. The converse occurs at point B, where firms make losses.

## 1.2 Factor Prices and Income Distribution

Once we know factor prices, how do we get the distribution of income? Obviously, we just have to apply equation (1.1), but we have to take a stand on how the $h_i$s are determined. If the vector of inputs supplied by workers to the labor market is multidimensional, there is no obvious choice and it depends on the problem at hand.

In many cases we will deal with simple models with two categories of workers: skilled and unskilled. In such a case there are two characteristics: $h_1$ and $h_2$, which we relabel $h$ and $l$. An unskilled worker $i$ is endowed with $l_i$ units of "labor"—where $l_i$ thus potentially differs across workers. A skilled worker is endowed with $h_i$ units of "human capital." Throughout the book, we will denote by $w$ the price of labor and by $\omega$ the price of human capital. In such a case, the wage of an unskilled worker is simply equal to $wl_i$, and that of a skilled worker to $\omega h_i$.

In other cases, workers provide a whole vector of characteristics. Each of these characteristics is a separate input into the production function and is rewarded at its marginal product, independent of the worker's endowment in other characteristics. In such a case, one just applies (1.1) mechanically. We will refer to this case as the *nonspecialization model.*

Note that while this approach is formally impeccable, from an economic viewpoint it is somehow controversial. Suppose that there are two characteristics, beauty and strength. Then it must be the case that a firm's output depends only on the total quantity of beauty and the total quantity of strength that are present in its employees, irrespective of how these characteristics are distributed across them. Thus, a firm in which half of the workers are beautiful and strong and the other half weak and ugly will have the same output as a firm in which half of the workers are ugly and strong and the other half beautiful and weak. Clearly, one could speculate that in the second situation, the firm would be more productive by assigning beautiful workers to beauty-intensive communication tasks and strong workers to strength-intensive physical tasks.[3] The reason this achieves greater output than in the first situation is that people have *time constraints*, which prevents a beautiful-and-strong worker from producing as much as a pair of workers who are jointly endowed with the same vector of characteristics.

Once the time constraint is reintroduced, one cannot sum the returns to all individual characteristics. Instead, we have to modify the problem by casting it in terms of tasks performed rather than inputs brought to the market. One way of doing so is to reinterpret the aggregate labor inputs $H_j$ as tasks and individual endowments $h_{ij}$ as the individual's *full-time* production of task $j$.[4] Normalizing total time endowment to 1, individual $i$'s income is determined as the solution to the following maximization problem:

$$z_i = \max_{\tau_{ij}} \sum_{j=1}^{J} \omega_j h_{ij} \tau_{ij},$$

$$\text{s.t.} \sum_{j=1}^{J} \tau_{ij} = 1,$$

where $\tau_{ij}$ is the fraction of time devoted by individual $i$ to task $j$.

In general, the individual will specialize solely in the task that yields the highest return. Thus, he will pick $j^*(i) = \arg\max_j \omega_j h_{ij}$, and set $\tau_{ij^*(i)} = 1$. Thus, the distribution of income is determined by a different logic from simply applying (1.1). We will refer to this approach as the *Roy specialization model.*

A simple illustration is the Roy (1951) model of comparative advantage. Assume that people are endowed with $h_i$ units of human capital and $l_i$ units of raw labor. Each of these endowments is equal to the individual's productivity at a corresponding task. Then an individual will specialize in human capital if and only if $\omega h_i > w l_i$, i.e.,

$$\frac{h_i}{l_i} > \frac{w}{\omega}.$$

This is just Ricardo's law of comparative advantage applied to an individual instead of a nation. An interesting case is when $h_i$ and $l_i$ derive from an underlying individual parameter, "skill," which is unidimensional. Thus, an individual with skill $s$ has human capital $h(s)$ and labor

[3] Another issue is that for a single price of a given characteristic to hold across firms and sectors, it must be that a worker can supply beauty to one firm and strength to another firm. This assumption is challenged in chapter 6.

[4] $h_{ij}$ may in turn be related to the individual's characteristics by some mapping that we do not need to specify.

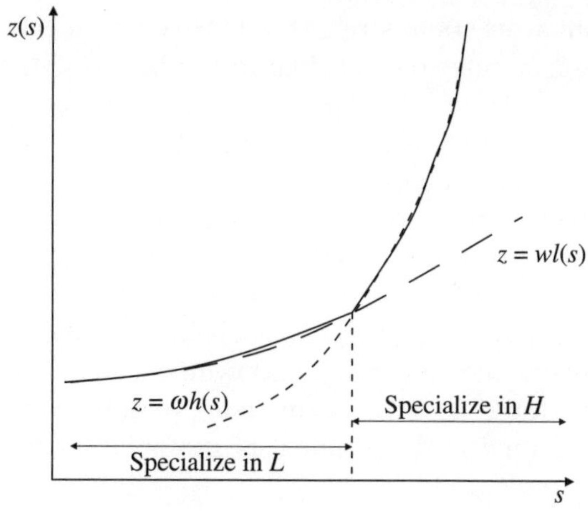


**Figure 1.2.** Occupational choice and the wage schedule.

endowment $l(s)$. We assume that both $h$ and $l$ are increasing functions of $s$: more skilled workers are better endowed in both dimensions. Furthermore, another natural assumption is that human capital is more responsive to skill than labor is:

$$\frac{h'(s)}{h(s)} > \frac{l'(s)}{l(s)}. \tag{1.5}$$

A consequence of this is that the function $h(s)/l(s)$ is increasing in $s$. Therefore, people will specialize in human capital if and only if $s \geqslant s^*(w/\omega)$, where $s^*$ is the threshold skill level determined by $h(s^*)/l(s^*) = w/\omega$. There is *sorting* by skills into the two alternative activities.

For a given value of the relative wage $w/\omega$, the distribution of income is determined as in figure 1.2. The solid line depicts the *wage schedule,* $z(s)$, which tells us how much a worker with skill $s$ earns. The dashed lines, defined by $z = \omega h(s)$ and $z = wl(s)$, tell us the level of earnings if one were to specialize in either activity. The wage schedule is the upper envelope of these two lines, and has a kink at their crossing point. Low-skill people provide labor and high-skill people provide human capital. The kink implies that there is a jump in the returns to skill, $z'(s)$, when one goes through the specialization threshold $s^*$. This jump reflects the fact that human capital is more sensitive to skill than labor is. Roughly speaking, this sorting model thus predicts higher return to skill for skilled workers than for unskilled workers.

The aggregate supplies of labor and human capital are determined endogenously. An increase in the skill premium, $\omega/w$, reduces the threshold skill level beyond which people specialize in human capital.

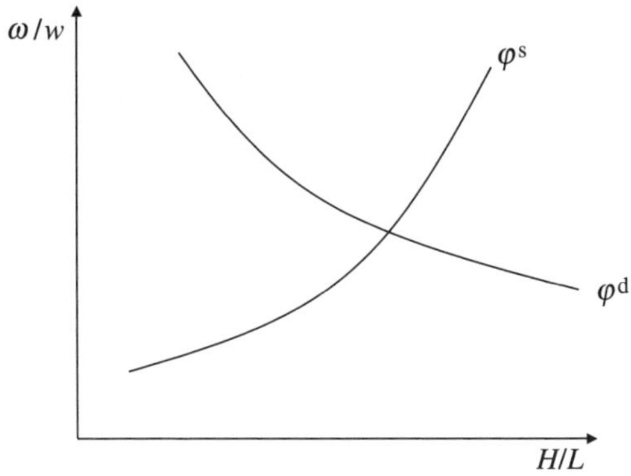


**Figure 1.3.** Equilibrium determination of the skill premium.

Thus, in the aggregate $H$ goes up and $L$ goes down. Denoting total population by $P$ and the distribution of skills by $g(\cdot)$, we have that

$$H = P \int_{s^*(w/\omega)}^{+\infty} h(s)g(s)\,\mathrm{d}s = H\left(\frac{\omega}{w}\right), \quad H' > 0, \tag{1.6}$$

$$L = P \int_{0}^{s^*(w/\omega)} l(s)g(s)\,\mathrm{d}s = L\left(\frac{\omega}{w}\right), \quad L' < 0. \tag{1.7}$$

This in turn determines the relative supply of $H$ with respect to $L$, $H/L$, as an increasing function of the skill premium:

$$\frac{H}{L} = \frac{H(\omega/w)}{L(\omega/w)} = \varphi^{\mathrm{s}}\left(\frac{\omega}{w}\right), \quad \varphi^{\mathrm{s}\prime} > 0.$$

At the same time, the relative demand is derived from cost minimization:

$$\frac{H}{L} = \frac{c_\omega}{c_w} = \varphi^{\mathrm{d}}\left(\frac{\omega}{w}\right), \quad \varphi^{\mathrm{d}\prime} < 0.$$

Thus, the equilibrium skill premium is uniquely determined by equating relative supply with relative demand, as illustrated in figure 1.3. The skill premium in turn pins down $H$, $L$, from (1.6) and (1.7), then $\omega$ and $w$, from (1.3), and finally the distribution of income, from the above considerations.

In this framework, any shift in labor demand that increases the skill premium $\omega/w$ will increase any measure of inequality (such a shift is illustrated in figure 1.4, where for the sake of clarity we have kept $w$ unchanged). To see this, consider any pair of workers with skills $s$ and $s'$ such that $s' > s$. Denote by $\omega_0$ and $w_0$ the initial values of $\omega$ and $w$, and by $\omega_1$ and $w_1$ their final values. Denote by $s_0^*$ and $s_1^*$ the initial and final values of the critical skill level. Since $\omega_1/w_1 > \omega_0/w_0$, $s_1^* < s_0^*$. Denote

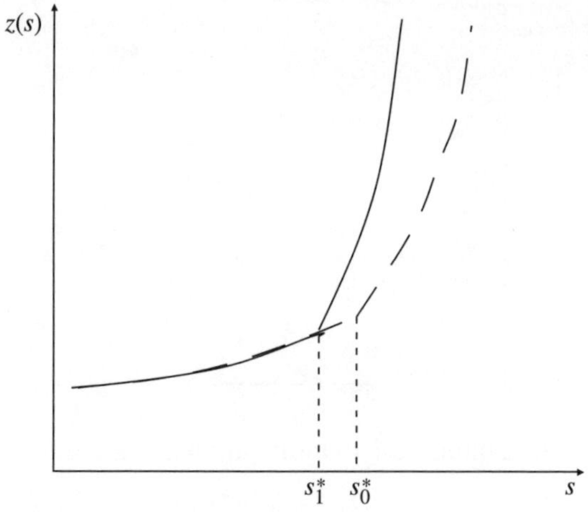


**Figure 1.4.** The impact of an increase in the skill premium on the distribution of wages.

by $z_0$, $z_0'$ the initial income levels of $s$ and $s'$, and by $z_1$ and $z_1'$ the final levels. There are five possible cases:

- If $s < s' < s_1^* < s_0^*$, both workers supply raw labor before and after the shift. Thus, $z_1'/z_1 = z_0'/z_0 = l(s')/l(s)$. Inequality between the two workers does not change.

- If $s < s_1^* < s' < s_0^*$, then worker $s$ supplies labor before and after the change, while worker $s'$ moves from labor to human capital. Therefore, $z_0'/z_0 = l(s')/l(s)$, and $z_1'/z_1 = \omega_1 h(s')/w_1 l(s)$. By revealed preference, $\omega_1 h(s') > w_1 l(s')$; otherwise, it would not pay for worker $s'$ to specialize in human capital after the change. Therefore, $z_1'/z_1 > l(s')/l(s) = z_0'/z_0$. Inequality between the two workers goes up.

- If $s_1^* < s < s' < s_0^*$, then both workers move from specializing in labor to specializing in human capital as a result of the shift. Therefore, $z_0'/z_0 = l(s')/l(s)$ and $z_1'/z_1 = h(s')/h(s)$. Since $h(s')/l(s') > h(s)/l(s)$, it must be that $z_1'/z_1 > z_0'/z_0$.

- If $s_1^* < s < s_0^* < s'$, then worker $s$ moves from labor to human capital, while worker $s'$ supplies human capital before and after the shift. Thus, $z_0'/z_0 = \omega_0 h(s')/w_0 l(s)$, and $z_1'/z_1 = h(s')/h(s)$. Again by revealed preference, $w_0 l(s) > \omega_0 h(s)$, as it is optimal for worker $s$ to specialize in labor before the change; substituting this inequality into the expression for $z_0'/z_0$, we again get that $z_0'/z_0 < z_1'/z_1$.

- Finally, if $s_1^* < s_0^* < s < s'$, then both workers always supply human capital, and $z_0'/z_0 = z_1'/z_1 = h(s')/h(s)$.

To summarize, inequality between two arbitrary workers must either go up or stay constant as $\omega/w$ goes up. Consequently, any aggregate measure of relative inequality will go up.

A similar result is obtained when (1.1) applies, i.e., in the nonspecialization model, provided that $h$ and $l$ are again functions of an underlying skill $s$ that satisfy (1.5). The income of an individual with skill $s$ is then

$$z(s) = wl(s) + \omega h(s),$$

so that for $s' > s$ we have

$$\begin{aligned}\frac{z(s')}{z(s)} &= \frac{wl(s') + \omega h(s')}{wl(s) + \omega h(s)}\\ &= \frac{l(s') + (\omega/w)h(s')}{l(s) + (\omega/w)h(s)}.\end{aligned}$$

Clearly, this is an increasing function of the skill premium $\omega/w$ if and only if (1.5) holds. In this case too, a higher skill premium unambiguously raises any relative inequality measure.

A special case of this arises when all workers are endowed with the same quantity of raw labor but different levels of human capital. This is equivalent to assuming that $h(s) = s$ and $l(s) = l = \text{const}$. Equation (1.5) then clearly holds, and a higher skill premium clearly increases inequality.

Things are more complex, obviously, if the underlying distribution of skills is multidimensional. It may then be the case that some workers who supply human capital have a lower income than some other workers who supply labor. An increase in the skill premium will then reduce inequality between these workers, while at the same time possibly increasing inequality between other types of workers. Some measures of aggregate inequality may go up while others may go down.

## 1.3 Factor Accumulation

The preceding analysis allows us to determine the distribution of income at a point in time, given the distribution of factor endowments. From a dynamic perspective, however, this distribution is partly endogenous, because some factors can be accumulated over time. To assess the effect of technical change on the distribution of income in the long run, we need to know how factor accumulation reacts to a shift in technology.

For our purposes, the two main accumulable factors are physical and human capital.

The two most popular models of capital accumulation are the Ramsey growth model and the Diamond overlapping-generations (OLG) model. We only provide a concise treatment here, as most readers are familiar with them. For the purpose of this book we need only focus on these models' predictions for the long-run level of the capital stock.

### 1.3.1 The Ramsey Growth Model

In the Ramsey growth model, there is a single representative consumer who lives for an infinitely long time. Capital is a productive asset that allows transfer of consumption between dates. The consumer maximizes the present discounted value of utility. The model is typically cast in continuous time, in which case the consumer's problem is

$$\max \int_0^{+\infty} U(C_t)\mathrm{e}^{-\rho t}\,\mathrm{d}t. \tag{1.8}$$

However, for our purposes, we can deal with a discrete-time equivalent:

$$\max \sum \frac{U(C_t)}{(1+\rho)^t}\,\mathrm{d}t.$$

The consumer is endowed with a fixed labor supply $L$. At date $t$ the stock of capital is equal to $K_t$. The total output at a given date is given by the production function, where we allow for technical progress by introducing a shift factor $A_t$:

$$Y_t = F(K_t, L; A_t). \tag{1.9}$$

Both $U$ and $F$ have the usual properties: concavity, constant returns (for $F(\cdot)$), and differentiability.

Finally, the final good can be used either for consumption or investment purposes. Capital depreciates at rate $\delta$. Therefore, it accumulates according to

$$K_{t+1} = Y_t - C_t + (1-\delta)K_t. \tag{1.10}$$

We maximize the consumer's utility under the physical constraints of equations (1.9) and (1.10).[5] The key optimality condition can be obtained by using the following thought experiment. Suppose the consumer decides to increase $C_t$ and to reduce $C_{t+1}$, so as to maintain the subsequent path of capital and consumption unchanged. Call $\Delta C_t$

[5] This can be understood as looking for either a social optimum or a competitive equilibrium. If there is perfect competition, standard results tell us that the equilibrium is a Pareto optimum. In a representative agent model there is generically only one Pareto optimum: the one which maximizes the utility of the representative agent.

the increment in $C_t$ and $\Delta C_{t+1}$ the corresponding negative increase in $C_{t+1}$. Capital at $t+1$ changes by $\Delta K_{t+1} = -\Delta C_t$. This in turn raises $Y_{t+1}$ by $\Delta Y_{t+1} = -F'_{Kt+1}\Delta C_t$. Finally, the change in $K_{t+2}$ is $\Delta K_{t+2} = \Delta Y_{t+1} - \Delta C_{t+1} + (1-\delta)\Delta K_{t+1}$. Since the path of capital is assumed to be unchanged from $t+2$ on, we must have $\Delta K_{t+2} = 0$. Therefore,

$$\Delta C_{t+1} = -(1 + F'_{Kt+1} - \delta)\Delta C_t.$$

At the optimum, such a marginal change must leave the consumer's utility unchanged. Hence, the utility gain from consuming more at $t$ must be offset by the discounted disutility from consuming less at $t+1$. Therefore,

$$U'(C_t) = \frac{1 + F'_{Kt+1} - \delta}{1+\rho} U'(C_{t+1}).$$

This optimality condition for consumption—called both the Ramsey condition and the Euler equation—determines the long-run stock of capital. If there is no growth in technology, then the economy is in steady state in the long run, with $C_t = C_{t+1}$. The preceding expression then yields the steady-state form of the Ramsey condition, which implies that capital is accumulated up to the point where its net marginal product is equal to the rate of time preference:

$$F'_K = \rho + \delta. \tag{1.11}$$

Hence, the long-run real interest rate is pinned down by the rate of time preference. In response to a shock, the marginal product of capital cannot deviate permanently to its long-run level.

What if productivity grows? We can show that under certain conditions, the economy converges to a balanced-growth path, i.e., a trajectory where all variables grow at a constant rate. This will be the case, in particular, if utility is isoelastic,

$$U(C_t) = \frac{C_t^\gamma - 1}{\gamma}, \quad \text{for } \gamma < 1,$$

or

$$U(C_t) = \ln C_t,$$

and if technology $A_t$ is labor-augmenting, i.e., the production function can be written as $Y_t = F(K_t, A_t L_t)$, and grows at a constant rate $g$. In the long run, $C$, $K$, and $Y$ all grow at rate $g$, and the Ramsey condition (1.11) must now be replaced by

$$F'_K = (1+g)^{1-\gamma}(1+\rho) + \delta - 1. \tag{1.12}$$

Trend growth now affects the marginal product of capital in the long run. But it remains true that any technological shock other than a permanent shift in trend growth leaves it unaffected.

### 1.3.2 The Diamond Overlapping-Generations Model

An alternative model of capital accumulation is the Diamond (1965) overlapping-generations model. Its two-period overlapping-generations structure yields a very simple optimization problem. This feature may be quite valuable when it comes to analyzing heterogeneity across people in accumulation patterns.

In this model, people live for two periods. In the first period of their life they work and in the second period they are retired. In order to finance their consumption when old, they accumulate wealth. In the version of the model that is of interest to us in this book, the only asset is physical capital. At each date a new generation is born, thus the old generation, born at $t-1$, coexists at date $t$ with the young generation, born at $t$. We assume that the young are endowed with one unit of labor and that the size of each cohort is normalized to $L$. The young thus maximize their utility function $u(c_{yt}, c_{ot+1})$, where $c_{yt}$ is their consumption when young (at date $t$) and $c_{ot+1}$ their consumption when old (at date $t+1$), subject to their budget constraint

$$c_{ot+1} = (1 + r_{t+1})(w_t - c_{yt}).$$

In this formula, $r_{t+1}$ is the net rate of return to capital between $t$ and $t+1$, which must be equal to its marginal product at $t+1$ net of depreciation. Assuming that the utility function is homothetic, it follows that the savings of the young can be written as

$$w_t - c_{yt} = w_t s(r_{t+1}),$$

where $s(\cdot)$ is the savings function. We can now aggregate and get the savings of the whole young cohort:

$$S_t = w_t L s(r_{t+1}).$$

The young are the only people who are holding assets at the end of period $t$. Furthermore, the only asset is the capital stock. Consequently, capital must be equal to the total asset holdings of the young generation, which (in the absence of bequests) is just $S_t$:

$$K_{t+1} = S_t. \tag{1.13}$$

The model is then closed by assuming a standard production function, and that competitive firms equalize factor prices with their marginal product. Assuming a production function $Y = F(K, AL) = ALf(K/AL)$, the long-run capital stock is then determined by the following condition:

$$K = Ls\left(f'\left(\frac{K}{AL}\right)\right)\left(f\left(\frac{K}{AL}\right) - \frac{K}{AL}f'\left(\frac{K}{AL}\right)\right).$$

This condition is more complex than in the Ramsey model, and the long-run marginal product of capital is no longer pinned down. For example, a once-and-for-all change in $A$ can either increase it or reduce it.

### 1.3.3 Human Capital Accumulation

Unlike with physical capital, there is no standard way of embodying human capital in growth models. Therefore, we will not discuss the determinants of human-capital accumulation in this book. One can note, however, that the OLG model can also be useful for modeling human-capital accumulation. For this, we can assume that instead of investing in capital, people have offspring and invest in their human capital. A simple way to proceed is to assume that people work and consume in the first period of their life and derive utility from their offspring's human capital in the second period of their life. Thus, they maximize $u(c_t, h_{t+1})$, where $c_t$ is their consumption and $h_{t+1}$ their offspring's human capital. Their income is $\omega_t h_t$, where $\omega_t$ is the price of human capital at $t$. One then has to specify some equation for human-capital accumulation, for example $h_{t+1} = \omega_t h_t - c_t$. If utility is homothetic, we simply get that $h_{t+1}$ will be proportional to $\omega_t h_t$. The model can then be completed with some production function, say $Y = F(H, AL)$.

## 1.4 Endogenous Technical Change

This book is chiefly concerned with the effect of technical change on inequality; however, in several instances, interesting effects derive from the observation that the level and structure of technical change are themselves responsive to economic conditions. For example, once we identify the conditions under which technological progress increases inequality, we may want to know whether these conditions are made more or less likely by different economic environments. For this purpose we need a theory of endogenous technology.

In the above formulation, technology is summarized by a parameter $A$ which shifts the production function. The large endogenous growth literature has proposed a number of approaches to make it endogenous. One of the simplest ones, which is rooted in a long tradition of theoretical and empirical work, consists in assuming that productivity grows because of learning by doing. The more one produces a good, the better one becomes at doing so. This could be summarized by a learning function $\Phi(A_t, Y_t)$ such that $\Phi'_Y > 0$ and

$$\frac{\mathrm{d}A_t}{\mathrm{d}t} = \Phi(A_t, Y_t).$$

This process may lead to sustainable growth depending on the parameters of the model. For example, if labor is the only factor of production, $Y_t = A_t L$, and $\Phi(A_t, Y_t) = A_t^{\gamma} Y_t^{\varepsilon}$, then there is a balanced-growth path with a positive growth rate if $\gamma + \varepsilon = 1$. For a thorough discussion of these issues, we refer the reader to Barro and Sala-i-Martin (2003) and Aghion and Howitt (1997).

One problem with the learning-by-doing approach is that technical progress is a mechanical process. In particular, it is independent of prices. More sophisticated approaches, following Romer (1990), Grossman and Helpman (1991), and Aghion and Howitt (1992), take into account the fact that innovation is the outcome of a research and development (R&D) process that is responsive to economic incentives. One distinguishes two formalizations:

- the "horizontal innovation" approach of Romer and Grossman/Helpman, where innovators introduce new goods; and
- the "vertical innovation" approach of Aghion and Howitt, where new technologies associated with an increase in $A_t$ are introduced.

For our purposes, the horizontal approach is simpler, and, under some interpretations, can also be considered as a model of productivity improvements—we will therefore use it throughout the book. Its starting point is the Dixit and Stiglitz (1977) model of endogenous product diversity. In the version that we will use, at any point in time there is a continuum of products whose total mass is $N$. The consumers' instantaneous utility is given by

$$U_i = U(C_i) = U\left[\int_0^N x_{ij}^{\varepsilon}\, \mathrm{d}j\right]^{1/\varepsilon}, \quad 0 < \varepsilon < 1. \tag{1.14}$$

In this formula, the consumer $i$ consumes a quantity $x_{ij}$ of the atomistic individual good $j$. These consumption levels enter a composite consumption index $C_i$. This index is of the constant elasticity of substitution (CES) type and it is homogeneous of degree one. An important aspect of this utility function is that there is taste for diversity, in that people value an increase in $N$ for a given physical purchasing power. If, for example, the consumer's income is $z_i$ and all goods are priced at $p_0$, the composite index when one consumes the same amount of each good is given by

$$C_i = \left[N\left(\frac{z}{pN}\right)^{\varepsilon}\right]^{1/\varepsilon} = N^{(1-\varepsilon)/\varepsilon}\frac{z_j}{p_0}. \tag{1.15}$$

This is clearly increasing in $N$: with the same budget in "real" terms, people buy less of each good but a greater variety of goods when $N$ goes up, and that makes them better-off.

This utility function yields the demand for each good $j$ if its price is $p_j$, for a consumer $i$ with nominal income $z_i$. Maximizing $U$ with respect to the budget constraint $z_i = \int_0^{N_t} p_j x_{ij}\,\mathrm{d}j$ yields

$$x_{ij} = \frac{z_i}{p}\left(\frac{p_j}{p}\right)^{-\eta}. \tag{1.16}$$

In this formula, $\eta$ is the elasticity of substitution between goods, $\eta = 1/(1-\varepsilon) > 1$, and $p$ is the aggregate price index for the composite index $C$ and is given by

$$p = \left(\int_0^N p_j^{1-\eta}\,\mathrm{d}j\right)^{1/(1-\eta)}. \tag{1.17}$$

One can straightforwardly check that the consumer's aggregate consumption index is indeed given by

$$C_i = \frac{z_i}{p}.$$

Furthermore, the taste for diversity is reflected in the aggregate price index. If all goods are priced at $p_0$, one has $p = p_0 N^{(\varepsilon-1)/\varepsilon} = p_0 N^{1/(1-\eta)}$, which falls with $N$. In hedonic terms, the "cost of living" falls.

The smaller the elasticity of substitution between goods, the greater the effect of product variety on welfare.[6] This makes sense: if new goods are very good substitutes for existing goods, consumers are not very interested in increasing the number of different goods available. In the limit case where $\eta = +\infty$, the composite consumption index is linear, all goods are perfect substitutes, and diversity is not valued.[7]

The demand system (1.16) has two very convenient properties. First, demand can be aggregated across consumers with different incomes. In other words, the demand curve for each good is independent of the distribution of income. This is due to the fact that preferences are homothetic. Consequently, denoting by $Z = \sum_i z_i$ the economy's aggregate nominal income, the aggregate demand curve for good $j$ is simply given by

$$X_j = \frac{Z}{p}\left(\frac{p_j}{p}\right)^{-\eta}. \tag{1.18}$$

---

[6] It is, however, possible to disentangle the two by introducing $N$ directly into the utility function (see Bénassy 1996).

[7] Note that we have assumed that $\varepsilon > 0$, i.e., $\eta > 1$. There are at least two reasons for this. The first is that if $\eta < 1$, complementarities between goods are so strong that increases in $N$ actually make people less happy, as evidenced by (1.15). With $\eta < 1$, not consuming a good at all would yield $C = 0$, the lowest possible welfare level. On the other hand, $C$ could be strictly positive if instead all the goods for which the quantity consumed is zero did not exist at all. Thus, when $\eta < 1$, the equivalence between not consuming a good and that good not existing is broken. That does not make much economic sense, and that is why we assume that $\eta > 1$. The other reason is that we need the price elasticity of demand to be grater than 1 for monopoly pricing to make sense, as will be clear below.

Second, the price elasticity of demand for each good, holding $p$ constant, is constant and equal to $-\eta$. It is also the same for all goods.

Moving now to the determination of prices, each atomistic good is produced by a monopoly. The idea is that this monopoly holds a patent on this good, either because it has invented it or because it has purchased the patent. Thus, monopoly power derives from intellectual property. Assuming a constant marginal cost $c_j$ for good $j$,[8] the monopoly sets its price by maximizing its profits:

$$\begin{aligned}\pi_j &= (p_j - c_j)X_j \\ &= \frac{Z}{p}\left(\frac{p_j}{p}\right)^{-\eta}(p_j - c_j).\end{aligned} \tag{1.19}$$

Given the atomistic nature of the firm, its pricing decisions have a negligible effect on the aggregate price level $p$. Thus, it treats it as constant when maximizing $\pi_i$, and one simply finds that the price is determined by adding a constant markup over the marginal cost:

$$p_i = \mu c_i, \quad \mu = \frac{\eta}{\eta - 1}.$$

In the simpler case where all firms have the same cost $c$, we have $p_i = \mu c$, $p = \mu c N^{1/(1-\eta)}$, and, from (1.19),

$$\begin{aligned}\pi_i &= \pi \\ &= \frac{\mu - 1}{\mu}\frac{Z}{N}.\end{aligned} \tag{1.20}$$

By symmetry, each firm gets an income $Z/N$, and a fraction $(\mu - 1)/\mu$ of that income goes to the owner.

To transform this model to a model of endogenous product variety, one can simply assume that new varieties are invented at some cost, and that the reward to invention of a new good is the monopoly profit associated with it. For example, assume that the only input is labor and that total labor endowment in the economy is equal to $L$. Take the wage $w$ as the numéraire ($w = 1$), and assume that one needs one unit of labor to produce one unit of any good, thus $c = 1$. Assume that one can introduce a new good $j$ at a fixed cost $f$ in terms of labor, and that there is free entry in that process. In equilibrium, monopoly profits must be dissipated in the fixed costs, otherwise more people would pay $f$ to create new goods:

$$\pi = fw = f.$$

[8] As long as the production function for good $j$ has constant returns to scale, the marginal cost does not depend on the output level, and is just determined by the cost function, $c_j = c_j(\omega_1, \dots, \omega_K)$. Because firms are atomistic, the effect of their decisions on factor prices is negligible. They therefore treat $c_j$ as a constant.

Since profits pay the $f$ units of labor necessary to create the new good, all income goes to labor. Aggregate income is just

$$Z = Y = wL = L.$$

Substituting into (1.20) yields the equilibrium number of varieties:

$$N = \frac{\mu - 1}{\mu} L.$$

In the endogenous growth literature, this model is dynamic. Instead of being determined statically, $N$ now depends on time $t$ (and we therefore append a time index to it) and it grows over time because at each date some workers engage in R&D activities that increase the number of goods, $N$. One can, for example, assume that if, at $t$, $H_t$ workers do research, then they produce a flow of $bH_t$ new products:

$$\frac{\mathrm{d}N_t}{\mathrm{d}t} = bH_t. \tag{1.21}$$

The difficulty with this formulation is that $N_t$ cannot grow at a sustained rate unless $H_t$ grows, which rules out long-run growth in a stationary population. We do not want to enter into this complex debate here. Typically, people have assumed that a higher value of $N_t$ increases the productivity of the R&D sector through some sort of unspecified knowledge spillover, so that instead of (1.21) one would have something like

$$\frac{\mathrm{d}N_t}{\mathrm{d}t} = bN_t^{\upsilon} H_t. \tag{1.22}$$

If $\gamma = 1$ and $H_t$ equals a constant $H$, then $N_t$ grows at constant rate $bH$; the economy grows faster when more people devote themselves to R&D. An alternative route is to assume exogenous progress in the productivity of researchers, so that instead of a constant $b$ one would have $b_t = b_0 \mathrm{e}^{gt}$. For a constant $H$, $N_t$ would eventually grow at rate $g$ in the long run. This option ignores the determinants of the long-run growth rate, as an increase in $H$ would increase the number of goods but not its growth rate, but may yield useful insights.

How, then, is $H_t$ determined? The typical approach is to assume that R&D firms compete to hire intellectual workers, and that the value of the patents produced is dissipated in the wages of the researchers. Assume again free entry of firms into the R&D sector, and denote by $\omega_t$ the wage of R&D workers. Denoting by $V_t$ the value of a patent, the researchers get the whole value of the patents created:

$$\omega_t = bN_t^{\upsilon} V_t. \tag{1.23}$$

Finally, if one assumes for simplicity that patents hold forever, $V_t$ will simply be the present discounted value of monopoly profits. Assuming a constant interest rate $r$, we obtain

$$V_t = \int_t^{+\infty} \pi_s \mathrm{e}^{-r(s-t)}\,\mathrm{d}s.$$

It is often more convenient to differentiate this expression with respect to $t$, yielding

$$rV_t = \pi_t + \frac{\mathrm{d}V_t}{\mathrm{d}t}, \tag{1.24}$$

which is sometimes referred to as the "Bellman equation."

Consider a simple case where $\upsilon = 1$, the total labor force is $L$, and people can either work in the production sector or in the R&D sector. That is, the supply of research workers is infinitely elastic (later in the book we will consider a more general case). This implies that

$$\omega = w = 1,$$

where we again use wages as a numéraire. Consequently, from (1.23):

$$V_t = \frac{1}{N_t b}.$$

Substituting into (1.24), and noting again that $Y = L$, we obtain

$$\frac{r}{b} = \frac{\mu - 1}{\mu} L - \frac{\dot{N}}{bN},$$

where, throughout the book, the dot denotes the derivative with respect to time. This determines the growth rate of $N$:

$$g_N = \frac{\mu - 1}{\mu} hL - r.$$

This expression is a relationship between the growth rate $g_N$ and the nominal interest rate $r$. In most models, the model is closed by deriving another relationship between $g_N$ and $r$ from the consumers' intertemporal optimization. Suppose that, as in the Ramsey model, consumers maximize (1.8), with $C$ defined by (1.14). In steady state,

$$C_t = \frac{Z_t}{p_t} = \frac{L}{\mu} N_t^{1/(\eta - 1)}.$$

Therefore, consumption grows at rate $g = g_N/(\eta - 1)$. The long-term interest rate is determined by the first-order condition (FOC) for the intertemporal allocation of consumption, i.e., the equivalent of (1.12). The marginal product of capital $F'_K$ must be replaced by the intertemporal rate of transformation of the aggregate consumption basket $C_t$. One can easily see that it is equal to $r + g$. Postponing consumption tomorrow yields two benefits: a financial benefit $r$, and the ability to consume a greater variety of goods from a given budget, captured by $g$.[9] Therefore, the condition (1.12) now reads[10]

$$r + g = (1 - \gamma)g + \rho.$$

In this model, there is no growth in productivity. The economy grows only in the sense that people are made happier because they can consume an ever-widening range of products. Because productivity does not grow, people also consume less of each product.

It is possible, however, to reinterpret the model as a model of productivity growth. To do so, just assume that $C_i$ is not an aggregate consumption index but that it is instead a homogeneous final good consumed by consumer $i$. This final good is produced from intermediate inputs. There is a continuum of such intermediate inputs, indexed by $j$, and there is a total of $N$ of them. The production function for the final good is

$$Y = \left[\int_0^N X_j^{\varepsilon}\,\mathrm{d}j\right]^{1/\varepsilon}.$$

Thus, we have reinterpreted the aggregate consumption index as a constant-returns production function for the final good, with a continuum of intermediate inputs. It is easy to see that very little has changed. We assume that producers of the intermediate goods have a monopoly but that the final good is produced by competitive firms. Thus, denoting by $p$ the price of the final good, they maximize their profit,

$$\Pi = \max p\left[\int_0^N X_j^{\varepsilon}\,\mathrm{d}j\right]^{1/\varepsilon} - \int_0^N p_j X_j\,\mathrm{d}j,$$

and this yields a demand for each good which is exactly the same as (1.18), with $Z/p$ replaced by $Y$. Furthermore, the zero-profit condition for the final good sector yields a relationship between $p$ and the $p_j$s which is exactly identical to (1.17). Thus, none of the analytics has changed.

Innovation, i.e., increases in $N$, is now viewed as a change in the production process toward greater sophistication: that is, the use of a greater number of intermediate products. Romer (1990) interprets it as advances in the division of labor. Whatever the interpretation, an increase in $N$ is now translated into higher total factor productivity in

---

[9] If, instead, the aggregate price level $p_t$ had been normalized to 1, then wages, now expressed in hedonic terms, would grow with time, and the interest rate $r$ would then reflect the effect of product diversity; it would thus be equal to the $r + g$ in the text.

[10] We have $\delta = 0$ since the stock of blueprints does not depreciate, and the approximation $(1 + g)^{1-\gamma}(1 + \rho) \approx 1 + (1 - \gamma)g + \rho$ becomes exact in continuous time, since the length of the period becomes infinitesimal.

the aggregate production function, rather than greater happiness. Taking the symmetrical case where all intermediate goods have the same price and are used in the same quantities, and assuming again that each of them only uses labor as an input, with a unit coefficient, we see that if $L$ people work in the production sector, $L/N$ of each intermediate good is produced and

$$Y = N^{(1-\varepsilon)/\varepsilon} L.$$

This relationship is the aggregate production function, which relates final output to the labor input. Total factor productivity is $A = N^{(1-\varepsilon)/\varepsilon}$ and goes up with $N$.

# 2

# Productivity and Wages in Neoclassical Growth Models

The natural starting point for discussing the effect of technical progress on wages is the neoclassical growth model discussed in the previous chapter. We have seen that technical progress can be represented by an increase in total factor productivity $A$, and that if this quantity grows at a constant rate $g$, the economy converges to a balanced-growth path, provided that utility is isoelastic and that $A$ is multiplicative in labor.

Why do growth theorists traditionally focus on such balanced-growth paths? One reason is that it allows us to have a tractable framework for analytical purposes (we can then talk about a well-defined long-run level for any variable, and perform comparative statics with that outcome). Another reason is that balanced-growth paths match the influential "Kaldor stylized facts of growth." As you will see in any textbook, these are the following:

- output per capita and capital intensity keep increasing;
- the capital–output ratio is constant;
- wages keep increasing;
- the rate of profit is constant; and
- the share of labor income in GDP is constant.

One can readily check that these properties are true in the case of the Ramsey growth model. It is interesting to understand why. The answer is that these properties only depend on the existence of a balanced-growth path, not on the specific behavior of consumers. Therefore, they hold for other models as well (such as the Diamond overlapping-generations model).

As noted in the preceding chapter, in such a path, $C$, $Y$, and $K$ must grow at a common rate $g$. The reason being that the equation for capital accumulation is $K_{t+1} = (1 - \delta)K_t + Y_t - C_t$, i.e., there is an additive relationship between these three variables. In a balanced-growth path

(BGP), each of these variables must by definition grow at a constant rate. For this relationship to hold at all dates, the growth rates of the three variables must be equal. With labor-augmenting technical progress, this common growth rate must in turn be equal to that of technology, $g$. With a production function $Y = F(K, AL)$,[1] because of constant returns to scale, to increase $K$ and $Y$ by the same proportional amount, $A$ must also grow by that amount.

It is then easy to check all the "Kaldor stylized facts." In particular, along the BGP wages are given by

$$w = \frac{\partial F}{\partial L} = AF_2'(K, AL).$$

Because of constant returns, we have $F(K, AL) = ALf(K/AL)$, and $F_2' = f(K/AL) - (K/AL)f'(K/AL)$. Hence, $f_2'$ only depends on the ratio $K/AL$, which is constant in a BGP. Consequently, wages are proportional to $A$ and grow at rate $g$. The other stylized facts can be checked in a similar fashion.

In a BGP, therefore, technical progress is associated with growing wages. One cannot therefore replicate a negative association between the two.

In this chapter, we come back to the neoclassical growth model, under assumptions that do not necessarily imply that there will be a BGP, and look for conditions under which technical progress might reduce wages.

Productivity is again thought of as a shift factor in the production function:

$$Y_t = \mathcal{F}(A_t, K_t, L_t),$$

where $Y_t$ is output at date $t$, $K_t$ is capital, $L_t$ is labor, and $A_t$ is technical progress. $\mathcal{F}$ has the standard properties—concavity and constant returns with respect to $K$ and $L$—and technical progress clearly must increase output to deserve its name:

$$\frac{\partial \mathcal{F}}{\partial A} > 0.$$

We make the following standard assumptions: the labor force is fixed, $L_t = L$; capital is accumulable but treated as fixed at any point in time; markets are competitive and they clear (i.e., supply equals demand); $A_t$ is an exogenous variable; and the price of output is normalized to 1. The first-order condition for labor demand determines the equilibrium wage:

$$\frac{\partial \mathcal{F}(A_t, K_t, L)}{\partial L} = w. \tag{2.1}$$

[1] If there is population growth, the same properties apply to per-capita growth, per-capita GDP, etc.

This basic formula allows us to discuss how technical progress affects wages. To analyze this, consider a once-and-for-all increase in $A$. Upon impact (i.e., at the exact time the shock occurs), $K$ is fixed, and the effect on wages is straightforwardly obtained from this formula. In the long run, $K$ adjusts through the response of savers to the shock. To take its effect on wages into account, it is useful to remember that because of constant returns and concavity, $\mathcal{F}''_{KL} > 0$; more capital always increases the marginal product of labor and hence the wage.[2]

## 2.1 The Short Run

First we discuss the impact of $A$ on wages when $K$ is held constant, and then we analyze how the conclusions can be altered by taking into account the adjustment of capital. Economists have traditionally made three assumptions about the way technical progress enters the production function:

(1) $A_t$ can be *output augmenting*, i.e., the production function is given by

$$Y_t = A_t F(K_t, L_t). \tag{2.2}$$

In this case, it is straightforward that, for a given value of $K_t$, technical progress increases wages.

(2) $A_t$ can be *capital augmenting*, i.e.,

$$Y_t = F(A_t K_t, L_t),$$

and an increase in $A$ is equivalent to an increase in $K$. Again, as $F_{KL} > 0$, wages must go up with $A$.

(3) $A_t$ can be *labor augmenting*, in which case we have

$$Y_t = F(K_t, A_t L_t),$$

so that $w = A_t F_2$, where $F_2$ is the derivative of $F$ with respect to its second argument. Here technical progress has two conflicting effects. First, it endows each worker with a greater amount of labor, in efficiency units. This effect tends to increase wages. Second, it increases the labor/capital

[2] A simple proof is as follows. Write down the Euler theorem for $\mathcal{F}$:

$$K\frac{\partial \mathcal{F}}{\partial K} + L\frac{\partial \mathcal{F}}{\partial L} = \mathcal{F}.$$

Differentiating both sides of this formula with respect to $L$ yields $\mathcal{F}_{KL} = -L(\mathcal{F}''_{LL}/K) > 0$.

ratio, expressed in efficiency units. That pushes labor down its marginal product curve, thus tending to reduce wages. Differentiating, we see that wages do fall if and only if

$$F_2' + ALF_{22}'' < 0.$$

If, for example, one has $F(K, AL) = K\varphi(AL/K)$, this is equivalent to

$$\frac{l\varphi''(l)}{\varphi'(l)} < -1$$

at $l = AL/K$, which states that the elasticity of the marginal product of labor with respect to $l$ must be larger than 1 in absolute value. If this condition holds, then the production function has such strong curvature (i.e., capital is strongly complementary to labor) that wages must fall for capital to absorb the increase in worker productivity. For example, with a CES production function given by

$$F(K, AL) = [K^{\varepsilon} + (AL)^{\varepsilon}]^{1/\varepsilon}, \quad -\infty < \varepsilon < 1,$$

we get that $\mathrm{d}w/\mathrm{d}A < 0$ if and only if

$$\varepsilon < -\left(\frac{AL}{K}\right)^{\varepsilon}.$$

Wages are more likely to fall with productivity, the more labor and capital are complementary ($\varepsilon$ negative), and the less capitalized the economy is ($(K/AL)$ small).

## 2.2 The Long Run

Let us now discuss the long-run effect of productivity, i.e., its effect on wages when capital is adjusted. As $\mathcal{F}_{KL}'' > 0$, capital adjustment tends to increase wages if capital goes up, and to reduce wages if it falls.

To analyze capital adjustment, we need a model of capital accumulation. Let us start with the Ramsey model, described in the preceding chapter. Assuming, for simplicity, that $A$ does not grow, in the long run the stock of capital will be such that its marginal product, net of depreciation, is equal to the consumer's rate of time preference, denoted by $\rho$. Assuming zero depreciation, we get that in the long run the capital stock adjusts so that

$$\frac{\partial \mathcal{F}(A, K, L)}{\partial K} = \rho. \tag{2.3}$$

Let us look again at our three specifications for technical progress.

(1) Under output-augmenting technical progress, the preceding formula is equivalent to

$$AF'_K(K,L) = \rho.$$

Clearly, as $F''_{KK} < 0$, an increase in $A$ is matched by an increase in $K$, which reinforces the initial increase in wages. Thus, the positive effect on wages is not overturned: wages actually rise more in the long run than in the short run.

(2) Under capital-augmenting technical progress, we now have

$$AF'_1(AK,L) = \rho.$$

Differentiating, we get

$$\mathrm{d}K = -\frac{F'_1 + AKF''_{11}}{A^2F''_{11}}\,\mathrm{d}A \lesseqgtr 0.$$

Capital now need not go up. The reason is similar to the analysis of wages in the labor-augmenting case: if complementarities are strong, then technical progress, which increases the total number of efficiency units of capital, will, when all effects are taken into account, reduce its marginal product. In order to restore equilibrium, savers will gradually reduce the capital stock, so as to bring the marginal product in line with the rate of time preference. Therefore, if complementarities are strong, the response of the capital stock runs counter to (and potentially overturns) the impact effect of productivity on wages. Otherwise, the impact effect is reinforced. An obvious question is now, can wages fall in the long run? To answer it, we need to fully differentiate wages with respect to $A$:

$$\begin{aligned}\frac{\mathrm{d}w}{\mathrm{d}A} &= F''_{12}\left(A\frac{\mathrm{d}K}{\mathrm{d}A} + K\right)\\ &= -\frac{F'_1F''_{12}}{AF''_{11}} > 0.\end{aligned}$$

Therefore, any fall in the capital stock cannot be strong enough to reduce wages in the long run. The reason being that total capital in efficiency units, $AK$, has to go up; otherwise, the marginal product of capital would go up in the long run—as there are fewer efficiency units of capital, while each piece of capital embodies more efficiency units—which is incompatible with the Ramsey condition (2.3). And the rise in $AK$ increases the marginal product of labor.

(3) Under labor-augmenting technical progress, one has $F_1'(K, AL) = \rho$, so that

$$\frac{\mathrm{d}K}{\mathrm{d}A} = -\frac{LF_{12}''}{F_{11}''} > 0.$$

The impact effect of $A$ is to raise the marginal product of capital; thus $K$ increases in the long run. Can this offset any potential short-run fall in wages? The answer is yes. To see this, compute $\mathrm{d}w/\mathrm{d}A$ again:

$$\begin{aligned}\frac{\mathrm{d}w}{\mathrm{d}A} &= (F_2' + ALF_{22}'') + AF_{12}''\frac{\mathrm{d}K}{\mathrm{d}A} \\ &= F_2' + AL\frac{F_{22}''F_{11}'' - (F_{12}'')^2}{F_{11}} \\ &= F_2' = \frac{w}{A} > 0,\end{aligned}$$

as the term $F_{22}F_{11} - F_{12}^2$ must be equal to zero because of constant returns to scale.[3] Thus, in the long run, wages go up proportionally to the increase in productivity. This is because capital must adjust proportionally too, as $K/AL$ must be unchanged for the Ramsey condition to hold. With the same capital–labor ratio in efficiency units, the wage per efficiency unit is unchanged, and the wage per unit of labor increases in proportion to $A$. We have just rediscovered the standard property that with labor-augmenting technical progress there exists a BGP where capital, wages, and other variables grow at a common rate, equal to the growth rate of $A$.

Therefore, in all three models wages must go up in the long run. This property is more general and must hold in the Ramsey model for any arbitrary specification of the production function $\mathcal{F}(A, K, L)$. This is because the wage $w$ and the interest rate $r$ must lie on the *factor-price frontier* (FPF), which is a downward-sloping relationship.

In the Ramsey model the long-run interest rate is pinned down; here we have $r = \rho$ in the long run. The wage is determined by the intersection between the FPF and a horizontal line at $r = \rho$ (figure 2.1). An increase in $A$ reduces costs: the $c(\cdot)$ function shifts down, and the FPF shifts out (figure 2.2). Wages must necessarily go up, regardless of the production function.

Wages could only fall in the long run if technical progress was associated with such a severe depletion in the capital stock that the required return to capital would go up by enough to offset the positive effects of technical change on wages (figure 2.3). For this to occur, we need a model

[3] To check this, differentiate the Euler condition $KF_1' + ALF_2' = F$ on both sides with respect to $AL$.

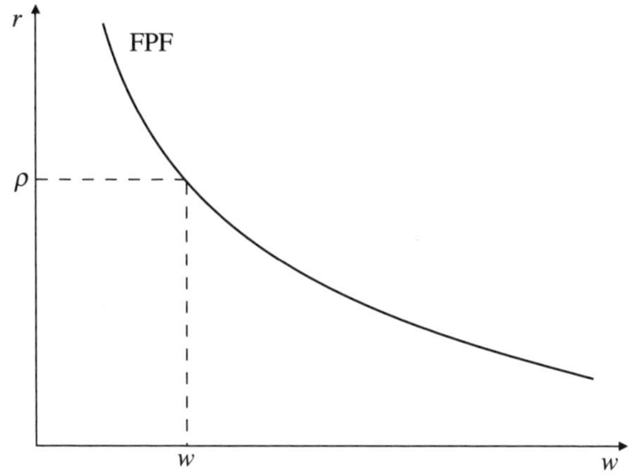


**Figure 2.1.** Long-run determination of wages in the Ramsey model.

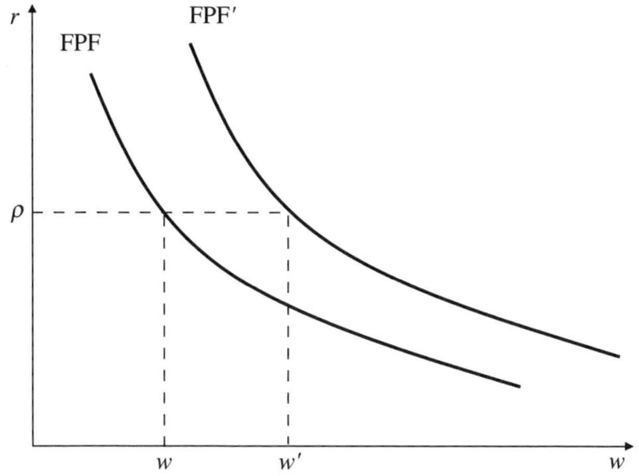


**Figure 2.2.** Long-run impact of technical progress on wages in the Ramsey model.

where an increase in the return to capital induces people to save less, i.e., where the "income effect" dominates the "substitution effect." This cannot happen in the Ramsey model, but it may happen in models where people have finite lives, such as the Diamond overlapping-generations model. In chapter 1 we have seen that capital is accumulated according to

$$K_{t+1} = w_t L s(r_{t+1}), \tag{2.4}$$

where $s$ is the savings function, defined as the share of savings out of total labor income $w_t L$, and $r_{t+1}$ is the rate of return to capital. Consider

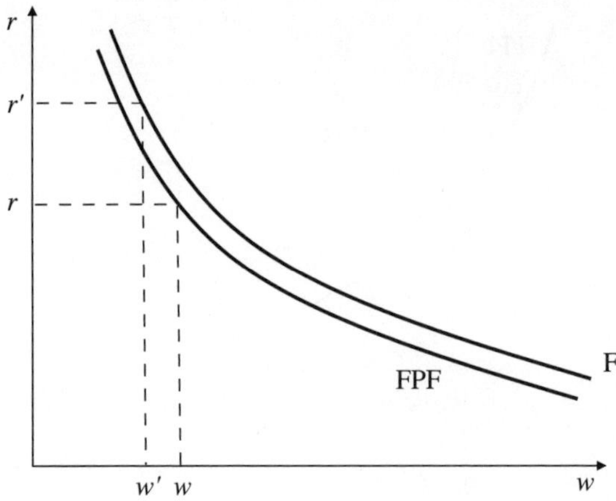


**Figure 2.3.** Wages may fall if the marginal product of capital goes up by a lot.

the case of output-augmenting technical progress, given by (2.2). Then,

$$r_{t+1} = A_{t+1} \frac{\partial F}{\partial K}(K_{t+1}, L). \tag{2.5}$$

In a steady state with constant $A$, $K$ and $w$ are also constant and are given by the following equations:

$$\begin{aligned} K &= wLs(r), \\ r &= AF'_K(K, L), \\ w &= AF'_L(K, L). \end{aligned}$$

Using these we can compute the full effect of $A$ on $w$:

$$\frac{\mathrm{d}w}{\mathrm{d}A} = \frac{F'_L(1 - Aws'LF''_{KK}) + AF''_{KL}F'_K ws'L}{1 - Aws'LF''_{KK} - AsLF''_{KL}}.$$

It is easy to show that for the local dynamics around the steady state to be stable, the denominator must be positive, which in itself prevents the income effect from being too large.[4] However, one can construct examples where this stability condition holds, while the numerator is

[4] Differentiating (2.1)–(2.5) we find that

$$\frac{\mathrm{d}K_{t+1}}{\mathrm{d}K_t} = \frac{AF''_{KL}Ls}{1 - AwLs'F''_{KK}}.$$

Assume that the denominator is positive. We have that $\mathrm{d}K_{t+1}/\mathrm{d}K_t > 0$. Furthermore, $\mathrm{d}K_{t+1}/\mathrm{d}K_t$ is lower than 1 if and only if $1 - AwLs'F''_{KK} > AF''_{KL}Ls$.

The case $1 - AwLs'F''_{KK} < 0$ is intuitively unappealing, for the following reason. An increase in the expected rate of return on capital would then trigger such a strong reduction in savings that the expected return would go up by even more. In other words, the intra-period determination of $r_{t+1}$ and $K_{t+1}$ would be unstable in the "eductive" sense (see Guesnerie 2005).

negative. One may check that this is the case by constructing a steady state with $F(K,L) = \sqrt{KL}$, $K = L = 1$, $s(r) = \frac{1}{2} + \gamma(1 - r)$ *locally*, $A = 2$, $r = w = 1$, for $1 < \gamma < \frac{3}{2}$.

Of course, this mechanism of very strong income effects is not very appealing: most economists would not find it plausible.

## 2.3 Conclusion

The standard neoclassical growth model with homogeneous labor leaves very little room for technical progress to reduce wages. The reason being that the economy must lie on the FPF and that technical progress moves that frontier up. Wages can fall only if there is a very strong increase in the rate of return to capital. This may occur under two circumstances:

- In the long run, if savings fall very drastically in response to the initial increase in the rate of return to capital.
- In the short run, if there are very strong complementarities between labor and capital and if technology is labor augmenting. In such a case, the economy moves up and to the left along the new FPF. But, in the Ramsey model, that move is defeated in the long run as savers respond to the initial increase in the rate of return by accumulating more capital.

# 3
# Heterogeneous Labor

If it is difficult for technology to reduce wages in a world of homogeneous labor, can it reduce the wages of *some* workers? To answer this question, we need to extend the neoclassical growth model to take into account heterogeneity among workers.

## 3.1 Skill-Biased Technical Progress

A simple way to introduce labor heterogeneity is to assume that there are two types of workers, skilled and unskilled. We denote by $H$ and $L$ the total supply of skilled and unskilled labor, and assume that these are fixed (we shall relax that assumption in chapter 5 when dealing with supply responses). The production function can now be written as

$$Y = \mathcal{F}(K, H, L; A).$$

With three inputs in the production function, the FPF is no longer a curve in a two-dimensional space. Rather, it is now a surface in a three-dimensional space (figure 3.1). Its equation is

$$\tilde{c}(r, w, \omega; A) = 1,$$

where $\tilde{c}(\cdot)$ is the cost function, $r$ the rate of return to capital, $w$ the wage of the unskilled, and $\omega$ the wage of skilled labor.

Assume that we are again in the context of the Ramsey growth model, and that capital is accumulated up to the point where its marginal product is equal to the rate of time preference $\rho$. Then this condition no longer pins down the equilibrium wage. Rather, it constrains $w$ and $\omega$ to lie on a "partial" FPF, which is the intersection between the FPF and the plane defined by $r = \rho$ (figure 3.2).

How are $w$ and $\omega$ determined on this locus? We know from chapter 1 that the demand for unskilled labor relative to skilled labor, at the optimum factor mix, is given by $c_w/c_\omega$. Equilibrium between supply and demand in factor markets then requires that

$$\frac{c_w}{c_\omega} = \frac{L}{H}. \tag{3.1}$$

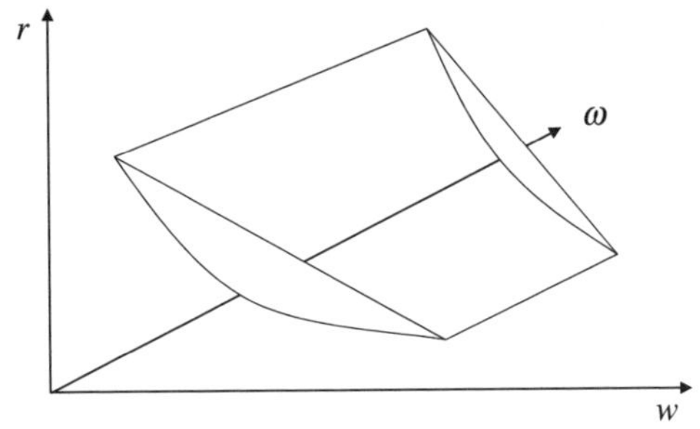


**Figure 3.1.** The FPF with three factors.

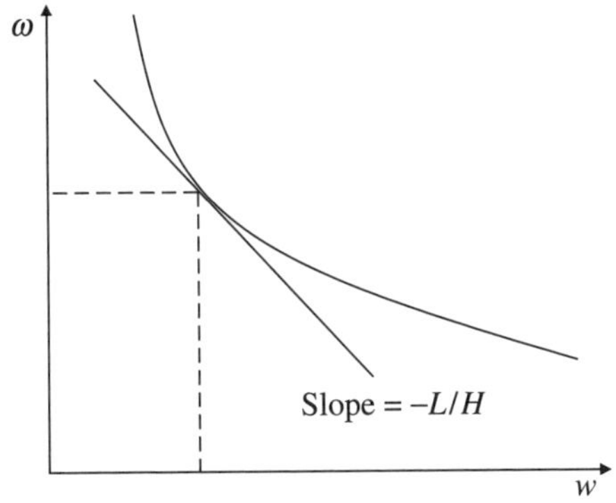


**Figure 3.2.** The partial FPF: the relationship between $w$ and $\omega$ for a given $r$.

This condition is illustrated in figure 3.2: the slope of the partial FPF must be equal to the $L/H$ ratio. As the FPF is convex, the smaller this ratio, the greater $w$ and the smaller $\omega$.

Again, technical change shifts the FPF, and thus the partial FPF, out. Consequently, the wages of at least one category of worker must go up.

In figure 3.3 we depict the case in which the wages of both categories of workers go up. Such a case would prevail if technical change had a small impact on the marginal rate of substitution between skilled and unskilled labor. Only a small change in the wage ratio $w/\omega$ is required for the relative demand for unskilled workers to remain equal to the relative supply, $L/H$. And for that ratio not to change too much, both wages must go up.

An important special case obtains if the partial FPF shifts homothetically as $A$ goes up, i.e., $c_w/c_\omega$ depends only on $w/\omega$. This case prevails when $H$ and $L$ enter the production function through a constant-returns labor aggregate, which is *independent* of $A$. In such a case the production function can be written as

$$\mathcal{F}(K, L, H; A) = F(K, \Phi(L, H); A).$$

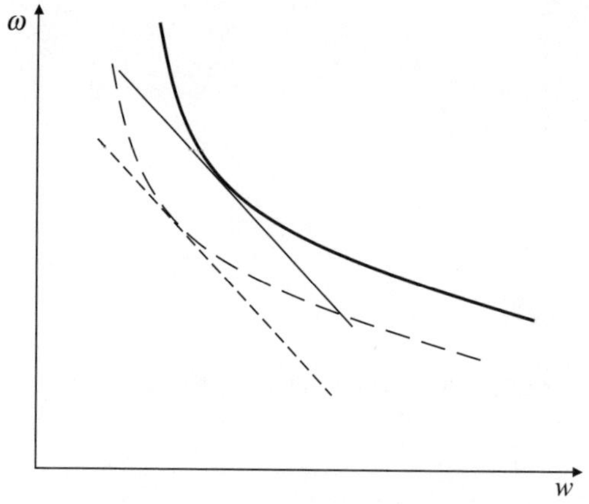


**Figure 3.3.** Technical change with little bias: both wages increase.

The cost function associated with $\mathcal{F}$ is

$$\tilde{c}(r, w, \omega; A) = c(r, c_\Phi(w, \omega); A),$$

where $c_\Phi$ is the cost function associated with production function $\Phi(\cdot)$ and $c(r, p_X; A)$ is the cost function associated with production function $F(K, X; A)$, where $p_X$ is the price of the composite labor input $X$. The partial FPF equation $\tilde{c}(\rho, w, \omega; A) = c(\rho, c_\Phi; A) = 1$ pins down the value of $c_\Phi$ as a function $\varphi(\rho, A)$, $\varphi_1' < 0$, $\varphi_2' > 0$. Thus, the partial FPF is characterized by

$$c_\Phi(w, \omega) = \varphi(\rho, A).$$

Because of constant returns to scale in $\Phi$, $c_\Phi$ is homothetic; consequently, $c_{\Phi w}/c_{\Phi\omega}$ depends only on $w/\omega$. This ratio is therefore pinned down by (3.1) and a shift in $A$ cannot affect it. Technical progress must therefore increase the wages of each type of worker by the same amount.

A further special case is when capital is absent from the production, $L$ and $H$ are the only inputs, and technical progress is output augmenting. Again, both wages must then increase proportionally to $A$.

In general, though, one cannot rule out a negative effect of an increase in $A$ on either $w$ or $\omega$. Figure 3.4 depicts a case where technical change reduces the wage of the unskilled. The partial FPF shifts up but becomes much flatter at the initial $w/\omega$ ratio. The marginal rate of substitution between skilled and unskilled workers falls sharply; to restore equilibrium, $w$ must fall in both relative and absolute terms. This is what is referred to as "skill-biased technical change."

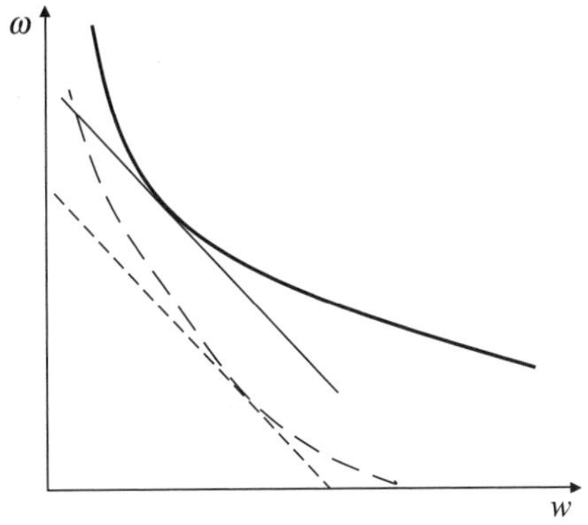


**Figure 3.4.** Technical progress with a strong bias against unskilled workers: $w$ falls.

## 3.2 Capital–Skill Complementarity

Skill-biased technical change occurs when the marginal product of skilled labor rises more than that of unskilled labor (and the latter may even fall, as we have just seen). That is, technology is complementary with skilled labor and substitute with unskilled labor. An appealing specification, as proposed by Krusell et al. (2000), who build on Stokey (1996), is to assume that capital and unskilled labor are substitutes, that they are both complements to skilled labor, and that $A$ is capital augmenting:

$$Y = F(AK + L, H). \tag{3.2}$$

For example, if $K$ represents "computers" and $L$ "secretaries," I can either ask my secretary to type my papers or type them myself. As word processors are more efficient (automatic spelling correction, handling of mathematical formulas, graphics, font choice, translation, etc.), $A$ goes up and a computer gives me more secretarial services. Either way, whether these services come from my computer or from my secretary, both output and my productivity as an economist go up when I use more secretarial services.

Under this specification, technical change unambiguously reduces the wages of unskilled workers in the short run, when $K$ is held constant. The first-order conditions for optimization are

$$\left.\begin{aligned} r &= \frac{\partial F}{\partial K} = AF_1'(AK + L, H), \\ w &= \frac{\partial F}{\partial L} = F_1'(AK + L, H), \\ \omega &= \frac{\partial F}{\partial H} = F_2'(AK + L, H). \end{aligned}\right\} \tag{3.3}$$

Clearly, $\mathrm{d}w/\mathrm{d}A = KF_{11}'' < 0$. Improvements in word processing reduce the marginal product of secretaries by making the total supply of word processing services more abundant, and reduce their wages, which, under standard assumptions, would even tend to zero as $A$ tends to infinity.

The same occurs if $K$ goes up: capital accumulation harms substitute workers just like capital-augmenting technical progress does. This means that it is possible for inequality to go up even though there is no shift in the production function, just a change in the input mix. In a two-factor model, for the skill premium to go up without technical change, skilled labor must become scarcer relative to unskilled labor. This is empirically implausible since the trend in all developed countries is for more people to acquire higher education. In a three-factor model, however, the skill premium increases with the stock of capital if it is complementary with skilled labor and substitute with unskilled labor.

What happens in the long run? Capital adjusts so that $r = \rho$. Depending on the elasticity of $F_1$ with respect to $AK$,[1] $K$ may go either up or down with $A$. If it goes up, $w$ falls more in the long run than in the short run. If it does not, $w$ falls less in the long run, but still falls: one must have $w = r/A = \rho/A$. In the long run, the wages of unskilled workers fall *proportionally* to $A$. Because of perfect substitutability between unskilled labor and capital, the marginal product of unskilled labor must be equal to that of capital divided by the productivity of capital. But the response of savers prevents the marginal product of capital from increasing beyond $\rho$ in the long run; therefore, there is no hope of the unskilled being compensated for the negative impact effect of technical progress on their productivity by capital scarcity.

In their empirical work, Krusell et al. (2000) estimate a different production function from (3.2), given by[2]

$$Y = A(\theta L^{\sigma} + (1-\theta)(\lambda K^{\varepsilon} + (1-\lambda)H^{\varepsilon})^{\sigma/\varepsilon})^{1/\sigma}. \tag{3.4}$$

Note that here capital and skilled labor are combined into a composite input, while in (3.2) capital is combined with unskilled labor. In (3.4), capital is complementary with skill provided $\varepsilon < \sigma$. Krusell et al. argue that this way of nesting the three inputs is empirically more plausible than

[1] Differentiating, we get

$$\frac{\mathrm{d}K}{\mathrm{d}A} = -\frac{F_1'}{A^2 F_{11}''} - \frac{K}{A}.$$

That is, $\mathrm{d}K/\mathrm{d}A > 0$ if and only if $|AKF_{11}''/F_1'| > 1$.

[2] Their specification is actually more complex, as it distinguishes between structures and equipment capital. We ignore this distinction here.

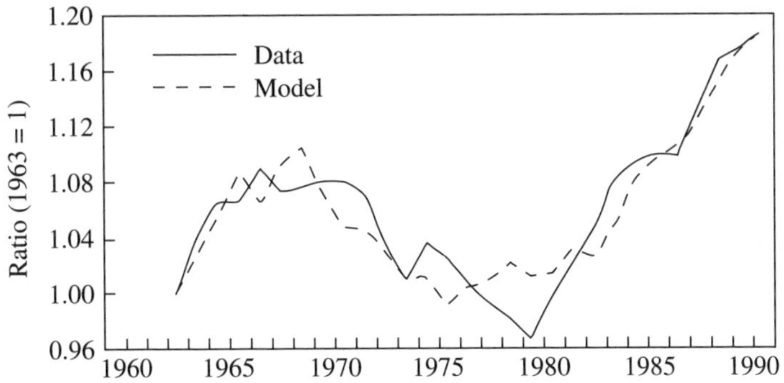


**Figure 3.5.** Actual versus matched skill premium in the Krusell et al. model. *Source*: Krusell et al. (2000). © The Econometric Society.

having a composite of raw labor and capital. This is somewhat surprising, intuitively: the specification in (3.2) suggests that skilled workers may either use a computer or a secretary as complementary inputs, or indeed a combination of the two—they may use their computer for word processing and their secretary to purchase air tickets, for example. By contrast, the specification in (3.4) suggests that one may undertake the same tasks (if $\sigma = 1$), or at least "similar tasks" (if $\sigma < 1$), with either raw labor or a combination of skilled labor and capital.

Krusell et al. then estimate the parameters in (3.4) by using the first-order conditions for optimization—that is, the equivalent of (3.3), with U.S. time-series data. Their estimates are $\varepsilon = -0.5$ and $\sigma = 0.4$, which imply substantial complementarity between skill and capital, and substitutability between unskilled labor and capital. Furthermore, their model does quite well at tracking the evolution of the skill premium in the United States over the 1962–92 period, as shown in figure 3.5, which is borrowed from Krusell et al.'s paper. This means that instead of ascribing the rise in inequality to a shift in the production function, they are able to explain it solely by the changes in the input mix. According to their results, the driving force for the increase in inequality is the sharp increase in (quality-adjusted) equipment investment starting in 1975.[3] This does not mean, however, that technical progress is not at the root of the phenomenon. Rather, it means that what has improved is the technology for producing capital goods (measured in units of "quality"),[4] an important fraction of which is computers, rather than the technology for

[3] Goldin and Katz (1998) present historical evidence of capital–skill complementarity, arguing that the phenomenon is quite general.

[4] An alternative source of growth in equipment capital could be a drop in global real interest rates and/or an increase in the U.S. national savings rate. Such changes are not observed during the relevant period.

producing the final goods. The increase in the skill premium is the joint result of the technology-driven fall in the relative price of capital goods and of the fact that these goods are complementary with skilled labor in the production of final goods.

## 3.3 Unbalanced Growth

Similar issues of complementarity and substitutability arise in a two-sector model in which labor cannot relocate between sectors in the short run. A productivity shock in one sector but not the other will always increase inequality upon impact. Furthermore, if complementarities in demand are sufficient between the two sectors, real wages may well fall in the sector in which productivity increases. These issues have been analyzed by Baumol (1967); here we reconsider them with an emphasis on complementarities, labor adjustment costs, and the distribution of earnings.

Consider the following simple, static model, based on Cohen and Saint-Paul (1994). There is a continuum of goods, indexed by $j \in [0,1]$. All agents have the same homothetic utility given by

$$U = \left[\int_0^1 x_j^{\varepsilon}\,\mathrm{d}j\right]^{1/\varepsilon},$$

with $-\infty < \varepsilon \leqslant 1$. Each good is produced with a linear production function $y_j = a_j l_j$, where $l_j$ is labor employed in sector $j$. Maximization of utility implies that (for any consumer) the ratio of marginal utilities is equal to the price ratio:

$$\frac{x_i^{\varepsilon-1}}{x_j^{\varepsilon-1}} = \frac{p_i}{p_j},$$

where $p_j$ is the price of good $j$. Competition among firms implies that

$$p_j = \frac{w_j}{a_j}, \tag{3.5}$$

where $w_j$ is the wage in sector $j$. As labor is not perfectly mobile across sectors, wages potentially differ. Equilibrium in goods markets implies that $y_j$ is the sum of the $x_j$s across consumers. Since $x_i/x_j = (p_i/p_j)^{-1/(1-\varepsilon)}$ is the same across consumers, this common ratio is also equal to $y_i/y_j$. Hence,

$$\frac{y_i}{y_j} = \frac{a_i l_i}{a_j l_j} = \left(\frac{w_i a_j}{w_j a_i}\right)^{-1/(1-\varepsilon)}.$$

This, for a given distribution of the $l_j$s, allows us to compute any relative wage $w_i/w_j$:

$$\frac{w_i}{w_j} = \left(\frac{l_i}{l_j}\right)^{-1/\eta} \left(\frac{a_i}{a_j}\right)^{(\eta-1)/\eta}, \tag{3.6}$$

where $\eta = 1/(1-\varepsilon)$ is the elasticity of substitution between the two goods. This expression, which we will discuss shortly, determines relative wages. What about absolute wages? In order to express them in terms of utility, we normalize the price of the aggregate basket of goods to 1. Using equations (1.17) and (3.5) we obtain

$$\begin{aligned} 1 &= \int_0^1 p_j^{1-\eta}\,\mathrm{d}j \\ &= \int_0^1 w_j^{1-\eta} a_j^{\eta-1}\,\mathrm{d}j. \end{aligned} \tag{3.7}$$

Substituting (3.6) into (3.7) we can solve for absolute wages:

$$w_i = a_i^{(\eta-1)/\eta} l_i^{-1/\eta} \left(\int_0^1 (a_j l_j)^{(\eta-1)/\eta}\,\mathrm{d}j\right)^{1/(\eta-1)}. \tag{3.8}$$

### 3.3.1 The Long Run

We are now able to discuss the effect of technical change on living standards. In this subsection, we focus on the long run, i.e., a situation where labor is perfectly mobile across sectors, so that wages are equalized. Substituting $w_i = w_j$ into (3.6) we get

$$\frac{l_i}{l_j} = \left(\frac{a_i}{a_j}\right)^{\eta-1}. \tag{3.9}$$

An implication of this is that if goods are substitutes ($\eta > 1$), more productive sectors employ more workers; the increase in demand associated with a fall in prices is larger, proportionally, than the fall in prices. Hence, when productivity grows, demand grows by more than productivity, so employment goes up. The opposite occurs if goods are complements ($\eta < 1$). More productive sectors employ fewer people; otherwise, their price would have to fall below the cost of labor for the market to absorb their extra output.

To proceed, we simply assume full employment and normalize the workforce to 1:

$$\int_0^1 l_j\,\mathrm{d}j = 1.$$

Substituting (3.9) into this formula, we can get the employment level in each sector:

$$l_i = \frac{a_i^{\eta-1}}{\int_0^1 a_j^{\eta-1}\,\mathrm{d}j}. \tag{3.10}$$

This long-run equilibrium distribution of employment may be substituted into (3.8) to get the equilibrium wage:

$$w_i = w = \left( \int_0^1 a_j^{\eta} \, \mathrm{d}j \right)^{1/\eta}.$$

Clearly, this is an increasing function of all the $a_j$s: technical progress raises living standards regardless of how it is distributed across sectors.

### 3.3.2 The Short Run

We now consider the short run, assuming that labor cannot be reallocated across sectors upon the impact of a productivity shock. To compute the effect of technical change on the distribution of wages, we can just use equation (3.8), taking the $l_j$s as exogenous.

Consider first an equiproportional improvement in productivity such that all the $a_j$s are multiplied by the same factor $\gamma$. Clearly, (3.8) implies that all wages are multiplied by $\gamma$. Technical progress benefits all workers proportionally if it is symmetrical across sectors. Furthermore, if the economy was in a long-run equilibrium, then it is still there, as the corresponding allocation of labor, given by (3.10), does not depend on $\gamma$. Wages remain equal across sectors and go up by a factor $\gamma$.

Now assume that technical progress is asymmetrical; to simplify, assume that only an infinitesimal interval of sectors $\mathrm{d}j$ around some value of $j$ have their productivity multiplied by $\gamma$. Because only an infinitesimal number of sectors are affected, the term $(\int_0^1 (a_j l_j)^{(\eta-1)/\eta} \, \mathrm{d}j)^{1/(\eta-1)}$ in equation (3.8) only changes infinitesimally. For the sectors that experience technical progress, all that matters is the change in the term $a_j^{(\eta-1)/\eta} l_j^{-1/\eta}$. Therefore,

- if the goods are substitutes ($\eta > 1$), workers in these sectors experience an increase in wages, and are therefore better-off;
- if the goods are complements ($\eta < 1$), wages fall in the sectors where productivity goes up.

We therefore again have a case where technical progress can reduce wages. Here it reduces wages *in the sector where it takes place*, provided there is *sufficient complementarity between this sector and other sectors* and provided that *workers cannot move from this sector to other sectors.*

Upon impact, prices would have to fall proportionally to the increase in $a_j$ to maintain constant wages. Because of complementarities, however, such a fall would trigger an increase in demand less than proportional to the increase in $a_j$. To maintain equilibrium, either employment has to fall—but that is ruled out by the fact that labor cannot relocate to other sectors—or prices have to fall further below that level, which can only take place if wages fall.

What happens to workers in other sectors? Their wages only change infinitesimally, due to the term $(\int_0^1 (a_j l_j)^{(\eta-1)/\eta}\,\mathrm{d}j)^{1/(\eta-1)}$. This quantity is increasing in the $a_j$s regardless of the value of $\eta$. Thus, other workers benefit from technical progress whether the goods are complements or substitutes. This is because they can buy the goods whose productivity has gone up at a lower price.

If goods are substitutes, all workers gain from asymmetric technical progress. If they are complements, those working in the sectors that experience the shock lose, while the others gain. There is a consensus in favor of technical progress, regardless of how asymmetric it is, in the substitutes case. By contrast, uneven technical progress is a source of conflict in the complements case.

*Relative* inequality always goes up if one starts from a long-run equilibrium, since wages are equalized in such an equilibrium. A wider distribution of wages gives the right signal to induce labor to migrate to the sectors where its use is economically most beneficial. Under substitutability, these are the sectors whose productivity has improved. Under complementarity, labor must move to the sectors where productivity has not improved.

## 3.4 Conclusion

The general theme of this chapter is that a type of labor can lose from technical progress if it is complementary with another type of labor that becomes neither more productive nor more abundant. This is what happens in the Cohen and Saint-Paul model, where, when $\eta < 1$, the negative effect of complementarities on the sector's relative price is stronger than the direct positive effect of greater productivity. In the Krusell et al. model, things are even worse for unskilled workers: instead of being pushed down their marginal product schedule by a shift that raises their own productivity, the driving force is a change in the productivity (or the amount) of a substitute input. Thus, unskilled workers bear the full costs of an increase in the supply of the tasks they perform, without being compensated by an increase in their own productivity.

# 4
# Competing Technologies

In the preceding chapter, we saw how technical progress can shift the production function in such a way that it reduces the marginal productivity of unskilled workers while increasing that of skilled workers. In that framework, the new production function replaces the old one. This chapter considers an alternative route: what if one can continue to use the old technology instead of the new one?

It may be that the new technology is so productive that the old technology is certain to be abandoned. If this is so, we are back to the analysis of the preceding chapter. This will be the case if the new technology (with cost function $c_{\mathrm{N}}(r, w, \omega)$) entirely dominates the old one (with cost function $c_{\mathrm{O}}(r, w, \omega) > c_{\mathrm{N}}$). In this case, the FPF corresponding to the new technology must lie above that corresponding to the old technology. The economy cannot lie on the two frontiers at the same time, meaning that one of the two technologies must be abandoned. It must be the old one, otherwise one could make strictly positive profits by using the new technology with the factor prices associated with the old technology, as we showed in chapter 1 when discussing figure 1.1.

Therefore, in this chapter we analyze how the distribution of income evolves when the two technologies are simultaneously in use. This pattern can arise under two circumstances:

- The new technology dominates the old one, but transferring inputs from one technology to another is costly; therefore, the old technology is still in use, at least in the short run.
- The new technology does not totally dominate the old one, it dominates it only for some input mixes. Depending on the economy's factor endowment, one may use the old technology, the new technology, or both.

We analyze these two cases in turn. A key message is that despite the fact that people go on using the old technology, some workers may experience an absolute wage loss as a result of the introduction of the new technology. The reason for this is that those workers who remain in the old technology work with a lower amount of complementary factors (such as capital), which reduces their productivity.

## 4.1 Learning the New Technology Is Costly

Following Caselli (1999), let us assume that learning the new technology is costly and that workers differ in their learning cost. At the same time, let us assume that capital can be relocated between the two technologies at no cost.

There are two factors of production: capital and labor. At a given date $t$, the supply of capital $K_t$ is given, and there are $L$ workers, each endowed with one unit of labor. Initially, the production function is

$$Y = A_0 K^{\alpha} L^{1-\alpha},$$

where $A_0$ is total factor productivity in the old technology. If the old technology prevails, the wage is given by

$$w = \frac{\partial Y}{\partial L} = (1-\alpha) A_0 \left(\frac{K}{L}\right)^{\alpha}$$

and the return to capital by

$$r = \frac{\partial Y}{\partial L} = \alpha A_0 \left(\frac{K}{L}\right)^{-(1-\alpha)}.$$

Consider a "technological revolution": one may now also use a new technology to produce the good. The new technology allows us to produce according to

$$Y = A_1 K^{\alpha} L^{1-\alpha},$$

with $A_1 > A_0$. Note that the new technology entirely dominates the old one: one produces more for the same input mix. Furthermore, the new technology is "unbiased": the ratio of marginal products is unchanged for the same input mix. Consequently, in the absence of mobility costs, all factors would switch from the old technology to the new technology, and wages and the rate of return to capital would both increase proportionally to $A_1/A_0$. In the long run, more capital would be accumulated, thus further raising wages.

Assume now that workers need to pay a training cost $e$ in order to be able to work with the new technology. Assume that $e$ is distributed among workers with cumulative distribution function (c.d.f.) $G(e)$. Clearly, if $G$ has full support over $[0, +\infty)$, some workers will work with the new technology and others with the old technology. Therefore, both technologies will simultaneously be in use. There will be a critical learning cost $e^*$ such that workers are employed in the new technology, if and only if $e < e^*$. It must be that

$$w_1 - w_0 = e^*, \tag{4.1}$$

where $w_i$ is the wage earned by workers who use technology $i$. Therefore, there will be $L_1 = G(e^*)L$ workers in the new technology and $L_0 = (1 - G(e^*))L$ workers will remain in the old technology. The corresponding allocation of capital between the two technologies is determined by the equilibrium requirement that it yield the same return in both:

$$\begin{aligned} r &= r_1 \\ &= \alpha A_1 \left( \frac{K_1}{LG(e^*)} \right)^{-(1-\alpha)} \\ &= r_0 \\ &= \alpha A_0 \left( \frac{K - K_1}{L(1 - G(e^*))} \right)^{-(1-\alpha)}, \end{aligned}$$

where we have used the condition that $K_0 + K_1 = K$. An important aspect of the model is that capital is perfectly mobile between the two sectors, while labor is not. The returns to capital must be equalized, but the wages need not be. More generally, the results remain qualitatively valid to the extent that capital remains more mobile than labor.

The model is completed by writing down the marginal product conditions for labor:

$$w_1 = (1 - \alpha)A_1 \left( \frac{K_1}{LG(e^*)} \right)^{\alpha}, \tag{4.2}$$

$$w_0 = (1 - \alpha)A_0 \left( \frac{K - K_1}{L(1 - G(e^*))} \right)^{\alpha}. \tag{4.3}$$

The preceding set of equations allows us to compute the endogenous variables $w_1$, $w_0$, $r$, $K_1$, and $e^*$.

### 4.1.1 Effects on the Distribution of Income

The question of interest is, how does the introduction of the new technology affect the distribution of income? Here, the only dimension of inequality is that between those workers who adopt the new technology and those who do not. We already know, from (4.1), that the former earn more, since they need to be compensated for the training cost. A more interesting question is, can it be that workers who still work with the old technology earn less than they would in the absence of the new technology?

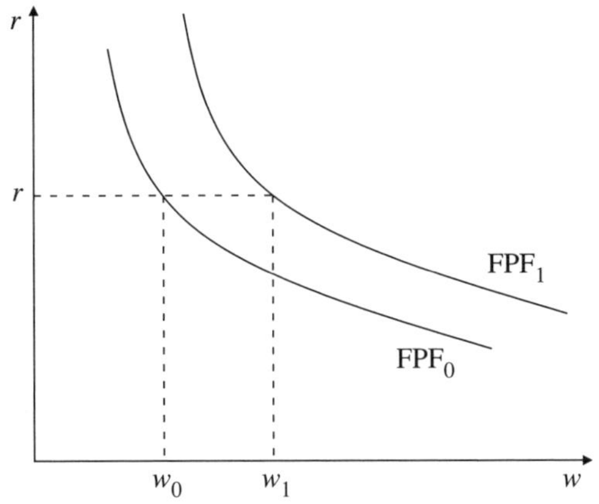


**Figure 4.1.** The determination of wages in each technology.

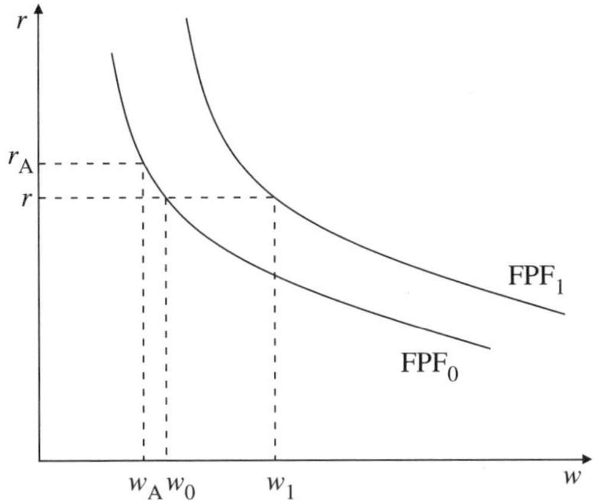


**Figure 4.2.** Configuration I: both wages go up.

The answer is that this will indeed be the case. This can be checked algebraically, but it is better to use a graphical argument, which is illustrated in figures 4.1–4.4. Because capital is mobile between the two sectors, there is a single rate of return $r$ in the economy. The wage in technology $i$ is then determined by the intersection of a horizontal line at $r$ with the corresponding FPF (figure 4.1). In the absence of the new technology, there is a single wage $w_{\mathrm{A}}$ determined by the intersection of the FPF for technology 0 and the horizontal line at the corresponding rate of return, called $r_{\mathrm{A}}$.

There are three possible configurations: (i) $r$ falls and both wages increase (figure 4.2); (ii) $r > r_{\mathrm{A}}$ and $w_0 < w_1 < w_{\mathrm{A}}$ (figure 4.3); (iii) $r > r_{\mathrm{A}}$ and $w_0 < w_{\mathrm{A}} < w_1$ (figure 4.4).

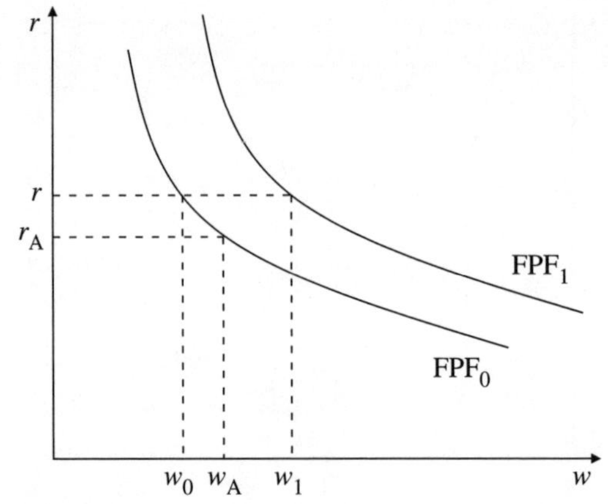


**Figure 4.3.** Configuration II: wage divergence.

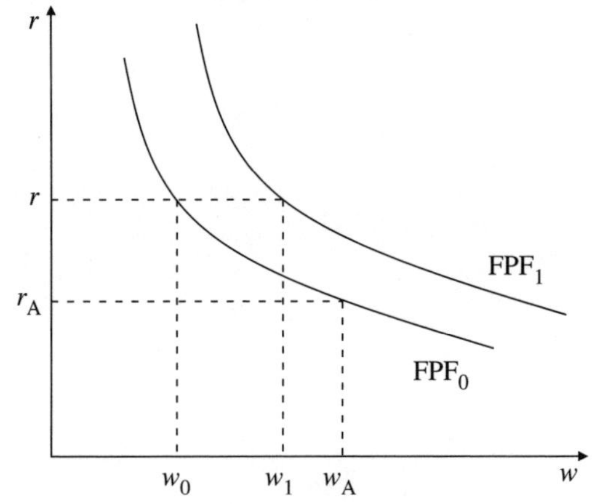


**Figure 4.4.** Configuration III: both wages fall.

Let us show that only case (iii) is relevant. Suppose first that $r < r_A$. Then it must be the case that

$$\frac{K - K_1}{L(1 - G(e^*))} > \frac{K}{L}.$$

As technology 0 is used in both cases, the only way for the technological revolution to reduce $r$ is by increasing the capital–labor ratio in technology 0. Then, since the economy-wide capital–labor ratio is unchanged, it must be the case that

$$\frac{K_1}{LG(e^*)} < \frac{K}{L},$$

which, as $A_1 > A_0$, clearly implies that $r_1 > r_A$; this contradicts the equilibrium condition that $r_1 = r_0 = r$.

Let us now rule out case (ii) in the same fashion. For the revolution to reduce wages in technology 0, the capital–labor ratio must fall. Consequently, the ratio must go up in technology 1, which, along with the fact that $A_1 > A_0$, implies that $w_1 > w_A$.

To conclude, the technological revolution necessarily reduces wages for those workers who still use technology 0 and necessarily increases them for those workers who use technology 1. Note, however, that workers who use technology 1 have to pay the training cost, so their net welfare does not necessarily increase. We return to this later.

How can we explain this diverging pattern? The explanation is as follows. Because the new technology is more productive, it generates a greater return to capital, for the same capital–labor ratio, than the old technology. It will therefore attract more capital up to an equilibrium point such that

$$\frac{K_1}{LG(e^*)} > \frac{K}{L} > \frac{K - K_1}{L(1 - G(e^*))}.$$

In this equilibrium, workers in technology 0 work with less capital; their marginal product is lower, and so is their wage. The technological revolution has sucked capital out of the old technology into the more profitable new technology. The effect on inequality is greater, the greater $\alpha$ is, i.e., the greater the common capital intensity of the two technologies. To see this, simply note that the relative wage must be equal to

$$\frac{w_1}{w_0} = \left(\frac{A_1}{A_0}\right)^{1/(1-\alpha)} = \psi. \tag{4.4}$$

The relative wage only depends on the relative productivity level $A_1/A_0$. This is because capital is mobile between the two technologies, and because the intensity of capital $\alpha$ is the same. The FPF for technology 1 is homothetic to that of technology 0, so that equating the return to capital between the two determines the wage ratio. If the relative wage were, say, lower than the right-hand side of (4.4), the return to capital would necessarily be higher in technology 1; capital would flow there, thus depressing wages in technology 0 and raising them in technology 1, until equilibrium condition (4.4) is restored.

As (4.4) makes clear, the greater $\alpha$ is, the more sensitive the relative wage is to relative total factor productivity $A_1/A_0$. This is not surprising: the greater $\alpha$ is, the lower the effect of capital reallocation between the two technologies on the rate of return differential, and the greater the response of the allocation of capital to productivity differences. In the extreme case where $\alpha = 0$ (no capital), inequality goes up but there is no fall in the wages of those who go on using the old technology.

### 4.1.2 Welfare: Can All Workers Lose?

We have seen that workers with a high learning cost stay in the old technology and unambiguously experience a wage fall. While those who move to the new technology gain in terms of wages, they do have to pay the learning cost. It follows that these workers, if their learning cost is close to the critical level $e^*$, will also lose from the technological revolution. Winners must have a learning cost sufficiently below $e^*$. Under our assumption that $G$ has full support, there will always be winners—those with a learning cost sufficiently close to zero. However, relaxing that assumption, we can easily construct an example where *all* workers lose in welfare terms.

Assume that $e$ can only take two values, $e_L$ and $e_H$, with $e_L < e_H$. Let $\theta$ be the fraction of workers with learning cost $e_L$. For all workers to lose in welfare terms, it is enough to construct an equilibrium such that the marginal worker has a cost $e_L$. The welfare of workers with that learning cost will then be equal to $w_1 - e_L = w_0 < w_A$. Using (4.4), we can get the wages for both types of workers:

$$w_0 = \frac{e_L}{\psi - 1},$$
$$w_1 = \frac{\psi e_L}{\psi - 1}.$$

Denoting by $\varphi$ the proportion of workers in the new technology, normalizing $L$ to 1 and substituting these two equations into the equivalents of (4.2) and (4.3), we can solve for $K_1$ and $\varphi$:

$$K_1 = \frac{K - k_0}{1 - k_0/k_1},$$
$$\varphi = \frac{K - k_0}{k_1 - k_0},$$

where $k_i = w_i^{1/\alpha}$ is the capital–labor ratio in technology $i$.

For this to indeed be an equilibrium, we only require that $\varphi \in [0, \theta]$: that is,

$$k_0 < K < \theta k_1 + (1 - \theta) k_0.$$

Thus, it may be the case that introducing the new technology harms *all* workers. Those who do not adapt to the new technology suffer a wage loss, due to the exit of capital from that technology. The others have their wage gains more than entirely offset by the cost of acquiring the human capital needed to work with the new technology. Capital entirely appropriates the return from the technological revolution.

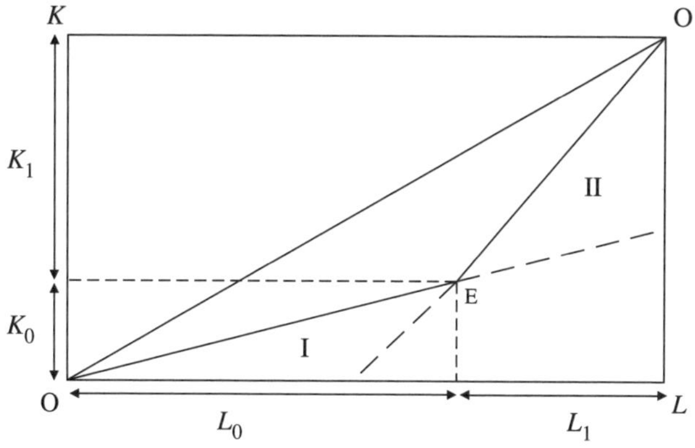


**Figure 4.5.** De-skilling technical progress moves the economy to region I.

### 4.1.3 De-skilling Technical Change

An interesting application of the above model is the analysis of *de-skilling* technical change. By this, we refer to a shift in the distribution of learning costs such that the new technology is easier to learn. This is reminiscent, for example, of the introduction of the assembly line by Henry Ford in 1927: while car production previously required complex skills, thus bringing relatively high wages to those who had acquired them, with the advent of the assembly line great numbers of workers could now work in car factories. The historical incidents associated with improvements in textile technologies that were mentioned in the introduction to this book can be interpreted in the same fashion.

How does such a change affect the distribution of income? To answer this question, we compare the structure of wages derived in the preceding section with the structure that we would see if learning costs were lower. Formally, this means that the distribution of learning costs, $G(\cdot)$, is replaced by another one, $\hat{G}(\cdot)$, such that $\hat{G} > G$ (i.e., $\hat{G}$ dominates $G$ in the "first-order stochastic dominance" sense[1]). How do the wages of workers using the old and new technologies, $w_0$ and $w_1$, evolve if $G$ is replaced by $\hat{G}$?

We already know from (4.4) that the $w_1/w_0$ ratio only depends on the parameters of the production function, and is therefore unaffected by the distribution of learning costs. Consequently, $w_1$ and $w_0$ must move in the same direction. Either wages in the two technologies both fall or they both go up. For this to be the case, it must be that the capital–labor ratio in both technologies moves in the same direction. This point is

[1] That is, weight is taken out of the density for the high values of $e$, and transferred to the low values of $e$.

illustrated in figure 4.5, which depicts the allocation of labor and capital between the two technologies. The economy is at point E. The horizontal distance OE is equal to $L_0$; the vertical distance OE is equal to $K_0$. The slope of OE is equal to the capital-labor ratio in the old technology, $K_0/L_0$. Similarly, the horizontal and vertical distances EO′ are equal to $L_1$ and $K_1$, respectively, and the slope of EO′ equals $K_1/L_1$. For the return to capital to be equal across the two technologies, despite the fact that $A_1 > A_0$, it must be that $K_1/L_1 > K_0/L_0$; hence E must lie below the diagonal.

When learning costs fall, the economy must necessarily move to one of the two regions marked I and II in figure 4.5. Otherwise the $K/L$ ratios would move in opposite directions and (4.4) would be violated. Furthermore, it is intuitively obvious that $K_1$ has to go up: a reduction in learning costs prompts more people to use the new technology, which will then attract more capital.

Therefore, the economy must move to region I. In that region, the capital-labor ratio falls in *both* technologies: this is the only way in which one can relocate resources to the technology with a greater capital-labor ratio, while maintaining the exogenous aggregate $K/L$ ratio unchanged—a type of effect not unfamiliar to students of international trade theory. Consequently, wages *fall* in the two technologies. Does this mean that all workers lose? No, it does not: the "de-skilling" technical change triggers a large movement of workers from the old to the new technology, and the wages of these workers go up. But it does reduce wages both for those who were already working with the new technology—they face a large inflow of competitors who previously could not learn it—and those who continue working with the old one—the capital with which they work is further reduced.

We showed that the economy moves to region I intuitively. It is easy to rule out a move to region II on a rigorous basis: in that region, both wages should go up, while keeping a constant ratio. Thus, the difference $w_1 - w_0 = e^*$ should go up, implying, since $\hat{G} > G$, that more people learn the new technology, so that $L_1$ goes up, which cannot be the case if the economy moves to region II.

### 4.1.4 Some Remarks on the Literature

Nelson and Phelps (1966) is one early influential paper that argues that new technologies have to be learned and that the skilled are better at doing this. While the preceding analysis is based on Caselli (1999), Greenwood and Yorukoglu (1997) have built a related model where only the skilled can learn a new technology. Their model is much more complex than that of Caselli and aims to explain the joint behavior of inequality, total factor productivity, and stock prices since 1974. On the other hand, the analysis of Greenwood and Yorukoglu lacks the simple wage-reducing effect of the allocation of capital highlighted in Caselli.

Along the same lines initiated by Nelson and Phelps are the models by Galor and Tsiddon (1997) and Aghion et al. (2002). See also Aghion (2002) for a concise, cohesive discussion.

An important implication of the Nelson–Phelps paradigm is that the rent earned by skilled workers due to their greater ability to implement new technologies is only *transitory*. As the new technology is in place, all workers eventually learn it and its impact on inequality vanishes. The general message is that inequality widens during periods of *fast* technological progress and is reduced during periods of slow technological progress. In the unbalanced-growth model of chapter 3, the rise in inequality is also transitory but for a slightly different reason: namely that labor mobility eventually eliminates wage differentials between sectors. Here it is the diffusion of the new technology that reduces the returns to being skilled. Once the technology is in place, there is not much left to implement. In the Caselli model, the effects of the technological revolution on inequality vanish if one assumes that the learning costs vanish for subsequent generations once the new technology is in place.

Interestingly, Bartel and Lichtenberg (1987) find some empirical support for the Nelson–Phelps view: using industry-level data, they find a negative association between the age of the capital stock (which is a proxy for the age of the technology used by the sector) and the demand for skilled workers.

Another implication, which is stressed by Galor and Tsiddon (1997), is that periods of fast technological change should also be associated with an increase in *intergenerational income mobility*. The reason for this is that the human capital of one's parents is more likely to become obsolete during such periods, so that its residual value to the child is lower. The same effect is discussed in Hassler and Rodriguez Mora (2000), who assume that general innate ability, which is easily transferable between technologies, is less heritable than parental human capital, which is more specific to a technology; but, if general innate ability is highly heritable, and if fast technical change makes the (nonheritable) skills acquired in the educational system obsolete, then it is easy to reverse the conclusion and instead predict that social mobility should fall when technical change accelerates (Rubinstein and Tsiddon 2004).

The Caselli model is also similar to the literature on *vintage human capital*, studied by, for example, Chari and Hopenhayn (1991), Violante

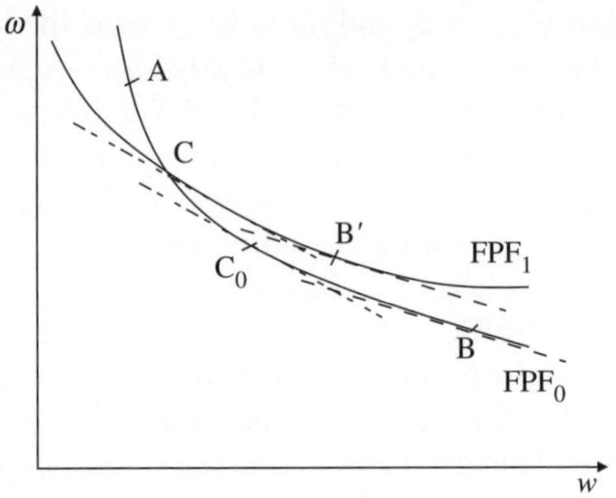


**Figure 4.6.** Introducing a skill-intensive technology.

(2002), and Hornstein et al. (2002), where workers become less productive if they move from an older to a newer technology—this loss of skills plays the same role as the learning cost in the Caselli model.

## 4.2 The New Technology Has Different Factor Intensities

Let us now consider the case where the new technology involves no learning cost, but may coexist with the old one because it has different factor intensities. Let us assume that there are two factors of production, skilled ($H$) and unskilled ($L$) labor. Initially, there is only one technology, the "old" one, denoted by subscript 0. In the $(w, \omega)$-plane, the economy lies at the point of the corresponding factor-price frontier ($FPF_0$), where the slope is equal to the $L/H$ ratio. Figure 4.6 depicts what happens if a new technology that is more intensive in skilled labor is introduced. Its FPF must be flatter: as it uses more skilled labor, a lower reduction in $\omega$ is needed to compensate for the same increase in $w$. The new FPF, which corresponds to the possibility of using either technology or both, is the upper envelope of $FPF_0$ and $FPF_1$. If, say, at a given value of $w$, $FPF_1$ lies above $FPF_0$, this means that under the value of $\omega$ corresponding to $w$ for technology 0, a firm using technology 1 could make strictly positive profits (see again figure 1.1).

If the $L/H$ ratio is high enough, as at point A in figure 4.6, then $FPF_1$ locally lies below $FPF_0$ and the new technology has no effect—in other words, the new FPF coincides with $FPF_0$ at point A, which is still the equilibrium point of the economy. There are not enough skills in the economy for the new technology to be profitable. If the $L/H$ ratio is high, then the economy initially lies at a point like B, where it is no longer profitable to use the old technology. It must move to a point on $FPF_1$.

Furthermore, the slope of $FPF_1$ at this new point B′ must be the same as the slope of $FPF_0$ at B, i.e., equal to the exogenous, aggregate $L/H$ ratio. As $FPF_1$ is flatter than $FPF_0$, B′ is necessarily above B and to its left. In this zone, the introduction of the new technology reduces the return to unskilled labor and increases the return to skilled labor. It is just another instance of skill-biased technical change, as studied in the preceding chapter. The fact that the old technology may still be used makes no difference, as it is nevertheless abandoned.

Finally, the economy may move to point C, which is the intersection between the two FPFs. This will happen if the $L/H$ ratio lies between the slopes of the two curves at C. This is the case if the economy initially lies between point C and point $C_0$ on $FPF_0$. Point $C_0$ is the point on $FPF_0$ where its slope is the same as that of $FPF_1$ at C. In such a case, both technologies are simultaneously in use, and this fact entirely determines $w$ and $\omega$, which are the coordinates of C. In particular, factor prices do not depend on the initial position of the economy between C and $C_0$, i.e., on the initial $L/H$ ratio. As $C_0$ is below C and to the right, we have the same qualitative pattern as if the old technology were abandoned: the wages of the unskilled fall, while the wages of the skilled go up. As the economy moves to point C, the $L/H$ ratio falls for workers who continue working with the old technology; unskilled workers work with less skilled workers, because these are attracted into the new technology which is more intensive in skilled labor. Consequently, their marginal product falls, while that of the skilled workers go up. As in the preceding analysis of technological revolutions, unskilled workers see their wages falling, despite continuing to work with the same technology as before, because they are deprived of the complementary factor, which gets better opportunities elsewhere.

The allocation of labor between the two technologies is determined by a diagram similar to figure 4.5, where one just has to replace $K$ with $H$. The $H/L$ ratio in any technology is determined by the inverse slope of the corresponding FPF at the intersection point C. The allocation of $L$ and $H$ between the two technologies is the only one that matches the aggregate $H/L$ ratio. It is again represented by point E on figure 4.5. Because the old technology is less skill intensive, the economy must again lie below the diagonal. The aggregate $H/L$ ratio, whose slope is equal to that of the diagonal, must be lower than that of the new technology at C but greater than that of the old technology. Otherwise, figure 4.5 cannot be constructed and the two technologies cannot be simultaneously in use. The greater the discrepancy between the two technologies, the more pronounced the kink of the upper envelope of the FPFs at C, and the

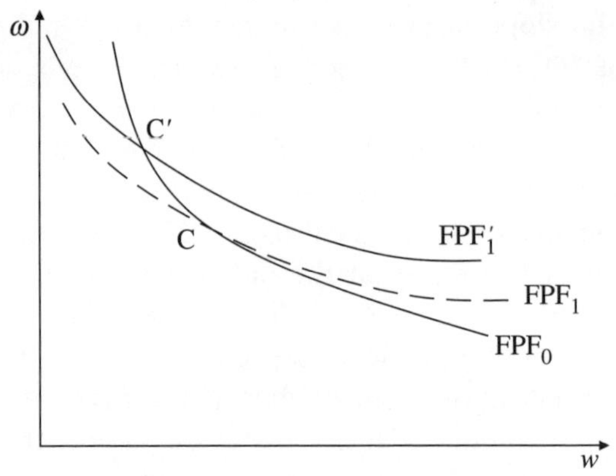


**Figure 4.7.** Technical progress in the skill-intensive technology.

greater the range of values of $H/L$ over which both technologies are simultaneously in use.

## 4.3 Asymmetric Technical Progress

An interesting aspect of the two-technology model is that technical progress in only one of the two technologies necessarily harms one category of workers. For example, if productivity grows in the skill-intensive technology, say by a multiplicative shift in its production function, its FPF shifts up (figure 4.7). The economy moves along the FPF of the old technology in such a way that $w$ falls and $\omega$ goes up. Thus, productivity growth in the technology intensive in one factor harms the other factor. Intuitively, the logic is again the same as in figure 4.5: both $H$ and $L$ move to the technology with the greater $H/L$ ratio, since that technology is more productive. To maintain the aggregate $H/L$ unchanged, it must be that $H/L$ *falls* in both technologies, so that $w$ must fall. This occurs despite the fact that unskilled workers in the new technology benefit from higher total factor productivity there. $H/L$ must fall by enough in the new technology to offset the direct positive effect of technical progress on $w$, and at the same time it must also fall in the old technology. If productivity growth is large enough, however, that pattern is not feasible, which simply means that the two technologies can no longer coexist and that everybody eventually works with the new technology—one is back to the case of a shift from B to B′ in figure 4.6.

The effects are similar to that of the nonneutral technical changes studied in the preceding chapters. For example, we have seen that if $K$ and $L$ are substitutes, capital-augmenting productivity growth reduces

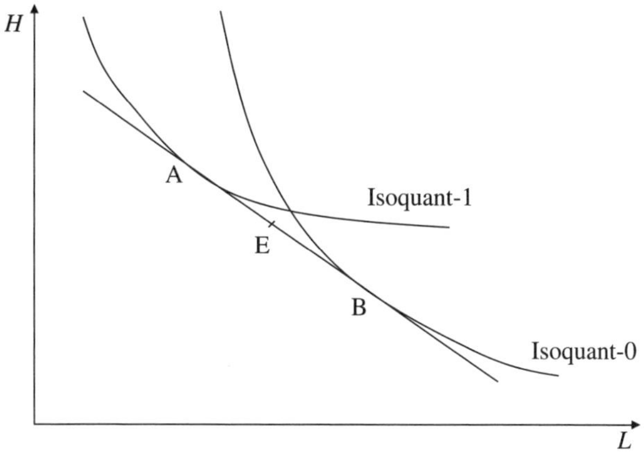


**Figure 4.8.** Representing the two technologies in the $(L, H)$-plane.

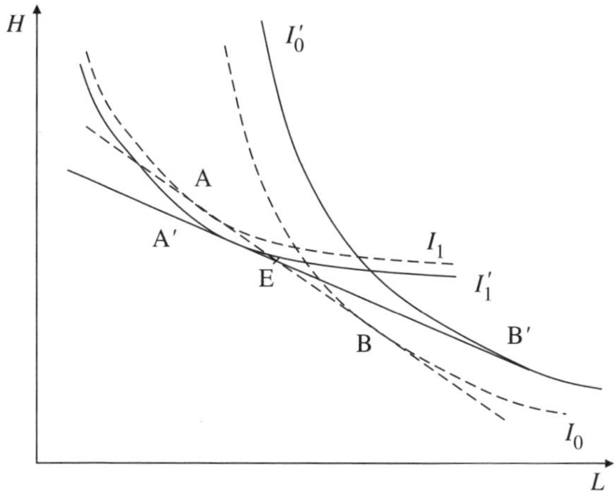


**Figure 4.9.** Technical progress in the skill-intensive technology in the $(L, H)$-plane.

$w$. Here, the coexistence of the two technologies increases the substitutability between the two factors, as in the familiar textbook diagram (figure 4.8). Over the segment [AB] where both technologies are used, one gets a constant marginal rate of transformation between $H$ and $L$ by just changing the proportions in which both technologies are used. Furthermore, if the point $\mathrm{E} = (L, H)$ describing the economy's endowment lies on [AB], then the two technologies are indeed used, and the share of output produced by the skill-intensive technology is equal to EB/AB. When productivity grows in only the skill-intensive technology, its own isoquant shifts down. Consequently, the isoquants of the aggregate production function become flatter: one needs more unskilled labor to make up for a given reduction in skilled labor (figure 4.9)—intuitively, skilled labor is more productive, relative to unskilled labor, than before, since the productivity of the technology that uses skilled workers relatively more has gone up. The $w/\omega$ ratio falls. Because the aggregate isoquant going through E is flatter, both A and B move to the right to A′ and B′, implying that the new technology is used to a greater extent. As the old technology's isoquant is flatter at B′ than at B, the $H/L$ ratio is lower, so $w$ must fall.

## 4.4 Conclusion

This chapter has shown that even if it is still possible to work with the old technology when the new one is introduced, this does not preclude wages from falling. The mechanism is that workers who continue to use the old technology are partially deprived of their complementary factors (at the micro level, they face a higher price for these factors). In the Caselli model of technological revolutions, capital moves to the new technology, which is used by workers who can afford the retraining cost. In the model where the new technology is more intensive in human capital, human capital moves to the new technology, where, everything being equal, it earns a higher return.

# 5
# Supply Effects

The rise in inequality that has been observed in the United States and other countries has taken place despite coinciding with a rise in the overall educational standards of the workforce. That is, the return to skill has increased while at the same time the supply of skills has increased. A conventional view (see, for example, Katz and Murphy 1992) is that relative demand shifts induced by technical change have been strong enough to offset these countervailing shifts in relative supply. It is tempting, however, to speculate that improvements in education levels have in fact *contributed* to the phenomenon of rising inequality, rather than dampened it. A simple explanation is as follows. A greater supply of skilled workers makes it worthwhile to adopt technologies and modes of organization that are intensive in skilled labor.[1] These changes, in turn, induce a fall in the relative demand for unskilled workers. According to this view, the rise in the supply of skilled workers is the event that triggers skill-biased technical change. Such a change is no longer exogenous but an outcome of changes in a country's aggregate factor endowment.

To make sense of such a view, we need a model that tells us why the introduction, or the adoption, of a technology intensive in a given factor of production is facilitated by increases in the supply of that factor. Furthermore, we require that the induced effect of that technological response on inequality is stronger than the direct effect of having more abundant skilled labor (overreaction).

If this view is correct, then human-capital accumulation, instead of being a welcome response to the increased relative demand for skills, is a mixed blessing: it further deepens inequality. Since human capital is an important engine for growth, one may then ask whether growth will inevitably increase inequality.

The answer is twofold.

First, beyond a certain level of human-capital accumulation, we expect the old technology to eventually be abandoned. The economy then

[1] While this chapter looks at technology, some of the literature, like Caroli and van Reenen (2001) and Thesmar and Thoenig (2000), is focused on modes of organization.

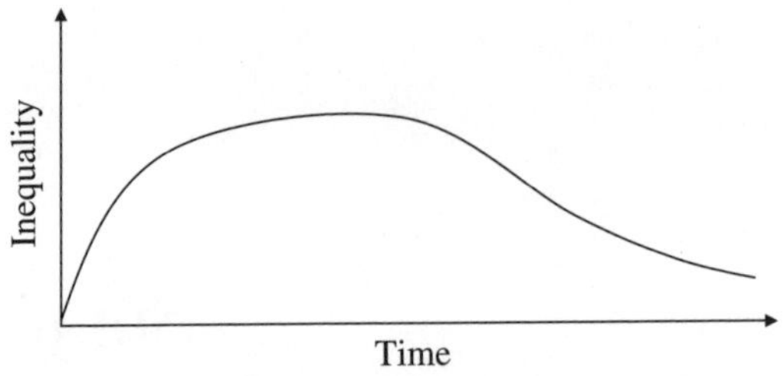


**Figure 5.1.** The Kuznets curve: the hump-shaped response of inequality to a technological breakthrough.

reverts to a "normal" regime where increases in skills reduce the skill premium. This argument suggests that technological revolutions could generate "Kuznets curves," as illustrated in figure 5.1. When introduced, the new technology triggers a hike in inequality, for the reasons explained in the preceding chapter. If people acquire better skills in response to the introduction of the new technology, inequality would continue to increase, due to the overreaction property. During this phase, resources are gradually reallocated away from the old technology into the new technology. The economy then reaches a stage where the old technology is abandoned and inequality starts falling, until the skill level in the workforce reaches a new equilibrium.

Second, along a growth path, the economy accumulates physical capital in addition to human capital; an interesting question is, then, how does physical-capital accumulation affect the distribution of income? Does it reinforce or offset the potentially negative effect of human-capital accumulation? To answer this question, we will study the effects of both physical capital and human capital in a two-technology model using the work of Beaudry and Green (2003).

## 5.1 Supply Effects and Competing Technologies

In order to capture the idea that increases in skill levels are inegalitarian because they favor skill-intensive technologies, it is natural to use the competing-technologies model described at the end of the preceding chapter. In this model, a human-capital-intensive technology may coexist with a labor-intensive technology. This model seems appropriate for the study of the effect of factor endowment on the technological mix: how does an increase in the aggregate $H/L$ ratio affect the relative use of each technology? If the skill-intensive technology is used more, can inequality go up?

As we have seen, if $H/L$ is low, only the labor-intensive technology will be used. If it is high, only the human-capital-intensive technology

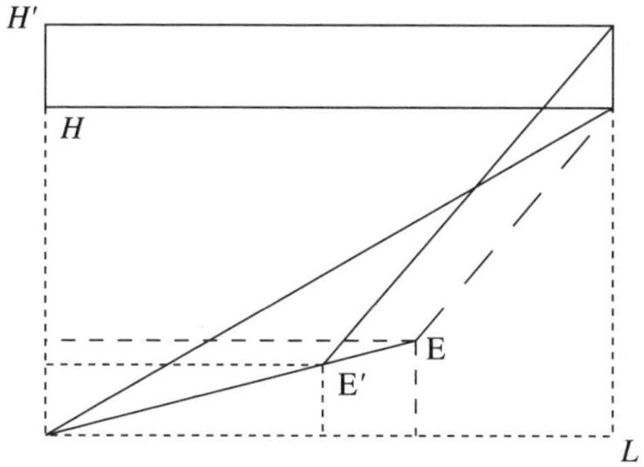


**Figure 5.2.** Impact of human-capital accumulation on the technology mix.

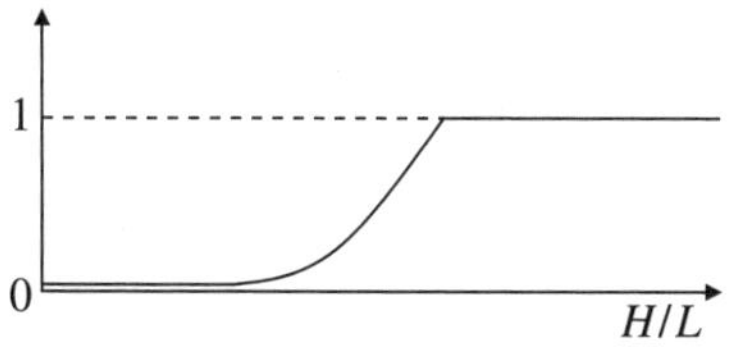


**Figure 5.3.** The evolution of the employment share of the new technology.

will be used. At intermediate levels, both technologies are used, and labor and human capital are allocated between the two as illustrated in figure 4.5. In this zone, when $H/L$ goes up, the economy evolves as in figure 5.2, where the impact of an increase in $H$ is shown: more resources are shifted to the new technology as the economy moves from E to E′.

Hence, in this simple model it is not difficult to get the first prediction that we need: the new technology is used more intensively as $H/L$ grows. Figure 5.3 illustrates this point: when $H/L$ goes past a threshold, the new technology starts being used, its share in total employment then steadily goes up, and after another threshold the economy only uses the new technology.

What happens to the distribution of income? In the zones where only one technology is used, $H/L$ has conventional effects on $\omega$ and $w$: the latter goes up and the former falls. Thus, increases in the supply of human capital cannot raise inequality. In the zone where both technologies are used, the supply of human capital has no impact on factor prices, which are determined by the intersection between the two FPFs. Thus, inequality stays constant when skills go up. This property brings us closer to, but falls short of, predicting an increase in inequality.

From a mathematical point of view, constancy of factor prices in this zone is due to the fact that the economy simultaneously lies on both

FPFs. This defines a two-equation system that has a unique solution for $(w, \omega)$. If there were more factors of production, $w$ and $\omega$ would not be pinned down and they would move in response to changes in $H/L$.

This suggests that if there are two technologies, to get a positive effect of the aggregate $H/L$ ratio on the skill premium we need to add a factor of production, namely capital. One modeling approach is to combine the two-technology model with the capital-sucking effect highlighted in the Caselli model: if greater use of the new technology makes capital scarcer in the old technology, then, instead of having a constant $\omega/w$ ratio when $H/L$ goes up, that ratio could go up as well. We then get an overreaction of the distribution of income to an increase in the supply of skills: the skill premium goes up, instead of falling.

The next question is, how can we implement this idea? In the Caselli model, "too much" capital was leaving the old technology, relative to labor, because capital was more mobile than labor and because the new technology was more productive than the old one. Here, all factors are perfectly mobile, and the new technology is not more productive than the old. Rather, it is more intensive in human capital. In order to get the capital-sucking effect, we require that, in some sense, the new technology is also more intensive in physical capital.

To get more precise predictions, we have to spell out the model explicitly. There are two technologies, old (O) and new (N), and we will limit the analysis to the case where both technologies are in use simultaneously. Each technology uses three factors of production: human capital $H$, labor $L$, and physical capital $K$. At the aggregate level, these three inputs are in fixed supplies: also denoted by $H$, $L$, and $K$. They are mobile between the two technologies, so there is a single price for each factor. These prices are denoted by $\omega$, $w$, and $r$ for $H$, $L$, and $K$, respectively. The cost function is $c_{\mathrm{O}}(w, \omega, r)$ for the old technology and $c_{\mathrm{N}}(w, \omega, r)$ for the new technology.

To solve the model, we will denote by $H_{\mathrm{O}}$, $K_{\mathrm{O}}$, $L_{\mathrm{O}}$ (respectively $H_{\mathrm{N}}$, $K_{\mathrm{N}}$, $L_{\mathrm{N}}$) the amount of each factor allocated to the old (respectively new) technology. The corresponding *unit* input requirement will be denoted with a hat. Hence, $\hat{H}_{\mathrm{O}} = H_{\mathrm{O}}/Y_{\mathrm{O}}$ (with $Y_{\mathrm{O}}$ being the output produced with the old technology), and so on. In particular, we know that $\hat{H}_{\mathrm{N}} = c'_{\mathrm{N}\omega}(w, \omega, r)$, and so on.

First of all, the economy must lie on the FPF for each technology, i.e.,

$$c_{\mathrm{O}}(w, \omega, r) = 1, \tag{5.1}$$

$$c_{\mathrm{N}}(w, \omega, r) = 1. \tag{5.2}$$

Next, the ratio of the cost functions' partial derivatives must be equal to the corresponding relative factor intensity:

$$\frac{c'_{O\omega}}{c'_{Ow}} = \frac{H_O}{L_O},$$
$$\frac{c'_{N\omega}}{c'_{Nw}} = \frac{H_N}{L_N} = \frac{H - H_O}{L - L_O}.$$

And similarly,

$$\frac{c'_{Or}}{c'_{Ow}} = \frac{K_O}{L_O},$$
$$\frac{c'_{Nr}}{c'_{Nw}} = \frac{K_N}{L_N} = \frac{K - K_O}{L - L_O}.$$

This is a six-equation system in the six unknowns $r$, $w$, $\omega$, $L_O$, $K_O$, and $H_O$, and $L_N$, $K_N$, and $H_N$ are then obtained straightforwardly.

We want to analyze how aggregate factor endowments affect inequality. To begin with, we assume that the new technology is more intensive in human capital, relative to labor, than the old technology. This is equivalent to

$$\frac{c'_{N\omega}(w,\omega,r)}{c'_{Nw}(w,\omega,r)} > \frac{c'_{O\omega}(w,\omega,r)}{c'_{Ow}(w,\omega,r)}, \quad \forall(w,\omega,r).$$

At this stage, this assumption is just a matter of labeling and entails no loss of generality.

Second, we will look at $\omega/w$ as our measure of relative inequality. As seen in chapter 1, under plausible assumptions, any measure of inequality will be increasing in that ratio, both in the nonspecialization model and in the Roy specialization model.

Finally, we are also interested in absolute wages, and will look at $w$ and $\omega$, in addition to their ratio, as factor endowments vary.

### 5.1.1 Comovements between Factor Prices

A number of interesting results can be obtained simply by using the first two equations (5.1) and (5.2). They imply that the vector of factor prices $(w,\omega,r)$ must lie on a one-dimensional curve in the three-dimensional space. Thus, if $r$ is given, we can compute $w$ and $\omega$:

$$w = w(r),$$
$$\omega = \omega(r).$$

Differentiating (5.1) and (5.2), we also find that

$$\frac{\mathrm{d}w}{\mathrm{d}r} = -\frac{c'_{\mathrm{O}r}/c'_{\mathrm{O}\omega} - c'_{\mathrm{N}r}/c'_{\mathrm{N}\omega}}{c'_{\mathrm{O}w}/c'_{\mathrm{O}\omega} - c'_{\mathrm{N}w}/c'_{\mathrm{N}\omega}} = -\frac{\hat{K}_{\mathrm{O}}/\hat{H}_{\mathrm{O}} - \hat{K}_{\mathrm{N}}/\hat{H}_{\mathrm{N}}}{\hat{L}_{\mathrm{O}}/\hat{H}_{\mathrm{O}} - \hat{L}_{\mathrm{N}}/\hat{H}_{\mathrm{N}}} \tag{5.3}$$

and

$$\frac{\mathrm{d}\omega}{\mathrm{d}r} = -\frac{c'_{\mathrm{N}r}/c'_{\mathrm{N}w} - c'_{\mathrm{O}r}/c'_{\mathrm{O}w}}{c'_{\mathrm{N}\omega}/c'_{\mathrm{N}w} - c'_{\mathrm{O}\omega}/c'_{\mathrm{O}w}} = -\frac{\hat{K}_{\mathrm{N}}/\hat{L}_{\mathrm{N}} - \hat{K}_{\mathrm{O}}/\hat{L}_{\mathrm{O}}}{\hat{H}_{\mathrm{N}}/\hat{L}_{\mathrm{N}} - \hat{H}_{\mathrm{O}}/\hat{L}_{\mathrm{O}}}. \tag{5.4}$$

These formulas allow us to analyze the comovements between factor prices. Given our assumption that the new technology is more intensive than the old in human capital relative to labor, the denominators in the preceding equations are positive, and we get the following taxonomy:

- If $\hat{K}_{\mathrm{O}}/\hat{H}_{\mathrm{O}} > \hat{K}_{\mathrm{N}}/\hat{H}_{\mathrm{N}}$, then the new technology is more intensive in human capital relative to physical capital than the old one is. This implies that $\mathrm{d}w/\mathrm{d}r < 0$. A rise in the cost of capital reduces the wage of raw labor.

- If $\hat{K}_{\mathrm{N}}/\hat{L}_{\mathrm{N}} > \hat{K}_{\mathrm{O}}/\hat{L}_{\mathrm{O}}$, then the new technology is more intensive in physical capital relative to raw labor than the old one is. This implies that $\mathrm{d}\omega/\mathrm{d}r < 0$. A rise in the cost of capital reduces the wage of human capital.

- Therefore, if

$$\frac{\hat{H}_{\mathrm{N}}}{\hat{H}_{\mathrm{O}}} > \frac{\hat{K}_{\mathrm{N}}}{\hat{K}_{\mathrm{O}}} > \frac{\hat{L}_{\mathrm{N}}}{\hat{L}_{\mathrm{O}}}, \tag{5.5}$$

  then these two inequalities hold. Labor and human capital are always "substitute," as their wages must vary in the same direction when factor endowments change. Furthermore, they vary negatively with the cost of capital: scarcer capital harms all workers. Intuitively, these inequalities mean that compared with the old technology, the new technology is most intensive in human capital and least intensive in labor, with physical capital falling between the two.

- If

$$\frac{\hat{H}_{\mathrm{N}}}{\hat{H}_{\mathrm{O}}} > \frac{\hat{L}_{\mathrm{N}}}{\hat{L}_{\mathrm{O}}} > \frac{\hat{K}_{\mathrm{N}}}{\hat{K}_{\mathrm{O}}},$$

  then $\mathrm{d}w/\mathrm{d}r < 0$ but $\mathrm{d}\omega/\mathrm{d}r > 0$. Changes in factor endowments affect the wages of skilled and unskilled workers in opposite directions. An increase in the cost of capital harms unskilled workers but benefits skilled workers.

**Table 5.1.** The effect of relative factor intensities in each technology on the degree of substitutability between factors in the aggregate production function.

| Condition | $K, L$ | $K, H$ | $H, L$ |
|---|---|---|---|
| $\dfrac{\hat{H}_N}{\hat{H}_O} > \dfrac{\hat{K}_N}{\hat{K}_O} > \dfrac{\hat{L}_N}{\hat{L}_O}$ | Complements | Complements | Substitutes |
| $\dfrac{\hat{H}_N}{\hat{H}_O} > \dfrac{\hat{L}_N}{\hat{L}_O} > \dfrac{\hat{K}_N}{\hat{K}_O}$ | Complements | Substitutes | Complements |
| $\dfrac{\hat{K}_N}{\hat{K}_O} > \dfrac{\hat{H}_N}{\hat{H}_O} > \dfrac{\hat{L}_N}{\hat{L}_O}$ | Substitutes | Complements | Complements |

- Finally, if

  $$\frac{\hat{K}_N}{\hat{K}_O} > \frac{\hat{H}_N}{\hat{H}_O} > \frac{\hat{L}_N}{\hat{L}_O},$$

  then the opposite occurs: more costly capital harms skilled workers but benefits unskilled workers.

So we get very strong predictions on the comovements between factor incomes from just the properties of the two technologies and the assumption that they are used simultaneously. We summarize our findings in table 5.1.

As the table makes clear, the factors that are used most intensively in each technology relative to the other technology are substitutes, while they are both complements to the third, intermediate, factor. This is a striking result, since it depends only on factor intensities in each technology and not on the degree of substitutability and complementarity within a technology.

The results can be easily understood using the partial FPF for each technology in the $(w, \omega)$-plane. A reduction in the cost of capital $r$ shifts both partials up: it is similar to technological progress in both technologies. If

$$\frac{\hat{L}_N}{\hat{L}_O} > \frac{\hat{K}_N}{\hat{K}_O},$$

then, relative to the old technology, the new one is even less intensive in capital than in labor. Consequently, it benefits very little from a fall in $r$. The partial FPF for the old technology shifts much more than the FPF for the new one, and the logic of the end of chapter 4 prevails: unskilled labor benefits and skilled workers lose out (figure 5.4). The economy evolves as if, in a two-factor model, there was productivity growth only in the labor-intensive technology—the opposite case of figure 4.7. Intuitively, a similar mechanism is at work. Both $H$ and $L$ are relocated to

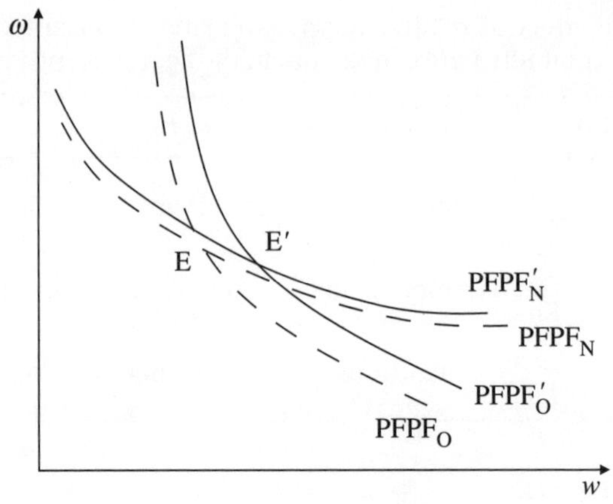


**Figure 5.4.** The impact of a fall in $r$ on wages in the case of capital–skill substitutability.

the old, labor-intensive technology. To compensate, the $L/H$ ratio has to fall in both technologies. This effect unambiguously increases $w$, which becomes scarce relative to the two other factors. As for $H$, it loses from greater scarcity in $L$ but gains from more abundant $K$. But that hardly matters in the new technology, which uses very little capital; therefore, overall the return to human capital falls.

On the other hand, if

$$\frac{\hat{K}_N}{\hat{K}_O} > \frac{\hat{H}_N}{\hat{H}_O},$$

one is in the opposite case where the partial FPF for the old technology shifts very little (figure 5.5), and $w$ falls while $\omega$ goes up.

Finally, if (5.5) holds, then there is enough similarity in capital intensity between the two technologies for the reduction in $r$ to trigger a rise in both wages.

A useful illustration is the extreme case in which the new technology does not use labor at all, while the old one does not use human capital:

$$Y_N = A_N H_N^{1-\alpha_N} K_N^{\alpha_N}, \tag{5.6}$$

$$Y_O = A_O L_O^{1-\alpha_O} K_O^{\alpha_O}. \tag{5.7}$$

In such a case, it must be that $H_N = H$ and $L_O = L$, and furthermore (5.5) is clearly satisfied. An increase in the capital stock will be allocated between the two technologies so that the marginal product of capital falls by the same amount, and this clearly induces an increase in the marginal product of $H$ and $L$; therefore, it is the case that $\mathrm{d}w/\mathrm{d}r < 0$ and $\mathrm{d}\omega/\mathrm{d}r < 0$; the economy moves along the FPF of each technology. An increase in $H$, upon impact, reduces its marginal product in the new technology, while

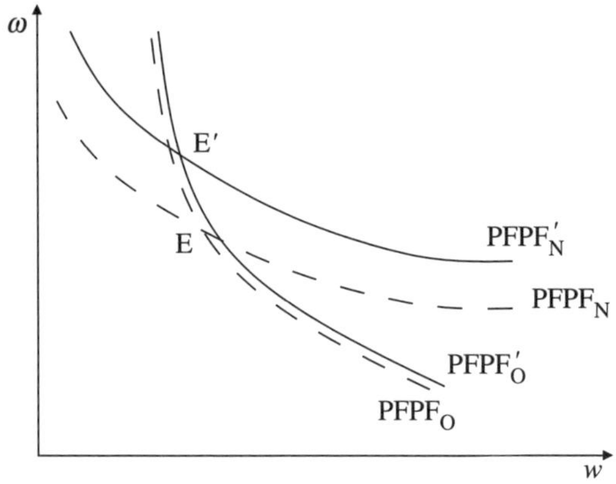


**Figure 5.5.** Impact of a fall in $r$ on wages in the case of capital–unskilled substitutability.

increasing that of capital. In response to this, capital is relocated to the new technology, so that $w$ must necessarily fall. Furthermore, capital movements cannot offset the negative impact effect on $\omega$, otherwise the marginal product of capital would go up in the old technology but down in the new technology, which violates arbitrage. Here, again, wages move in the same direction: both $w$ and $\omega$ fall. A similar argument applies to an increase in $L$.

### 5.1.2 Effects of Factor Accumulation on Absolute Wages

The preceding discussion goes a long way toward understanding the effect of factor accumulation on the absolute returns to human capital and labor. Despite the singularities introduced by the two-technology configuration, it is still true that a greater supply (weakly) reduces the price of that factor.[2] Consequently, we know how the accumulation of human capital and physical capital affects absolute wages. This is summarized in table 5.2.

If (5.5) holds, then physical-capital accumulation unambiguously increases the wage of all workers, while human-capital accumulation reduces the wage of all workers. While raw labor benefits from working with more human capital, this is more than offset by the movement of physical capital out of the old technology into the new technology.

[2] In a one-technology model, this is a straightforward consequence of the production function's concavity. When two technologies coexist, concavity still holds. A simple way to prove this is to note that under constant returns to scale, concavity of the production function is equivalent to convexity of the isoquants. The isoquants of the aggregate technology when both technologies can be used are the lower convex envelope of the corresponding isoquants for the two technologies, as illustrated in figure 4.8. Therefore, they are convex, implying that the aggregate production function is concave.

**Table 5.2.** The effect of human- and physical-capital accumulation on wages in the three configurations.

| Condition | $\dfrac{\partial w}{\partial(K/L)}$ | $\dfrac{\partial \omega}{\partial(K/L)}$ | $\dfrac{\partial w}{\partial(H/L)}$ | $\dfrac{\partial \omega}{\partial(H/L)}$ |
|---|---|---|---|---|
| $\dfrac{\hat{H}_N}{\hat{H}_O} > \dfrac{\hat{K}_N}{\hat{K}_O} > \dfrac{\hat{L}_N}{\hat{L}_O}$ | + | + | − | − |
| $\dfrac{\hat{H}_N}{\hat{H}_O} > \dfrac{\hat{L}_N}{\hat{L}_O} > \dfrac{\hat{K}_N}{\hat{K}_O}$ | + | − | + | − |
| $\dfrac{\hat{K}_N}{\hat{K}_O} > \dfrac{\hat{H}_N}{\hat{H}_O} > \dfrac{\hat{L}_N}{\hat{L}_O}$ | − | + | + | − |

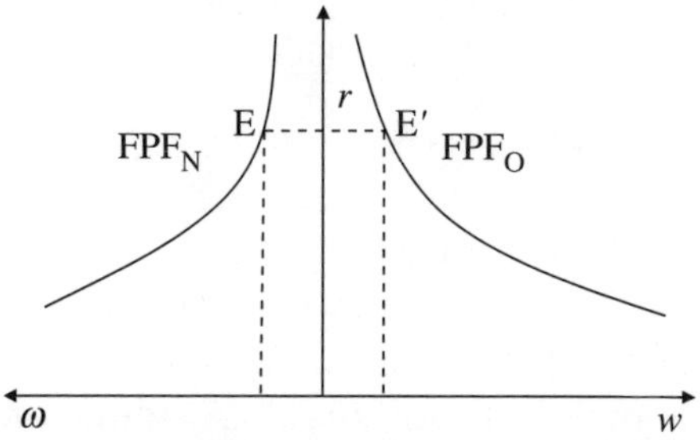


**Figure 5.6.** Factor price determination when each technology uses only one kind of labor.

Going back to the example of the preceding subsection, the determination of $w$ and $\omega$ can be illustrated on a graph with the FPF for each technology (figure 5.6). The economy is represented by points E and E′, which must have the same vertical coordinate for returns to capital to be equalized. An increase in the stock of physical capital must move both E and E′ up, so that both wages go up. An increase in $H$ must move E′ to the right, so that E must move to the left. Both wages fall, and $r$ goes up.

### 5.1.3 Neutral Factor Accumulation

An interesting property of the two-technology model is that there exists a path of factor accumulation such that $w$ and $\omega$ are unchanged. That is, given a change in $H$, we can offset it by a change in $K$ such that $w$ and $\omega$ remain constant. This property is just a consequence of the fact that $w$ and $\omega$ lie on a one-dimensional locus. If

$$dK = -\frac{\partial r/\partial H}{\partial r/\partial K}\, dH, \tag{5.8}$$

**Table 5.3.** Unless $K$ and $H$ are substitutes, an increase in $H$ must be matched by an increase in $K$ for factor prices to remain invariant.

| Condition | $\dfrac{\mathrm{d}(H/L)}{\mathrm{d}(K/L)}$ |
|---|---|
| $\dfrac{\hat{H}_{\mathrm{N}}}{\hat{H}_{\mathrm{O}}} > \dfrac{\hat{K}_{\mathrm{N}}}{\hat{K}_{\mathrm{O}}} > \dfrac{\hat{L}_{\mathrm{N}}}{\hat{L}_{\mathrm{O}}}$ | + |
| $\dfrac{\hat{H}_{\mathrm{N}}}{\hat{H}_{\mathrm{O}}} > \dfrac{\hat{L}_{\mathrm{N}}}{\hat{L}_{\mathrm{O}}} > \dfrac{\hat{K}_{\mathrm{N}}}{\hat{K}_{\mathrm{O}}}$ | − |
| $\dfrac{\hat{K}_{\mathrm{N}}}{\hat{K}_{\mathrm{O}}} > \dfrac{\hat{H}_{\mathrm{N}}}{\hat{H}_{\mathrm{O}}} > \dfrac{\hat{L}_{\mathrm{N}}}{\hat{L}_{\mathrm{O}}}$ | + |

then $\mathrm{d}r = 0$, implying that $\mathrm{d}w = \mathrm{d}\omega = 0$. Thus, a trajectory for $(H, K)$ which satisfies the differential equation (5.8) is a *neutral factor accumulation path*,[3] along which the return to each factor does not change.

This does not mean that the distribution of income is invariant: as human capital is embodied in people, they will get richer if they have more of it. But it implies that the returns to skill, both absolute and relative, are invariant; so is the wage curve, which determines an individual's wage as a function of his endowment in human capital and raw labor. Whether wage inequality rises or falls along that path clearly depends on how the increment in human capital is distributed between workers. With constant factor prices, an increase in human capital will reduce inequality if the least skilled benefit from it, while it will increase inequality if it is concentrated at the top of the distribution of income. As for total income inequality, it also depends on the distribution of claims to capital income and how it evolves through individual savings rates.

The neutral path is a useful benchmark: if the returns to different skills change, then by definition factor accumulation must have deviated from the neutral path. One can then analyze the rise in, say, the return to skills as the outcome of an imbalance between physical- and human-capital accumulation. Given the pattern of complementarities, it is easy to get the sign of the slope of the neutral path. It is described in table 5.3.

The neutral path is negatively sloped if and only if capital and skills are substitutes. In this case accumulation of both $K$ and $H$ cannot be neutral, and will lead to a fall in $\omega$ and a rise in $w$, which is an egalitarian outcome. Otherwise, the neutral path is upward sloping and factor accumulation can in principle proceed along this path.

[3] Here we differ from Beaudry and Green's terminology: they use the term "balanced-growth path," which we find ambiguous.

### 5.1.4 Effects on Relative Wages

The preceding discussion does not provide any result on relative wages. In the two cases where skilled and unskilled labor are complements, the effect of factor accumulation on the skill premium $\omega/w$ is obvious: human-capital accumulation unambiguously depresses it, while physical-capital accumulation increases it in one case (the case of capital–labor substitutability, $\hat{K}_N/\hat{K}_O > \hat{H}_N/\hat{H}_O > \hat{L}_N/\hat{L}_O$), and reduces it in the other (the case of capital–skill substitutability, $\hat{H}_N/\hat{H}_O > \hat{L}_N/\hat{L}_O > \hat{K}_N/\hat{K}_O$).

The case in which (5.5) holds is more difficult to analyze. We already know that $w$ and $\omega$ move in the same direction. How does $\omega/w$ evolve? An increase in the capital stock, which reduces interest rates, will reduce the skill premium if and only if

$$\frac{\partial(\omega/w)}{\partial r} > 0,$$

or, equivalently, using (5.3) and (5.4),

$$\frac{1}{w}\frac{\hat{K}_O/\hat{H}_O - \hat{K}_N/\hat{H}_N}{\hat{L}_O/\hat{H}_O - \hat{L}_N/\hat{H}_N} > \frac{1}{\omega}\frac{\hat{K}_N/\hat{L}_N - \hat{K}_O/\hat{L}_O}{\hat{H}_N/\hat{L}_N - \hat{H}_O/\hat{L}_O}. \tag{5.9}$$

Furthermore, if this inequality holds, it is also true that an increase in human capital increases the skill premium, since it must depress wages and therefore raise interest rates.

Beaudry and Green (2003) show that under (5.5) a sufficient condition for (5.9) to hold is that the new technology is more "capital efficient,"[4] i.e.,

$$\hat{K}_O > \hat{K}_N. \tag{5.10}$$

Intuitively, the factor which loses most is the one that is most vulnerable to an increase in the cost of capital; this will be labor if the old technology,

[4] To see this, note that homogeneity of cost functions then implies that $1 = r\hat{K}_O + w\hat{L}_O + \omega\hat{H}_O = r\hat{K}_N + w\hat{L}_N + \omega\hat{H}_N$, so that $w\hat{L}_N + \omega\hat{H}_N > w\hat{L}_O + \omega\hat{H}_O$. Furthermore, for (5.5) to hold along with (5.1) and (5.2) it must be that $\hat{L}_O > \hat{L}_N$ and $\hat{H}_N > \hat{H}_O$. Consequently, the inequality $w\hat{L}_N + \omega\hat{H}_N > w\hat{L}_O + \omega\hat{H}_O$ is equivalent to

$$w < \omega\frac{\hat{H}_N - \hat{H}_O}{\hat{L}_N - \hat{L}_O}.$$

A sufficient condition for (5.9) to hold is then

$$\frac{\hat{H}_N - \hat{H}_O}{\hat{L}_N - \hat{L}_O}\frac{\hat{K}_N/\hat{L}_N - \hat{K}_O/\hat{L}_O}{\hat{H}_N/\hat{L}_N - \hat{H}_O/\hat{L}_O} < \frac{\hat{K}_O/\hat{H}_O - \hat{K}_N/\hat{H}_N}{\hat{L}_O/\hat{H}_O - \hat{L}_N/\hat{H}_N}.$$

Rearranging and simplifying, one finds that it is equivalent to

$$(\hat{K}_O - \hat{K}_N)\left(\frac{\hat{H}_N\hat{L}_O}{\hat{H}_O\hat{L}_N} + \frac{\hat{L}_N\hat{H}_O}{\hat{H}_N\hat{L}_O} - 2\right) > 0,$$

which is true since $x + 1/x > 2$ for all $x > 0$, and $\hat{K}_O > \hat{K}_N$ by assumption.

where labor is used relatively more than human capital, is more intensive (in absolute terms) in physical capital than the new technology is.

Going back to our specific example of equations (5.6), (5.7), can we compute the effect of human-capital accumulation on the skill premium? The condition that the marginal product of capital must be equalized is

$$\alpha_N A_N H^{1-\alpha_N} K_N^{\alpha_N - 1} = \alpha_O A_O L^{1-\alpha_O} (K - K_N)^{-(1-\alpha_O)}.$$

Differentiating, we find that

$$(1 - \alpha_N)(\mathrm{d}\ln H - \mathrm{d}\ln K_N) = -(1 - \alpha_O)\,\mathrm{d}\ln(K - K_N). \tag{5.11}$$

The skill premium is

$$\frac{\omega}{w} = \frac{(1 - \alpha_N) A_N H^{-\alpha_N} K_N^{\alpha_N}}{(1 - \alpha_O) A_O L^{-\alpha_O} (K - K_N)^{\alpha_O}}.$$

Differentiating again,

$$\mathrm{d}\ln \frac{\omega}{w} = -\alpha_N\,\mathrm{d}\ln H + \alpha_N\,\mathrm{d}\ln K_N - \alpha_O\,\mathrm{d}\ln(K - K_N).$$

Clearly, the skill premium will go up only if the increase in $H$ induces a sufficiently strong movement of capital away from the old technology into the new technology. Using (5.11) and noting that $\mathrm{d}\ln(K - K_N) = -(K_N/K - K_N)\,\mathrm{d}\ln K_N$, we get

$$\frac{\mathrm{d}\ln(\omega/w)}{\mathrm{d}\ln H} = \frac{(\alpha_O - \alpha_N)K_N}{(1 - \alpha_N)(K - K_N) + (1 - \alpha_O)K_N}.$$

This is positive if and only if $\alpha_O > \alpha_N$, i.e., if the elasticity of output with respect to capital is greater in the old technology than in the new technology.

We can check that this condition is in fact equivalent to the capital efficiency condition (5.10). Writing down the dual optimization problem for firms using the new technology,

$$\min_{H,K} \omega H + rK,$$
$$\text{s.t. } Y = A_N H^{1-\alpha_N} K^{\alpha_N},$$

we get, from the first-order condition for $K$,

$$\hat{K}_N = \frac{\lambda_N \alpha_N}{r},$$

where $\lambda_N$ is the Lagrange multiplier, which must be equal to the marginal cost of output, i.e., computing $\lambda_N$ yields the cost function.[5] Similarly,

$$\hat{K}_O = \frac{\lambda_O \alpha_O}{r},$$

and again $\lambda_O = c_O(w, r)$. Since the two-technology case implies that $\lambda_O = \lambda_N$, it follows that $\hat{K}_N < \hat{K}_O$ if and only if $\alpha_O > \alpha_N$.

When $\alpha_O > \alpha_N$, if figure 5.6 were drawn on a logarithmic scale, i.e., if the axes were $(\ln w, \ln r)$ and $(\ln \omega, \ln r)$, the FPF would be flatter for the old technology than for the new technology. Consequently, the rise in $r$ associated with an increase in $H$ (or with a reduction in $K$), triggers a greater relative fall in $w$ (i.e., absolute fall in $\ln w$) than in $\omega$, which raises the skill premium.

### 5.1.5 Empirical Assessment

From the preceding discussion, the conditions under which human-capital accumulation raises the skill premium seem pretty stringent. First, one must be in a configuration where both technologies are simultaneously used. Second, the two technologies must be such that their joint use leads to substitutability between human capital and labor, i.e., (5.5) must hold. Third, the capital efficiency condition (5.10) must also hold. That is, the new technology must use less capital than the old one, but not to the point where (5.5) would be violated; it must therefore use even less labor.

Nevertheless, Beaudry and Green (2003) show that these conditions are testable and not rejected by their data. They use disaggregated data on the distribution of wages in Germany and the United States, and aggregate time-series data on factor inputs $(H, K, L)$ in each country. The idea is to estimate an earnings function for each country at each date, and regress the intercept and slope of this function on aggregate factor inputs. Beaudry and Green assume that an individual $i$ is characterized by a productivity $l_i$, which also defines his raw labor input. He has $e_i$ years of education, and his human capital is $h_i = l_i e_i$. In this nonspecialization model, workers earn the returns to all their characteristics. Hence, the income of individual $i$ is

$$z_i = (w + \omega e_i) l_i.$$

[5] In this particular case, algebraically,

$$\lambda_N = c_N(\omega, r) = \frac{\omega^{1-\alpha_N} r^{\alpha_N}}{A_N (1-\alpha_N)^{1-\alpha_N} \alpha_N^{\alpha_N}}.$$

This leads the authors to estimate a log-earnings function of the following form:

$$\ln z_i = \ln w + \frac{\omega}{w} e_i + \ln l_i,$$

where the approximation $\ln(1 + (\omega/w)e_i) \approx (\omega/w)e_i$ has been made. Thus, at any date, one runs a regression of earnings on years of education, with the individual-specific productivity term $\ln l_i$ being treated as an error term in the regression. We get estimates $a = \ln w$ of the "intercept" and $b = \omega/w$ of the slope. The theory discussed above implies that, since they depend only on factor prices, $a$ and $b$ can be expressed as functions of relative of factor endowments only:

$$a = a(K/L, H/L),$$
$$b = b(K/L, H/L).$$

These relationships can be estimated, and from the above discussion the estimates are subject to a number of restrictions. Assume, as Beaudry and Green do, that we use the following specification:

$$a = a_0 + a_1 \ln \frac{K}{L} + a_2 \ln \frac{H}{L},$$
$$b = b_0 + b_1 \ln \frac{K}{L} + b_2 \ln \frac{H}{L}.$$

A first restriction comes from the hypothesis that the two technologies are simultaneously in use. We then know that $w = w(r)$ and $\omega = \omega(r)$. Therefore, any function of the factor prices $\phi(w, \omega, r)$ can be written as a function of $r$ only, $\phi(w, \omega, r) = \phi(w(r), \omega(r), r) = \hat{\phi}(r)$. If we now express it as a function of the logarithms of the ratios of factor endowments, $\phi = \psi(\ln(K/L), \ln(H/L))$, it must be the case that

$$\frac{\partial \psi}{\partial(\ln(K/L))} = \hat{\phi}'(r) \frac{\partial r}{\partial(\ln(K/L))}$$

and

$$\frac{\partial \psi}{\partial(\ln(H/L))} = \hat{\phi}'(r) \frac{\partial r}{\partial(\ln(H/L))};$$

therefore,

$$\frac{\partial \psi/\partial(\ln(K/L))}{\partial \psi/\partial(\ln(H/L))} = \frac{\partial r/\partial(\ln(K/L))}{\partial r/\partial(\ln(H/L))},$$

which is independent of the particular function $\phi$ that we are using. Applying this result to $\phi = \ln w$ (i.e., $\psi = a$) and then to $\phi = \omega/w$ (i.e., $\psi = b$), we find that

$$\frac{\partial r/\partial(\ln(K/L))}{\partial r/\partial(\ln(H/L))} = \frac{\partial a/\partial(\ln(K/L))}{\partial a/\partial(\ln(H/L))} = \frac{a_1}{a_2}$$
$$= \frac{\partial b/\partial(\ln(K/L))}{\partial b/\partial(\ln(H/L))} = \frac{b_1}{b_2}.$$

Thus, the two-technology hypothesis has the testable implication that $a_1/a_2 = b_1/b_2$. This restriction is tightly satisfied by Beaudry and Green's estimates.

Another implication is that if (5.5) holds, then capital accumulation increases wages and human-capital accumulation reduces wages. One must then have $a_1 > 0$ and $a_2 < 0$ (implying also that $b_1 b_2 < 0$). This implication is also borne by Beaudry and Green's data. A consequence is that the neutral accumulation path is upward sloping.

Finally, if (5.10) holds, then human-capital accumulation increases the skill premium and physical-capital accumulation reduces it. This implies that $b_1 < 0$ and $b_2 > 0$, which is also true of their estimates.

The authors then argue that imbalances in the accumulation of human capital and physical capital explain why inequality has increased in the United States but not in Germany. Germany has more or less followed a neutral accumulation path, while the United States has deviated from it by accumulating too much human capital relative to physical capital. As a result, the United States has used the new technologies to a greater extent, with the mixed blessing of stagnant wages and a rise in the returns to skill. On the other hand, Germany has had constant relative wage inequality, and, if the model is to be believed, this is due to its greater balance between human and physical accumulation, which has prevented it from adopting the new technologies to the same extent as the United States.

Beaudry and Green's results are controversial, because many believe that Germany has escaped the rise in wage inequality—at the cost of higher unemployment—because of its rigid system of wage formation based on collective bargaining, which prevents the gap between skilled and unskilled wages from widening. Their explanation, in contrast, ignores institutions and ascribes all the differences between the two countries to different trends in factor inputs. That the data validates their tight restrictions, and in particular the two-technology hypothesis, is in itself a remarkable achievement.

## 5.2 Induced Bias in Innovation

Until now we have analyzed only the effect of the supply of skills on the relative use of the skill-intensive technology when two technologies are available. We now discuss how a greater supply of skilled workers may induce technological progress in a direction that shifts relative demand in their favor. To allow for such a possibility, we must have a model in which technical progress can be biased either in favor of skilled workers or in favor of unskilled workers.

The early literature on the "induced bias" in growth, starting with Hicks (1932), emphasized the role of "bottlenecks." The idea was that if technical progress increases the productivity of a factor too much relative to the complementary factors, these will be in ever greater demand, which will trigger compensating innovation that would raise their own productivity. One can then expect growth to proceed in a "balanced way," with different dimensions of productivity growing at the same rate. The more recent literature, building on endogenous growth theory, has highlighted "market-size" effects, which say that if a factor accounts for a greater share of value added, innovators that make that factor more productive will make higher profits (see Acemoglu 1998, 2002a). In the analysis below we show that the relative importance of bottlenecks and market-size effects depends on the extent to which skilled and unskilled workers are complements or substitutes in the aggregate production function. We first gain an intuitive understanding by looking at the marginal willingness to pay for technological improvements in one dimension or the other, then move to a more fully specified endogenous growth model along the lines of chapter 1.

### 5.2.1 The Relative Willingness to Pay for Technical Progress

A natural specification is a production function with two technical progress parameters:

$$Y = F(AL, BH). \tag{5.12}$$

In such a case, the wages of unskilled and skilled labor are given by, respectively,

$$\begin{aligned} w &= AF_1', \\ \omega &= BF_2'. \end{aligned}$$

With this framework, we can already ask how innovation in $A$ and $B$ will respond to changes in factor endowments. A heuristic way to tackle this problem is to compute firms' marginal willingness to pay for a unit increase in the productivity of labor versus a unit increase in the productivity of human capital. With the price of output again normalized to 1, let $c(w, \omega, A, B)$ be the cost function. Per unit of output, a firm is willing to pay $-\partial c/\partial A$ (respectively $-\partial c/\partial B$) to increase $A$ (respectively $B$) by one unit. The Lagrangian of the unit cost minimization problem is $\mathcal{L} = \omega H + wL - \lambda(F(AL, BH) - 1)$. By the envelope theorem,

$\partial c/\partial A = -\lambda L F_1'$. As seen in chapter 1, $\lambda = 1$ in equilibrium. Therefore,

$$\frac{\partial c}{\partial A} = -LF_1',$$
$$\frac{\partial c}{\partial B} = -HF_2'.$$

These equations define the firms' marginal willingness to pay, per unit of output, for an increase in the technological levels $A$ and $B$. A simple interpretation is as follows: upon an increase in $A$, firms can produce the same (unit) amount of output by decreasing $L$ proportionally. At the optimum, such a response is as good as any other marginal change in the input mix, since such changes only have second-order effects. The savings made by reducing $L$ proportionally are equal to $wL\,\mathrm{d}A/A = AF_1'L\,\mathrm{d}A/A = LF_1'\,\mathrm{d}A$.

If firms were "paying" for an improvement in $A$ and $B$, and if the "costs" of such improvements were the same for $A$ and $B$,[6] then the marginal willingness to pay would be equalized between the two types of improvements, implying the following simple relationship:

$$\frac{F_1'}{F_2'} = \frac{H}{L}. \tag{5.13}$$

Because of constant returns to scale, the left-hand side is an increasing function of the ratio $BH/AL$. The formula therefore pins down the equilibrium ratio $b = B/A$ as a function of the relative factor endowment $h = H/L$. If one were to start from a situation where the left-hand side was larger than the right-hand side, firms would get more out of an improvement in $A$ than out of an improvement in $B$. Innovation would only be labor augmenting, thus progressively reducing $F_1'$ and raising $F_2'$, until equality in (5.13) is reached.

How does the supply of human capital relative to labor affect the induced bias in innovation? Assuming that $F(AL, BH) = ALf(BH/(AL))$[7] and differentiating (5.13) we get that

$$\frac{\mathrm{d}b}{\mathrm{d}h} = -\frac{f'^2}{f''fh} - \frac{b}{h}. \tag{5.14}$$

This is positive if and only if

$$\frac{f''}{f'} > -\frac{f'}{fb}, \tag{5.15}$$

i.e., if the curvature of $f$ is not too strong. That is, if there is enough substitutability between the two factors, an increase in $H/L$ is matched by

[6] That this cost is the same is an unimportant assumption that just simplifies the derivations below.

[7] Equation (5.13) is then equivalent to $f'h(1 + b) = f$.

an increase in $B/A$. As human capital is more abundant relative to labor, firms are more willing to "invest" in increasing its productivity, since this investment boosts the productivity of more workers—Acemoglu's (1998) "market-size" effect; at the same time, it makes the bottleneck in unskilled labor worse, but that is not too much of a problem if there is enough substitutability between skilled and unskilled labor. On the other hand, if there is a lot of complementarity between $H$ and $L$, it is more profitable to boost the productivity of the scarce factor; $B/A$ will tend to compensate imbalances between $H$ and $L$, thus falling when $H/L$ goes up.

Consider, for example, the CES case:

$$F(AL, KH) = ((AL)^{\gamma} + (BH)^{\gamma})^{1/\gamma}. \tag{5.16}$$

Then (5.13) is equivalent to

$$\frac{B}{A} = \left(\frac{H}{L}\right)^{\gamma/(1-\gamma)}; \tag{5.17}$$

this function is increasing if $\gamma \in (0, 1]$ (substitutability), and decreasing if $\gamma < 0$ (complementarity).

That induced technical change favors skilled workers does not in itself imply that their relative wage has to go up. The effect has to be strong enough to offset the direct negative effect of $H/L$ on the marginal productivity of skilled workers and its positive effect on the marginal productivity of unskilled workers. We have that

$$\begin{aligned} \frac{\omega}{w} &= b\frac{F_2'}{F_1'} \\ &= \frac{b}{h}. \end{aligned} \tag{5.18}$$

Differentiating, we get

$$\frac{w}{\omega}\frac{\mathrm{d}}{\mathrm{d}h}\left(\frac{\omega}{w}\right) = \frac{\mathrm{d}b}{\mathrm{d}h} - 1.$$

Thus, we need a more than proportional response of the technological ratio to the factor endowment ratio for an increase in human capital to raise the return to skill. Using (5.14), we see that this will be the case provided that

$$\frac{f''}{f'} > -\frac{f'}{f(h+b)},$$

which is more stringent than (5.15) and implies a lower curvature, i.e., more substitutability between $H$ and $L$ than is implied by (5.15).

Going back to the CES example, (5.17) and (5.18) simply imply that

$$\frac{\omega}{w} = h^{(2\gamma-1)/(1-\gamma)}.$$

Hence, an increase in $h$ may indeed increase the return to skill, provided $\gamma > \frac{1}{2}$.

Essentially, when substitutability is large enough, the market-size effect dominates the effects coming from decreasing returns (i.e., the bottleneck effect in innovation and the direct negative effect of $h$ on $\omega/w$).

An important requirement for these effects to come into play is that technical progress can be *directed*. That is, one is able to decide, before making an innovation, whether it is more likely to increase $B$ or $A$.

### 5.2.2 A Model with Profit-Motivated Horizontal Innovation

The preceding analysis is of course loose, since it does not say what it means to "buy" an increase in productivity, nor does it explicitly formalize the R&D process. However, its essence is basically unchanged when we make the model more rigorous.

To do so, we can build on the endogenous growth literature described in chapter 1, and assume that technical change takes the form of a greater variety of intermediate inputs. Extending the analysis of chapter 1, we now assume that the final good is produced using two intermediate inputs, $Y_h$ and $Y_l$:

$$Y = F(Y_l, Y_h).$$

Each of these goods is produced using a continuum of differentiated inputs, produced by monopolies. The goods used to produce $Y_l$ are different from the goods used to produce $Y_h$. The input $Y_l$ uses differentiated goods of "$l$-type," available in total mass $N_l$ and indexed by $j$:

$$Y_l = \left[\int_0^{N_l} y_{lj}^{\varepsilon}\,\mathrm{d}j\right]^{1/\varepsilon}.$$

Similarly, $Y_h$ uses intermediate inputs of "$h$-type," whose total mass is $N_h$:

$$Y_h = \left[\int_0^{N_h} y_{hj}^{\varepsilon}\,\mathrm{d}j\right]^{1/\varepsilon}.$$

To produce the $l$-type varieties, one only uses labor, and the production function is

$$y_{lj} = l_j,$$

where $l_j$ is the labor input used in variety $j$. Similarly $h$-type goods only use human capital, with

$$y_{hj} = h_j.$$

As in chapter 1, people innovate by introducing new varieties, either of the $l$-type or of the $h$-type. As we have shown, we can rewrite an aggregate production function as (5.12), with

$$A = N_l^{1/(\eta-1)}, \tag{5.19}$$

$$B = N_h^{1/(\eta-1)}, \tag{5.20}$$

where $\eta = 1/(1-\varepsilon)$ is the elasticity of substitution.

Hence, inventing a new variety whose production uses a given factor is equivalent to increasing the productivity of that factor in the aggregate production function.

In order to determine whether technical progress will be biased toward increasing $A$ or toward increasing $B$, we have to compute the value of a patent—and therefore the monopoly profits—for each type of variety. To do so, we first compute prices, and then quantities.

Monopoly pricing implies that the price of an individual $l$-type good is

$$p_{lj} = \mu w,$$

where again $\mu = 1/\varepsilon = \eta/(\eta-1)$ is the markup. Similarly, for an $h$-type good,

$$p_{hj} = \mu\omega.$$

Profit maximization for the (competitive) producers of the intermediate aggregates $Y_l$ and $Y_h$ yields the equilibrium prices of these goods, denoted by $p_l$ and $p_h$:

$$\begin{aligned} p_l &= \left[\int_0^{N_l} p_{lj}^{1-\eta}\,\mathrm{d}j\right]^{1/(1-\eta)} \\ &= N_l^{1/(1-\eta)}\mu w \\ &= \mu\frac{w}{A}. \end{aligned}$$

Similarly,

$$p_h = \mu\frac{\omega}{B}.$$

Thus, the marginal cost of an aggregate intermediate input can be expressed as the price of the factor that it uses divided by the appropriate index of total factor productivity, and the price of an aggregate intermediate input is in turn equal to a markup over that marginal cost.

Finally, $p_l$ and $p_h$ must be equal to the marginal product of the corresponding composite inputs, which allows us to get $w$ and $\omega$ as functions of aggregate factor inputs $H$ and $L$:

$$p_l = F_1'(AL, BH) \quad \Longleftrightarrow \quad w = \frac{A}{\mu}F_1'(AL, BH)$$

and

$$\omega = \frac{B}{\mu}F_2'(AL, BH).$$

This completes the characterization of prices. Next, note that since the differentiated goods of each type are symmetrical, labor is uniformly allocated between them, implying that

$$y_{lj} = \frac{L}{N_l}$$

and

$$y_{hj} = \frac{H}{N_h}.$$

This allows us to compute profits in each sector:

$$\begin{aligned} \pi_{lj} &= y_{lj}(p_{lj} - w) = \frac{L}{N_l}\frac{\mu - 1}{\mu}AF_1' \\ &= L\frac{\mu - 1}{\mu}A^{2-\eta}F_1' = \pi_l \end{aligned} \tag{5.21}$$

and

$$\pi_{hj} = H\frac{\mu - 1}{\mu}B^{2-\eta}F_2' = \pi_h. \tag{5.22}$$

Suppose that the economy is in a steady state where a positive level of innovation takes place in each category of input. Then researchers must be indifferent between inventing an $l$-variety and an $h$-variety. Consequently, the value of a patent must be the same for both kinds of innovation. Calling these values $V_l$ and $V_h$, they must satisfy the Bellman equation (1.24),

$$rV_h = \pi_h + \mathrm{d}V_h/\mathrm{d}t, \tag{5.23}$$

and similarly for $V_l$. Equality between $V_h$ and $V_l$ at all dates clearly implies that $\pi_h = \pi_l$. Using the preceding formulas, we get that

$$\frac{F_1'}{F_2'} = \frac{H}{L}\left(\frac{B}{A}\right)^{2-\eta}. \tag{5.24}$$

We get something quite similar to the simple "willingness to pay approach" (i.e., (5.13)), but it is different in that we now have a term in $(B/A)^{2-\eta}$ on the right-hand side. The term in $H/L$ still reflects the market-size effects that are driving Acemoglu's unconventional results. When a factor is in greater supply, there is a larger market for any intermediate good that uses that factor, given the total number of such intermediate goods. Consequently, profits for the monopolies that produce these goods are higher, and so are the incentives to introduce new varieties of these goods. The term $(B/A)^{2-\eta}$ reflects two conflicting effects. First, productivity can be higher for one factor only if there is a greater number of intermediate inputs using that factor, which automatically reduces the profits of each of these individual firms. This effect is clearly specific to the "horizontal" approach to innovation that we use here. At the same time, a higher $A$ increases the wage $w$, which, given market size, increases prices and thus profits—an effect which is also neglected in the willingness to pay equations of the preceding subsection.

In this steady state, the relative bias in technology $B/A$ is therefore determined by equation (5.24). Limiting ourselves to the CES case defined by (5.16), we obtain

$$\frac{\pi_h}{\pi_l} = \left(\frac{H}{L}\right)^{\gamma} \left(\frac{B}{A}\right)^{1-\eta+\gamma}.$$

Intuitively, for this to determine a stable, interior value of $B/A$, we need the right-hand side to be falling with $B/A$, i.e.,

$$1 - \eta + \gamma < 0. \tag{5.25}$$

Otherwise, an increase in $B/A$ will increase the benefit of innovating in $h$-type goods relative to $l$-type goods, which will tend to further increase $B/A$. Such a possibility is analyzed in greater detail below when we deal with the dynamics. Assuming then that (5.25) holds, the equilibrium bias in technology is given by

$$\frac{B}{A} = \left(\frac{H}{L}\right)^{\gamma/(\eta-1-\gamma)}. \tag{5.26}$$

As the denominator of the exponent is positive, this has the same properties as (5.17): the bias favors the more abundant factor if the two composite inputs are substitutes ($\gamma > 0$) and will favor the scarce factor and offset bottlenecks if the two inputs are complements ($\gamma < 0$).

Similarly, looking at wages, we find that

$$\frac{\omega}{w} = \frac{BF_2'}{AF_1'} = \left(\frac{H}{L}\right)^{(\eta\gamma+1-\eta)/(\eta-1-\gamma)}.$$

We again find that $\omega/w$ increases with $H/L$ provided that

$$\gamma > \frac{\eta - 1}{\eta}. \tag{5.27}$$

Again, a positive effect of the supply of skilled workers on the skill premium is possible, but we need a greater degree of substitutability between $H$ and $L$ than is needed simply for $H/L$ to have a positive effect on the skill bias in technology.

### 5.2.3 Dynamics

We can then easily extend the model to characterize its dynamics. To do so, we assume a simple representation of the R&D process. Assume that there is a fixed supply $g$ of researchers, who can devote their time to inventing either an $h$-type good or an $l$-type good. To fix ideas, assume that there is no adjustment cost of switching between the two activities, and that competition between R&D firms means that the value of patents produced by a researcher equates with his wage. Finally, assume that the researcher's productivity is the same for both types of inventions.

At any date $t$, we define the total stock of knowledge to be

$$\begin{aligned} N_t &= N_{ht} + N_{lt} \\ &= A_t^{\eta-1} + B_t^{\eta-1}. \end{aligned}$$

We assume, as in chapter 1, that a researcher's productivity is proportional to $N_t$, with a fixed unit coefficient. Therefore, the total number of goods invented at $t$ must be equal to

$$\frac{\mathrm{d}N_t}{\mathrm{d}t} = gN_t,$$

so that $N_t$ grows at rate $g$. The new goods are allocated optimally between the two types, on the basis of profitability.

The allocation of researchers between the two kinds of innovations, must be such that we have the following situation.

- If $V_h > V_l$, only $h$-type goods are invented, implying, given (5.19) and (5.20), that

$$\begin{aligned} \frac{\mathrm{d}B}{\mathrm{d}t} &= \frac{1}{\eta - 1} N_{ht}^{(2-\eta)/(1-\eta)} \dot{N}_{ht} \\ &= \frac{g}{\eta - 1} B_t^{2-\eta} (A_t^{\eta-1} + B_t^{\eta-1}) > 0, \\ \frac{\mathrm{d}A}{\mathrm{d}t} &= 0, \end{aligned}$$

  and therefore $\mathrm{d}(B/A)/\mathrm{d}t > 0$.

- If $V_l < V_h$, only $l$-type goods are invented, so that $\mathrm{d}B/\mathrm{d}t = 0$,

$$\frac{\mathrm{d}A}{\mathrm{d}t} = \frac{g}{\eta - 1} A_t^{2-\eta} (A_t^{\eta-1} + B_t^{\eta-1}) > 0,$$

  and $\mathrm{d}(B/A)/\mathrm{d}t < 0$.

- If $V_l = V_h$, both types of goods are invented. Researchers are indifferent between the two activities, and there exists one allocation of research effort such that $\mathrm{d}\ln B/\mathrm{d}t = \mathrm{d}\ln A/\mathrm{d}t$, i.e., $\mathrm{d}(B/A)/\mathrm{d}t = 0$.[8]

It turns out that a convenient variable that we can use in order to analyze the dynamics is

$$\Delta_t = \frac{V_{ht} - V_{lt}}{N_t^{(2-\eta)/(\eta-1)}} = \frac{V_{ht} - V_{lt}}{(A_t^{\eta-1} + B_t^{\eta-1})^{(2-\eta)/(\eta-1)}}.$$

The ratio $b_t = B_t/A_t$ now depends on time. The preceding remarks allow us to draw a $\dot{b}_t = 0$ locus, denoted EE, in the $(b, \Delta)$-plane. It is horizontal and is defined by $\Delta = 0$. If the economy is above it, then $\dot{b}_t > 0$, if it is below it, then $\dot{b}_t < 0$.

The evolution equation for $\Delta_t$ is then obtained by using the Bellman equations (5.23) for $V_h$ and $V_l$ and substituting the formulas for profits, (5.21) and (5.22), yielding

$$\dot{\Delta}_t = r\Delta_t - \frac{\mu - 1}{\mu} \frac{1}{(1 + b_t^{\eta-1})^{(2-\eta)/(\eta-1)}} (Hb^{2-\eta}F_2' - LF_1').$$

In the CES case defined by (5.16), this can be rewritten as

$$\dot{\Delta}_t = r\Delta_t - \frac{\mu - 1}{\mu} L \frac{(1 + (bh)^{\gamma})^{(1-\gamma)/\gamma}}{(1 + b_t^{\eta-1})^{(2-\eta)/(\eta-1)}} (h^{\gamma} b_t^{1-\eta+\gamma} - 1). \tag{5.28}$$

This defines a $\dot{\Delta}_t = 0$ locus DD in the $(b, \Delta)$-plane. It crosses EE at a point $(b^*, \Delta^*)$ which satisfies $\Delta^* = 0$, i.e., $\pi_{ht} = \pi_{lt}$, and thus $h^{\gamma} b^{1-\eta+\gamma} = 1$, which is the same as (5.26). Thus, the steady state of this dynamical system is the one that has been analyzed above. Furthermore, if the stability

---

[8] This is determined as follows. Call $\theta$ the fraction of researchers seeking to invent the $h$-type goods. Then $\dot{N}_h = \theta g N$, and $\dot{N}_l = (1 - \theta) g N$. Therefore,

$$\frac{\dot{B}}{B} = \frac{1}{\eta - 1} \frac{\dot{N}_h}{N_h} = \frac{1}{\eta - 1} \frac{\theta g N}{B^{\eta-1}}$$

and

$$\frac{\dot{A}}{A} = \frac{1}{\eta - 1} \frac{(1 - \theta) g N}{A^{\eta-1}}.$$

The equilibrium value of $\theta$ is therefore

$$\theta = \frac{A^{1-\eta}}{A^{1-\eta} + B^{1-\eta}}.$$

The common growth rate of $A$ and $B$ is then $g/(\eta - 1)$, and the common growth rate of $N_h$ and $N_l$ is just $g$.

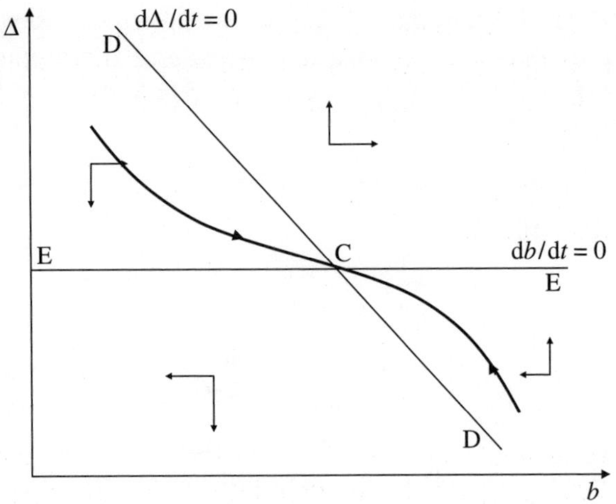


**Figure 5.7.** The dynamics of the technology bias.

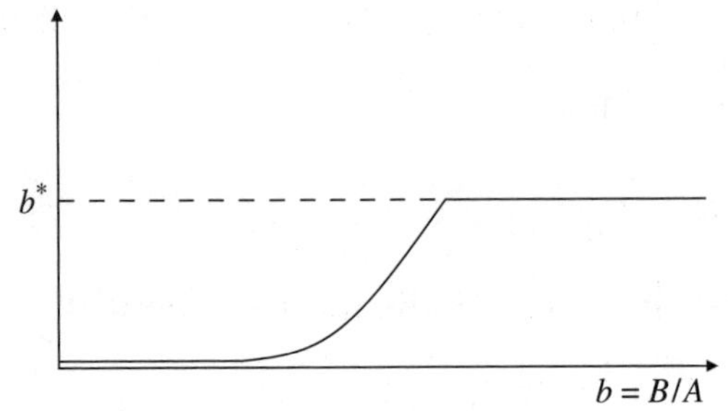


**Figure 5.8.** The convergence path of the technology bias.

condition (5.25) holds, then DD is locally downward sloping around the steady state, and must always be such that $\Delta < 0$ (respectively $\Delta > 0$) for $b > b^*$ (respectively $b < b^*$).

The dynamics are illustrated in figure 5.7.[9] The saddle-path property is satisfied.[10] If the initial value of $b$ is lower than $b^*$, then $\pi_{ht} > \pi_{lt}$; $\Delta$ jumps above zero, reflecting expectations of higher profits in the $h$-type goods for a while. Innovation only takes place in that sector, so $B$ grows while $A$ remains constant. At some point, then, $b$ is going to become equal to $b^*$; research workers then allocate themselves so as to satisfy (5.26) throughout. In figure 5.7 this takes place when (at a finite date) the economy hits the steady-state point C, where DD and EE cross. The

[9] For simplicity, DD has been drawn as downward sloping throughout.

[10] That is, given an initial value for $b$, there exists a unique initial value of $\Delta$ such that the subsequent trajectory for the economy is not explosive. This trajectory converges to the steady state and is called the "saddle-path."

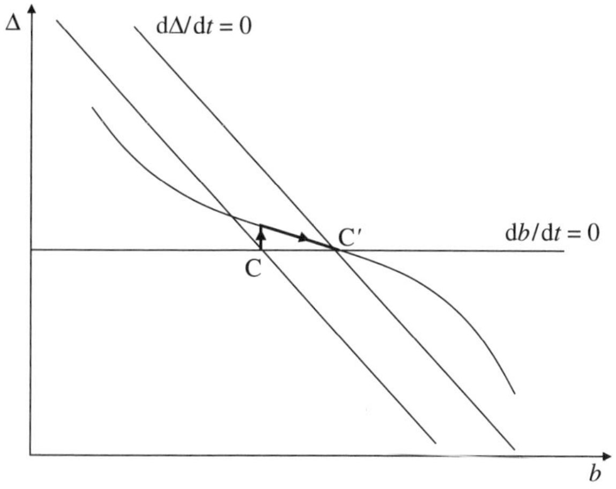


**Figure 5.9.** Response of the technology bias to an increase in $H/L$.

corresponding evolution of $b = B/A$ is represented in figure 5.8: it goes up and then stays constant.

The stability condition guarantees that $\pi_h$ falls relative to $\pi_l$ as $B$ grows relative to $A$. Consequently, $\Delta$ falls along the convergence path and the economy converges to the steady state.

Figure 5.9 shows the economy's response to a once-and-for-all increase in the relative supply of human capital, in the case where $\gamma > 0$. The DD locus shifts up: because market-size effects dominate, one has $\pi_{ht} > \pi_{lt}$ upon impact. Thus, $\Delta$ jumps to a positive value and adjustment proceeds as in figure 5.8, until the economy reaches a permanently higher level of $B/A$; the higher relative supply of skilled workers induces a permanently greater technological bias in favor of them.

Figure 5.10 shows the response of the skill premium, given, at any point in time, by

$$\frac{\omega_t}{w_t} = \left(\frac{H}{L}\right)^{\gamma-1}\left(\frac{B_t}{A_t}\right)^{\gamma}.$$

Upon impact, the increase in $H/L$ reduces the skill premium, as skilled workers are pushed along their marginal product schedule. Over time, however, $B$ grows, so that the skill premium gradually recovers. If (5.27) is violated, then the skill premium is permanently lower as the economy hits the new steady state (figure 5.10(a)). If it holds, then the response of the technological bias more than compensates for the direct depressing effect of relative labor supply, and the skill premium is permanently higher (figure 5.10(b)).

If $\gamma < 0$, then, as equation (5.28) makes clear, an increase in $H/L$ shifts DD to the left, and we get the opposite response of $b$.

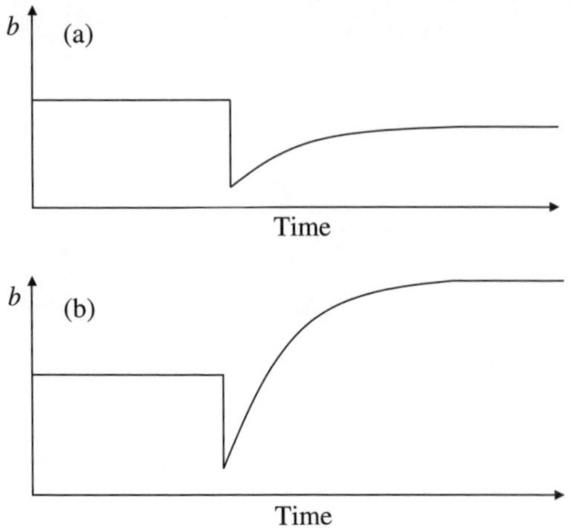


**Figure 5.10.** Response of the skill premium to an increase in $H/L$.

What happens if the stability condition is violated? Accumulation of knowledge in one type of goods further increases the relative profitability of inventing more such goods. Intuitively, we expect the bias of technology to be cumulative, and the economy will eventually only innovate in $h$-goods or in $l$-goods.

## 5.3 Conclusion

We have presented two models in which, upon an increase in the supply of skilled workers, more of the technologies intensive in skilled workers are used. In both cases, such a shift may paradoxically increase the skill premium. In the Beaudry and Green model, this is because physical capital moves away from the old labor-intensive technology into the new human-capital-intensive technology, and because capital is more important to the old technology than to the new one—therefore, the unskilled are more vulnerable to the relative scarcity of capital triggered by the increase in human capital. In the Acemoglu model, this is because there is a strong response of innovation in the technologies that use human capital, because the market size for such technologies is larger and bottleneck effects are unimportant, due to the relatively large substitutability between skilled and unskilled workers in production.[11]

[11] Note, however, that in other contexts, it is the bottleneck effects that can be inegalitarian. Zeira (1998) develops a model where innovation must be labor saving, and shows that more innovations will then be adopted in richer countries where wages are higher. Thus, the pattern of innovation amplifies the initial world inequality.

# 6

# Labor as a Quality Input: Skill Aggregation and Sectoral Segregation

The preceding chapters have analyzed how technical progress affects inequality in "neoclassical models." These models have the following characteristics:

- Workers bring to the firm a vector of characteristics.
- The production function depends on the aggregate vector of characteristics used by the firms and is independent of how they are embodied in its workers. That is, workers interact within the firm in a linear fashion. Their characteristics are added so as to determine the vector of the firm's inputs.
- The labor market makes individual firms and workers "irrelevant." A firm can purchase any vector of characteristics it wants, by paying a linear price for each characteristic. It does not care about which particular workers it will employ to get its preferred input vector. Consequently, in equilibrium the marginal product of each characteristic is equalized throughout the economy, and this defines the unique return to that characteristic. Similarly, workers disregard which particular firm they are working for. Their income is the sum of the return to each characteristic multiplied by the amount of that characteristic that they supply.

In this chapter and chapters 7 and 8 we depart from these assumptions and consider models where individuals cannot be aggregated into stocks of homogeneous labour inputs, so that their income is not a linear function of the vector of characteristics they are supplying to the market. This situation may arise if the assumptions described above fail to hold. This may happen under two sets of circumstances:

(1) Interactions between individuals at the firm level are not linear.

(2) The marginal product of a characteristic is not equalized throughout the economy, because equalization would not be compatible with equilibrium in the labor market. The price of a characteristic differs across activities. It is then optimal for workers to specialize in different activities depending on the vector of characteristics they are endowed with. Because different workers face different price vectors for their characteristics, the overall earnings schedule is not linear in characteristics.

This chapter builds on Rosen (1983) and Heckman and Scheinkman (1987) to analyze the second possibility, and its consequences for the distribution of income. Chapters 7 and 8 then elaborate on the first case by looking into the sources of nonlinearity more deeply.

## 6.1 Bundling and Pricing of Labor Market Characteristics

To highlight the main point, I consider the following model. Workers are endowed with two characteristics, human capital ($h$) and labor ($l$). There is a continuum of worker skill types indexed by $s$. A worker of skill $s$ is endowed with $l(s)$ units of labor and $h(s)$ units of human capital. Without loss of generality, we can order workers by comparative advantage and assume that $h(s)/l(s)$ is increasing with $s$.[1] The total labor force is normalized to 1 and $s$ is defined so as to be uniformly distributed over $[0,1]$. Furthermore, and importantly, workers do not choose to supply either $h$ *or* $l$, they come with both characteristics at the same time. Therefore, we are not in the context of the Roy model of specialization described in chapter 1. Nor, and equally importantly, can workers choose to supply one characteristic to one firm and another to a different firm. Firms matter because they are the places where workers are physically working with their whole bundle of characteristics. For this reason, the nonspecialization model of chapter 1 does not apply either.

Assume there is a single homogeneous consumption good, with the following production function:

$$Y = F(H, L),$$

where $H$ is the aggregate human-capital input, and $L$ the aggregate labor input.

[1] If workers are distributed over a two-dimensional set in the $(h, l)$-plane, we can simply aggregate together all workers who have the same $h/l$ ratio. We can then treat them as a single worker type, since, within such a set, workers will all make the same decisions.

We can show that in equilibrium, the earnings of a worker with skill $s$ are given by

$$z(s) = wl(s) + \omega h(s), \tag{6.1}$$

where $w$ and $\omega$ are the marginal products of labor and human capital at full employment, i.e.,

$$\begin{aligned} w &= F'_L(H, L), \\ \omega &= F'_H(H, L), \\ H &= \int_0^1 h(s)\,\mathrm{d}s, \\ L &= \int_0^1 l(s)\,\mathrm{d}s. \end{aligned}$$

In the nonspecialization model of chapter 1, this result was obvious since, by assumption, there was a separate, anonymous market for each characteristic—that is, people were allowed to *unbundle* their vector of characteristics and supply them to different firms. Here people cannot unbundle their characteristics and there is a single labor market for people. However, the result still holds. To see this, write the firm's optimization problem as follows:

$$\max_{g(\cdot)} F\left(\int_0^1 h(s)g(s)\,\mathrm{d}s, \int_0^1 l(s)g(s)\,\mathrm{d}s\right) - \int_0^1 z(s)g(s)\,\mathrm{d}s,$$

where $g(s)$ is the density of workers with skill $s$ employed by the firm. That is, the firm is simply maximizing profits with respect to the number of workers of each skill type that it wants to hire. The first-order condition for a worker type such that $g(s) > 0$ is

$$F'_H h(s) + F'_L l(s) = z(s). \tag{6.2}$$

Therefore, workers are paid the marginal product of the vector of characteristics they bring to the firm. Does that establish that (6.1) holds, thus completing the proof? The answer is no. In (6.2), $F'_H$ and $F'_L$ are the marginal products in the firm in which the worker is working. To complete the proof, we need to show that these marginal products are equalized throughout the economy. To do so, we show that in equilibrium all firms must have the same $H/L$ ratio, i.e., the same marginal products $F'_H$ and $F'_L$. This is due to the fact that a firm with a higher $H/L$ ratio has a higher marginal product of $L$, and therefore attracts workers with a relatively high $l$. In equilibrium, these workers must be employed by the firm, which contradicts the fact that the firm has a high $H/L$ ratio. To see this, assume that there are two firms, 1 and 2, with input vectors $(H_i, L_i)$, $i = 1, 2$, and assume that they have different $H/L$

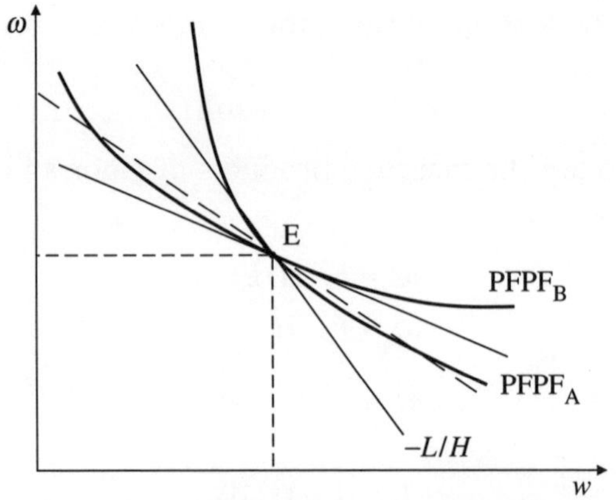


**Figure 6.1.** Factor-price equalization in the two-sector model.

ratios, say $H_1/L_1 > H_2/L_2$. Then $F_H'(H_1, L_1) = F_{H1}' < F_{H2}' = F_H'(H_2, L_2)$ and $F_L'(H_1, L_1) = F_{L1}' > F_{L2}' = F_L'(H_2, L_2)$. A worker's marginal product in firm $i$ is $F_{Hi}'h(s) + F_{Li}'l(s)$, and this is also his wage if firm $i$ employs workers of his type. A worker for whom

$$\frac{h(s)}{l(s)} = \frac{F_{L1}' - F_{L2}'}{F_{H2}' - F_{H1}'} = h(s^*)$$

has the same marginal product (i.e., would earn the same income in equilibrium) in both firms. Consequently, as $h(s)/l(s)$ grows with $s$, a worker for whom $s > s^*$ cannot work in firm 1. If he did, firm 2 could make a positive profit by hiring him since his marginal product in firm 2 would be greater than his wage. Conversely, a worker for whom $s < s^*$ cannot work in firm 2. Therefore, firm 2 only employs workers for whom $h/l \geqslant h(s^*)$, while firm 1 only employs workers for whom $h/l \leqslant h(s^*)$. But this contradicts the assumption that $H_1/L_1 > H_2/L_2$. Therefore, all firms have the same $H/L$ ratio, which must be the one that prevails in the economy. This proves that wages are uniquely determined by (6.1).

Now consider what happens when there are several goods in the economy. Assume that there are two goods, A and B, each with a different production function:

$$Y_A = F_A(H_A, L_A),$$
$$Y_B = F_B(H_B, L_B).$$

Let us normalize the price of good A to 1. Let $p$ be the price of good B. In the simple nonspecialization model where unbundling is allowed, the equilibrium returns to $H$ and $L$ are the same in both sectors as long as both goods are produced. As in the two-technology models analyzed in chapters 4 and 5, the returns are determined by the intersection of

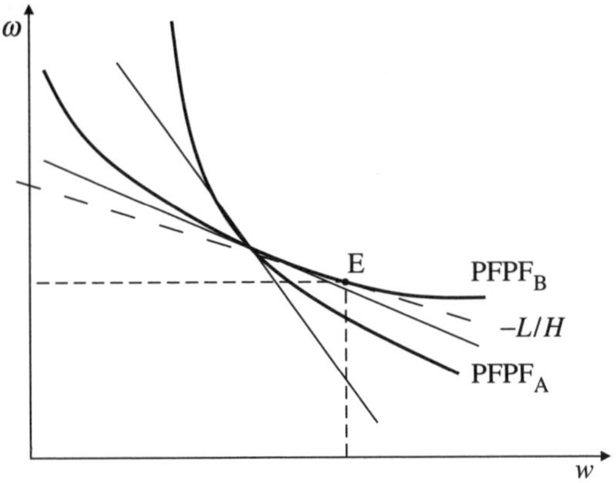


**Figure 6.2.** Full specialization under unbundling.

the FPFs for each good: see figure 6.1, which has been drawn assuming that good B is more intensive in human capital than good A. For both goods to be produced, the economy-wide ratio $H/L$ must be between the ones prevailing in each sector, i.e., a straight line with slope $-L/H$ must cut the equilibrium point between the two tangents, as illustrated in figure 6.1. If the economy-wide $H/L$ ratio is greater than, say, the $H/L$ ratio at the equilibrium point for good B, as illustrated in figure 6.2, then in equilibrium the economy entirely specializes in that good. The equilibrium E is now located to the right of the intersection between the two FPFs, at the point on the FPF for good B where the slope is equal to minus the aggregate $L/H$ ratio. In both scenarios, it is still the case that there is a unique price for each characteristic throughout the economy—the "factor-price equalization" (FPE) case. Of course, the exact position of the FPF for good B depends on $p$, i.e., on preferences. For example, if the marginal utility from consuming good B goes to infinity as the quantity goes to zero, the case of figure 6.2 cannot arise in general equilibrium.

In the case where both goods are produced, the equilibrium can be depicted by the standard Edgeworth box diagram of figure 6.3. This diagram is similar to figures 4.5 and 5.2. Each sector-specific $H/L$ ratio is determined by the slope of the corresponding FPF at the intersection point. The allocation of $H$ and $L$ between the two sectors is determined by the intersection of the two lines, whose slope relative to the relevant origin is equal to the $H/L$ ratio. This is the only allocation that matches the aggregate $H/L$ ratio with the sector-specific ones.

Can this allocation also be an equilibrium in the case where unbundling is impossible? For this to be the case, there must exist an allocation of *people* between the two sectors that yields the right aggregate values of $H_A$, $L_A$, $H_B$, and $L_B$. This raises the following question: what are the

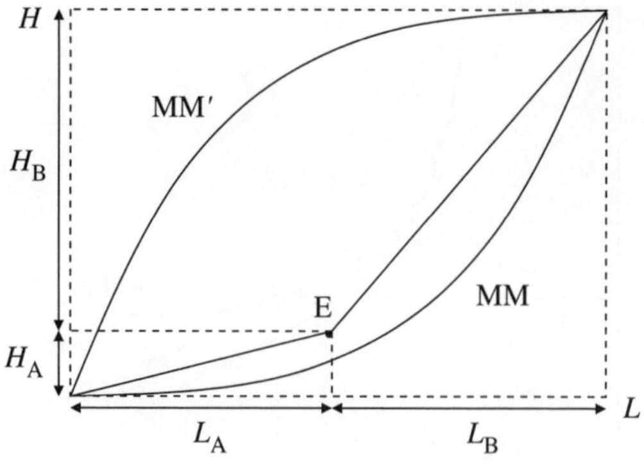


**Figure 6.3.** The allocation of labor and human capital.

*feasible* allocations of $H$ and $L$ between the two sectors, i.e., the feasible points on figure 6.3 such that there exists an underlying allocation of people which matches that allocation?

The answer is depicted by the two curves MM and MM′ in figure 6.3. Feasible allocations must lie within a "lens" of points, delimited by the curve of minimum human-capital intensity MM and its inverted image MM′. The lens depicts how the distribution of $h$ and $l$ across people imposes constraints on the aggregate allocation of $H$ and $L$ between the two sectors. The portion of the space between MM and MM′ is the set of macroeconomic allocations of characteristics to the two sectors that are supported by a microeconomic allocation of people between these sectors.

Suppose that I want to allocate labor to sector A while keeping the $H/L$ ratio in that sector to a minimum. How am I going to do it, and what is the lowest possible value of $H_A/L_A$ that I can achieve, given that a total raw labor input $L_A$ must be obtained? If I could unbundle characteristics, I could keep the ratio equal to zero by allocating just labor and no human capital to sector A. If unbundling is not possible, all I can do is allocate *people*, instead of characteristics, to sector A. These workers bring their human capital to sector A in addition to their labor. To keep $H/L$ at a minimum, the best I can do is to start allocating to that sector the workers with the lowest $h/l$ ratio, i.e., the "least skilled" people. However, the more I want to increase the number of people who are working in sector A, the more I need to add marginal workers who have a greater $h/l$ ratio than the inframarginal workers in the sector. In other words, when $L_A$ is greater I need to allocate more people to sector A and I have to be less picky regarding their $h/l$ ratio; therefore the minimum $H/L$ ratio in sector A must go up with $L_A$. This procedure defines a relationship between $L_A$ and $H_A$, the minimum-human-capital-intensity curve MM.

Since the workers who must be added to sector A in order to increase $L_A$ have a higher $h/l$ ratio than the inframarginal workers, it defines $H_A$ as an increasing, convex function of employment $L_A$. Algebraically, the minimum-capital-intensity allocation is such that

$$L_A = \int_0^{s^-} l(s)\,ds, \tag{6.3}$$

$$H_A = \int_0^{s^-} h(s)\,ds, \tag{6.4}$$

where $s^-$ is the skill of the marginal worker—the highest skill level allocated to sector A. We have that

$$\frac{dH_A}{dL_A} = \frac{h(s^-)}{l(s^-)},$$

which is indeed positive and increasing in $s^-$ (and thus in $L_A$), hence the convexity.

If, instead, I allocate the least skilled people to sector B, I am maximizing the $H_A/L_A$ ratio, and $(L_A, H_A)$ now lies on the MM′ curve, which is represented by the following equations:

$$L_A = L - \int_0^{s^+} l(s)\,ds = \int_{s^+}^1 l(s)\,ds,$$

$$H_A = H - \int_0^{s^+} h(s)\,ds = \int_{s^+}^1 h(s)\,ds,$$

where $s^+$ is now the lowest skill level allocated to sector A.

Geometrically, MM′ is symmetrical to MM with respect to the center of the box, i.e., it is its inverted image.

In any feasible allocation, the aggregate values of $L_A$ and $H_A$ must be such that $(L_A, H_A)$ lies above MM; otherwise, the distribution of $h/l$ in the population does not allow us to pick a set of workers whose aggregate characteristics match the desired ones. If, for example, $(L_A, H_A)$ is below MM, then even the least skilled workers with a combined labor supply equal to $L_A$ have a combined human capital greater than $H_A$. Similarly, for any value of $L_A$, $(L_A, H_A)$ must lie below MM′ in figure 6.3. Therefore, the economy must lie in the lens—which is the case in the configuration of figure 6.3.

Conversely, if $(L_A, H_A)$ is in the lens, then one can construct an allocation of people who bring aggregate levels of labor and human capital exactly equal to $L_A$ and $H_A$, respectively. To do so, just take the two points on MM and MM′ with the same value of $L_A$, and take a linear

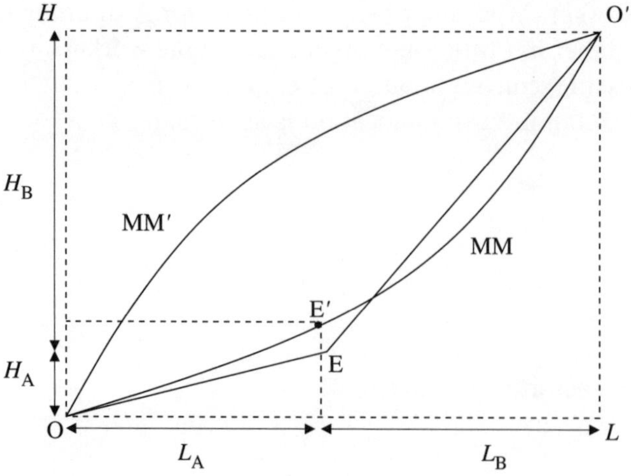


**Figure 6.4.** Equilibrium when E is outside the lens.

combination of their corresponding micro-allocations, with weights that yield the desired aggregate value of $H_A$.[2]

It is then easy to see that if the unbundling equilibrium E lies in the lens, it is also an equilibrium *with* bundling. With equal factor prices, workers are indifferent as to which sector they work in. And an allocation of workers which yields the corresponding allocation of $H$ and $L$ corresponding to E exists, since one is in the lens. Finally, as at point E firms cannot increase profits by changing their human capital and labor as they wish, a fortiori they cannot do so by changing them in the restricted way imposed by bundling. Therefore, point E remains an equilibrium.

Figure 6.4 represents the equilibrium if E is outside the lens. Since sector B is more intensive in human capital, E must lie below the diagonal, and must therefore be below the MM curve to be outside the lens. Factor-price equalization is now unfeasible because it would require too low an $H/L$ ratio in sector A; to reach it, one would have to transfer human capital from unskilled to skilled workers and labor from skilled to unskilled workers, but that is impossible since labor-market characteristics are embedded in people. Therefore, the equilibrium must be such that factor prices differ between the two sectors. Note, however, that within a

[2]Denote by $H_A^-$ and $H_A^+$ the vertical coordinates on MM and MM′ that correspond to $L_A$, and by $s^-$ and $s^+$ the corresponding critical skill levels. The weight on the micro-allocation that gives $(L_A, H_A^-)$ must be equal to $\theta = (H_A^+ - H_A)/(H_A^+ - H_A^-)$. The allocation of labor that yields $L_A$ and $H_A$ in the aggregate is then such that (i) a density $\theta l(s)$ is allocated to sector A for $s < \min(s^-, s^+)$; (ii) a density $(1-\theta)l(s)$ is allocated to sector A for $s > \max(s^-, s^+)$; (iii) all workers, i.e., a density $l(s)$, are allocated to sector A for $s \in [s^+, s^-]$ (which is nonempty only if $s^- > s^+$); and (iv) no worker is allocated to sector A for $s \in [s^-, s^+]$.

sector factor prices are still equalized and equal to the marginal value product: the above reasoning to rule out different factor prices in the one-sector case still applies. Therefore,

$$w_{\mathrm{A}} = F'_{\mathrm{A}L}(H_{\mathrm{A}}, L_{\mathrm{A}}), \tag{6.5}$$

$$w_{\mathrm{B}} = pF'_{\mathrm{B}L}(H_{\mathrm{B}}, L_{\mathrm{B}}), \tag{6.6}$$

$$\omega_{\mathrm{A}} = F'_{\mathrm{A}H}(H_{\mathrm{A}}, L_{\mathrm{A}}), \tag{6.7}$$

$$\omega_{\mathrm{B}} = pF'_{\mathrm{B}H}(H_{\mathrm{B}}, L_{\mathrm{B}}). \tag{6.8}$$

Intuitively, when factor prices differ across sectors, workers will fully specialize in one sector, since they typically get a different income in each sector. For both sectors to be able to attract workers, each must pay more than the other for one factor only. Therefore, either $w_{\mathrm{A}} < w_{\mathrm{B}}$ and $\omega_{\mathrm{A}} > \omega_{\mathrm{B}}$, or $w_{\mathrm{A}} > w_{\mathrm{B}}$ and $\omega_{\mathrm{A}} < \omega_{\mathrm{B}}$. In the former case, workers above a critical skill level will work in sector A and workers below that level will work in sector B. But this would imply a higher $H/L$ ratio in sector A than in sector B. Given that B is more intensive in human capital, this would imply a higher wage of human capital in sector B, which is a contradiction. Therefore, it must be that $w_{\mathrm{A}} > w_{\mathrm{B}}$ and $\omega_{\mathrm{A}} < \omega_{\mathrm{B}}$. The less skilled, with a lower $h/l$ ratio, specialize in sector A, while the more skilled specialize in sector B. The critical skill level which delimits the two groups, still denoted by $s^*$, is such that $w_{\mathrm{A}}l(s^*) + \omega_{\mathrm{A}}h(s^*) = w_{\mathrm{B}}l(s^*) + \omega_{\mathrm{B}}h(s^*)$, i.e.,

$$\frac{h(s^*)}{l(s^*)} = \frac{w_{\mathrm{A}} - w_{\mathrm{B}}}{\omega_{\mathrm{B}} - \omega_{\mathrm{A}}}. \tag{6.9}$$

Because of this specialization pattern, the least skilled all work in sector A; as this minimizes the $H/L$ ratio there, the economy must lie on the MM curve, at the point at which $s^- = s^*$. How is the equilibrium then determined? It is the unique allocation on MM such that the corresponding marginal worker indeed earns the same wage in both sectors. Algebraically, it is the solution to (6.3), (6.4), (6.9), and the sector-specific marginal product conditions.

Intuitively, when one moves up the MM curve, the $H/L$ ratio goes up in both sectors. This is because the marginal worker, who is transferred from sector B to sector A, has an $h/l$ ratio which is larger than average in sector A but smaller than average in sector B. Consequently, $\omega$ falls in both sectors, while $w$ goes up in both sectors. The first effect tends to harm the marginal worker, while the second one helps him. Furthermore, as $h/l$ goes up with $s^*$, the marginal worker's wage per unit of labor, $w + \omega h(s^*)/l(s^*)$, is also pushed up in both sectors.

This suggests that the evolution of that worker's wage differential between the two sectors as one moves along MM is a priori ambiguous. However, one can show that as one moves up the MM curve, the marginal worker's wage expressed per unit of labor goes up faster in the human-capital-intensive sector B than in sector A.

It is easy to see this algebraically. Using constant returns, rewrite $F_A(H_A, L_A) = L_A f(H_A/L_A)$ so that

$$\omega_A = f_A'\left(\frac{H_A}{L_A}\right) \tag{6.10}$$

and

$$w_A = f_A\left(\frac{H_A}{L_A}\right) - \frac{H_A}{L_A} f_A'\left(\frac{H_A}{L_A}\right). \tag{6.11}$$

Similarly, for sector B we have

$$\omega_B = p f_B'\left(\frac{H_B}{L_B}\right), \tag{6.12}$$

$$w_B = p\left(f_B'\left(\frac{H_B}{L_B}\right) - \frac{H_B}{L_B} f_B'\left(\frac{H_B}{L_B}\right)\right). \tag{6.13}$$

The wage per unit of labor of the marginal worker in sector $j$ is

$$\frac{z_j(s^*)}{l(s^*)} = w_j + \frac{\omega_j h(s^*)}{l(s^*)}.$$

Differentiating and using equations (6.10)–(6.13), we obtain

$$\frac{\mathrm{d}}{\mathrm{d}s^*}\left(\frac{z_A(s^*)}{l(s^*)}\right) = \frac{\mathrm{d}(H_A/L_A)}{\mathrm{d}s^*}\left[\frac{h(s^*)}{l(s^*)} - \frac{H_A}{L_A}\right] f_A'' + \omega_A \frac{\mathrm{d}}{\mathrm{d}s^*}\frac{h(s^*)}{l(s^*)},$$

$$\frac{\mathrm{d}}{\mathrm{d}s^*}\left(\frac{z_B(s^*)}{l(s^*)}\right) = \frac{\mathrm{d}(H_B/L_B)}{\mathrm{d}s^*}\left[\frac{h(s^*)}{l(s^*)} - \frac{H_B}{L_B}\right] f_B'' + \omega_B \frac{\mathrm{d}}{\mathrm{d}s^*}\frac{h(s^*)}{l(s^*)} + \frac{\mathrm{d}p}{\mathrm{d}s^*}\left(\frac{z_B(s^*)}{pl(s^*)}\right).$$

Since $H_A/L_A < h(s^*)/l(s^*) < H_B/L_B$, the first term is negative for $j = A$ but positive for $j = B$. As $\omega_B > \omega_A$, the second term is strictly greater for $j = B$ than for $j = A$. Finally, the terms-of-trade effect

$$\frac{\mathrm{d}p}{\mathrm{d}s^*}\left(\frac{z_B(s^*)}{pl(s^*)}\right)$$

is strictly positive, as an increase in $s^*$ relocates labor to sector A and must be matched by an increase in the relative price of good B for consumers to shift their expenditures accordingly. Consequently, along MM,

$$\frac{\mathrm{d}}{\mathrm{d}s^*}\left(\frac{z_B(s^*)}{l(s^*)}\right) > \frac{\mathrm{d}}{\mathrm{d}s^*}\left(\frac{z_A(s^*)}{l(s^*)}\right).$$

Therefore, there is at most one point on MM at which $z_B(s^*) = z_A(s^*)$, and this defines an equilibrium. This equilibrium is represented by point E′ in figure 6.4.[3]

[3] Nothing precludes E′ from being below the OEO′ broken line.

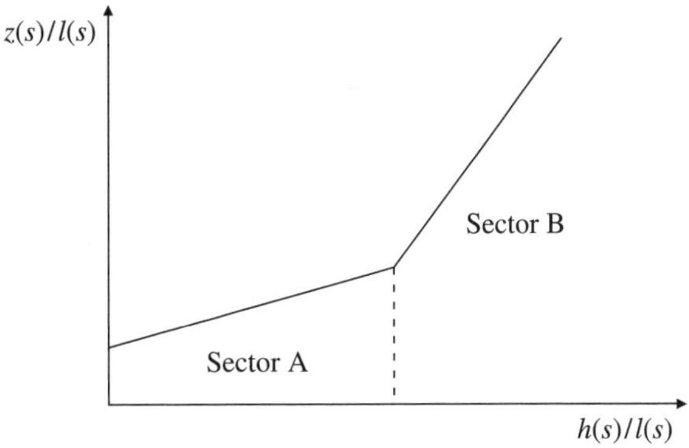


**Figure 6.5.** The distribution of income under full specialization.

Does such an equilibrium always exist? By continuity, it exists if $z_B(0) < z_A(0)$ and $z_B(1) > z_A(1)$. If these two inequalities do not hold, we can construct a corner equilibrium of the type shown in figure 6.2, in which all workers work in only one sector.[4]

To summarize, as labor is reallocated from sector B to sector A along MM, the marginal worker's income per unit of labor goes up by more in sector B than in sector A, which yields a unique equilibrium. There are three effects at work: (i) the (new) marginal worker now has more human capital relative to labor, and human capital is more valued in sector B; (ii) fewer people are working in sector B, and its relative price goes up; (iii) the change in factor prices—the rise in $w$ and the fall in $\omega$ in both sectors—hurts the marginal worker in sector A who has the largest relative endowment in human capital in that sector, while it benefits the marginal worker in sector B who has the lowest relative endowment of human capital in that sector.

Note that if E were in the lens, we could not construct an equilibrium on MM in the way we just have. In that case, any point F on MM would have a lower ratio $H_A/L_A$ and a greater ratio $H_B/L_B$ than E. Consequently, $w_A$ (respectively $w_B$) is smaller (respectively larger) at F than at E, while $\omega_A$ (respectively $\omega_B$) is larger (respectively smaller) at F than at E. Given that $\omega_A = \omega_B$ and $w_A = w_B$ at E, this implies that at F one must have $w_A < w_B$ and $\omega_A > \omega_B$. But this makes it suboptimal for low-skilled workers to choose sector A and for high-skilled workers to choose sector B, and therefore point F cannot be an equilibrium.

In some sense, the equilibria that we just discussed resemble the Roy model of specialization. In the Roy model, workers allocate their time to the activity in which they have a comparative advantage, given their

[4] It is quite possible to have such an equilibrium even though without bundling the two-sector factor-price equalization equilibrium depicted in figure 6.1 would arise.

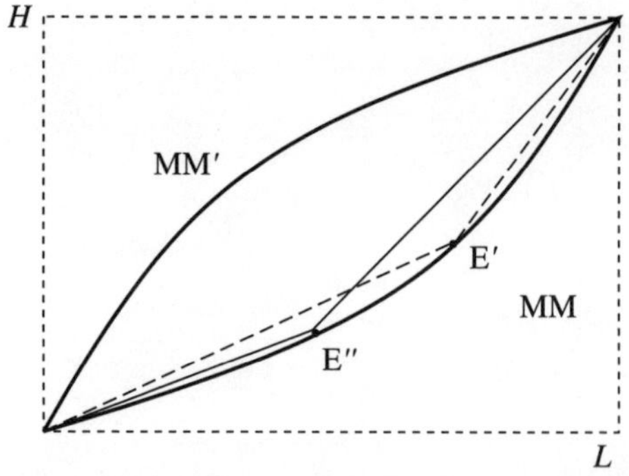


**Figure 6.6.** The effect of an increase in $p$ under full specialization.

relative productivity at various activities. Here, they cannot do so, but they can partly specialize by selecting the economic sector in which they have a comparative advantage, given their relative endowments of various characteristics. The familiar wage schedule (per unit of labor) arises, as seen in figure 6.5. Workers beyond the critical skill level get a greater return to skill by selecting the sector which rewards human capital better.

Let us now use this model to study the effect of an increase in demand for the skill-intensive good on the distribution of income and the allocation of labor. To simplify the analysis, we assume that the two goods are perfect substitutes, thus taking $p$ as exogenous, and we also assume that $p$ goes up. In the case of factor-price equalization, the effects of an increase in $p$ are very similar to the effects of technical progress in the skill-intensive technology, as depicted in figure 4.7. In both cases, the return to human capital goes up and the return to labor goes down, and people move to the technology (sector) which benefits from the positive shock.

In the case of complete specialization, the results are qualitatively similar. The shock tends to increase wages in sector B. To compensate, $s^*$ must fall, meaning that workers move to sector B. As illustrated in figure 6.6, the economy moves to the left along MM, from E′ to E″, implying a fall in $H/L$ in both sectors. Thus, we again get an increase in $\omega$ and a fall in $w$ in both sectors. However, the changes in $H/L$ are now constrained by the shape of the MM curve, i.e., by the distribution of skills in the economy. This is not the case in the FPE equilibria, where factor prices are only determined by technology. In particular, the more even the distribution of comparative advantage in the economy, i.e., the lower the elasticity of $h/l$ with respect to $s$, the flatter and closer to the diagonal the lens is, and the smaller the effect of a change in $p$ on factor prices is.

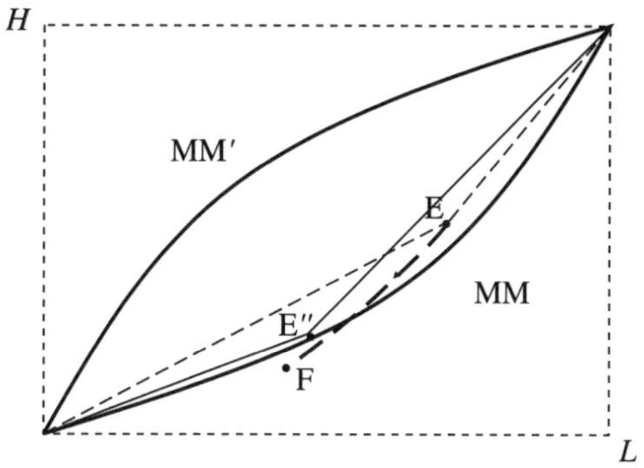


**Figure 6.7.** An increase in $p$ may trigger full specialization.

It is also possible that an increase in $p$ triggers a "catastrophe" in the distribution of income by moving the unbundling equilibrium point E out of the lens (figure 6.7). The allocation of labor then suddenly becomes segregated. All workers with a skill level lower than the critical level are reallocated from sector B to sector A, and those above the critical level migrate from sector A to sector B. The distribution of income (per unit of raw labor) shifts from a linear profile to a kinked one, as in figure 6.5.

To understand how segregation and inequality arise, it is useful to introduce some heuristic dynamics into the discussion. Until the economy reaches the MM frontier, the interpretation is the same as for figure 4.7: upon impact, sector B attempts to hire more workers in response to the increase in its relative price, while preserving its mix between human capital and labor. However, because its $H/L$ ratio is larger than in sector A, this depresses the $H/L$ ratio in that sector. As sector A tries to restore it, it bids for skilled workers, thus triggering an increase in $\omega$ and a fall in $w$. As sector B gradually grows, $\omega$ gradually goes up and $w$ gradually goes down, and the $H/L$ ratio falls in both sectors, while remaining higher in sector B. This defines a "target" adjustment trajectory EF, shown in figure 6.7. Along this trajectory, factor prices remain equalized in the two sectors, but sector B makes strictly positive profits and wants to expand further. As drawn, the target trajectory continues beyond the lens, as if unbundling were possible.

As sector B is more intensive in human capital, its costs rise faster, and the process eventually stops when its unit cost is again equal to $p$. What happens to the people during this process? They must move from sector A to sector B. But, as the latter is relatively intensive in human capital, the high-skill workers are more likely to already be in sector B. To maintain an $H/L$ ratio above that of sector A, as it grows it must attract the most skilled workers from sector A while releasing its less skilled workers to sector A. The economy may reach the new equilibrium while remaining within the lens. Otherwise, the growth of sector B pushes the economy to a point where all workers below a certain skill level work in A while all workers above it work in B, and sector B still makes strictly positive profits: that is, the economy is now at the point where EF intersects MM and is about to leave the lens. To attract new workers sector B must now reduce its $H/L$ ratio "below target," as the new workers are insufficiently endowed with $h$ relative to $l$ compared with the existing workers. To compensate for this, sector B offers a higher return to human capital (since newcomers depress $H/L$ below target, thus pushing the marginal return to $h$ up), which creates a wedge between the returns to human capital in sector B and in sector A. Conversely, as the marginal workers leave, sector A's $H/L$ ratio is above target, because less human capital leaves sector A, relative to labor, than if workers could unbundle their characteristics. For this reason, it is willing to pay less for human capital than sector B is. In other words, the marginal workers are not sufficiently endowed with human capital for their migration to preserve the equality in marginal returns between the two sectors.

## 6.2 Conclusion

This chapter has studied a first case in which "people matter" and labor can no longer be modeled as a vector of homogeneous input: the case in which labor-market characteristics are bundled in people in such a way that they cannot supply them to different firms. Despite this, from the firm's point of view each characteristic can be linearly aggregated into a homogeneous labor input, which has a well-defined price *within* the sector we are considering. The next two chapters study labor markets in which individual characteristics cannot all be aggregated at the firm level.

# 7
# The Economics of Superstars

In the labor market, one observes individuals whose earnings are orders of magnitude larger than any reasonable estimate of their opportunity cost of work. These people include top managers, media stars, and sportsmen. It seems difficult to explain such a phenomenon within the standard neoclassical framework. Furthermore, in many cases (as for the media) these supranormal returns seem to be associated with an information technology which allows these people to spread their talent over a large market. Understanding the superstars phenomenon may thus give some insights into how information technology affects the distribution of income.[1]

Rosen (1981) was the first to develop a theoretical analysis of the market for superstars. The two key mechanisms underlying it are the following.

First, labor is a "quality input." That means that instead of supplying a homogeneous factor to the labor market, people come with their own, unique skills. In particular, an individual cannot be replaced by another individual, or set of individuals, who would provide a perfect substitute for the tasks he is performing. One cannot replace a good journalist, a good footballer, or indeed a good physician with two bad ones. This quality effect is present to some extent in all professions, but is particularly salient in the ones where the superstar phenomenon is present. It is less present in occupations where skills are quantitative, rather than qualitative. For example, a mover with less physical strength could carry fewer items at the same time, thus producing a lower flow of value. If he takes 5% more time to move a given load, he will earn 5% less. On the other hand, a TV journalist who is 5% less popular will simply not get a slot on a major national TV channel, and would have to work on a small local channel, thus earning much less money. In some sense, each

[1] The superstars model also has implications for the profile of wages over the life cycle. For example, MacDonald (1998) develops a model where people are unsure about their talent and enter the market for a given occupation in the hope of becoming a star. A key prediction is that they initially earn returns below their alternative wage in other occupations, i.e., that there is *ex ante* dissipation of the rent earned by superstars.

individual owns a specific fixed factor, which is neither transferable nor tradeable, and we think of his earnings as the rent to that fixed factor.

Second, workers of higher quality have a larger market. Thus, better managers manage larger firms, better footballers play in higher-ranked leagues that are more widely broadcast, and so on. This effect acts as a multiplier which widens the income differences between high-quality and low-quality workers. In other words, the rent to a fixed factor is larger if it works with more complementary inputs, so as to produce more. Note that this effect depends on the nature of the technology used to produce the good. If the law of decreasing returns kicks in quickly, it will be costly to increase the output of a supplier, and that puts severe bounds on the earnings that can be made—as in the case of medical doctors or live theater. If technology allows the good to be produced in large quantities at a fairly constant marginal cost—as is the case with all informational goods such as TV shows, software, music, DVDs, and so on—then the best providers can obtain a huge market. As a consequence, we expect progress in information technology to exacerbate the superstar effect and to increase inequality among quality workers.

## 7.1 A Simple Model

We highlight these mechanisms in a simple partial equilibrium of the labor market. There is a continuum of workers, each endowed with one unit of raw labor and $q$ units of skills (or quality). The total mass of workers is normalized to 1 and $q$ is distributed with density $g(q)$ over $[q_{\min}, q_{\max}]$.

Firms produce a homogeneous good sold at price $p$. While $p$ will be determined by equilibrium in the market for that good, we first treat it as exogenous. To produce, a firm needs exactly one worker. Worker quality determines the productivity of the firm, so that if the worker's quality is $q$, the cost (in terms of a numéraire) of producing $y$ units of good 2 is $c(y)/q$, where $c$ is increasing and convex. A natural interpretation is that the worker is the firm's manager: better managers increase their firm's productivity proportionally, regardless of its size. But its size cannot become infinite, due to the decreasing returns captured in the convexity of the $c(\cdot)$ function. But, if $y$ is measured in units of utility, the individual can as well be interpreted as any supplier of information (footballer, journalist, consultant, problem solver, etc.) who increases the hedonic value of the firm's output. Therefore, this can be taken as any model of a sector where workers are not substitutable with one another and quality is crucial.

Because $q$ is a quality input, the earnings of a worker with skill $q$ cannot be written as the product of a single price for skill, $\omega$, times $q$. In a normal market, prices are linear because one can arbitrage out any nonlinearity by purchasing appropriate quantities of the appropriate bundles. Here, if there is a worker type who earns $\omega_1$ with skill $q_1$, I cannot get a skill input of $q_1/2$ at price $\omega_1/2$ by purchasing half the time of that worker. Nor can I get $2q_1$ at price $2\omega_1$ by employing two such workers instead of one. The quality inputs of different workers simply do not add up; each firm needs exactly one person and the intrinsic characteristics of that person determine productivity. Consequently, we are looking for a nonlinear wage schedule $\omega(q)$ which tells us how much a worker of skill $q$ earns.

The first question to be asked is, what are the equilibrium conditions determining $\omega(q)$? We assume that there is free entry of firms, at any worker quality level. Consider a firm with worker quality $q$. For an output equal to $y$, its profits are given by

$$\pi(y;q) = py - \frac{c(y)}{q} - \omega(q).$$

Therefore, the profit-maximizing level of activity for such a firm, $y(q)$, is such that

$$c'(y(q)) = pq. \tag{7.1}$$

Clearly, firms who hire a better worker produce more, since their marginal cost at any activity level is reduced proportionally.

Equilibrium in the labor market implies that all worker types are employed. Free entry implies that equilibrium profits for any existing firm are equal to zero. Therefore,

$$\omega(q) = py(q) - \frac{c(y(q))}{q}. \tag{7.2}$$

This can be rewritten, using (7.1), as

$$\omega(q) = \int_0^{y(q)} \left(\frac{c'(y(q)) - c'(y)}{q}\right) \mathrm{d}y,$$

i.e., the worker's wage is equal to the Ricardian rent on his specific factor.

It is straightforward to check that wages grow with skills. Differentiating (7.2) and using (7.1), we get

$$\omega'(q) = \frac{1}{q^2} c(y(q)) > 0. \tag{7.3}$$

How much inequality does this process generate, and how is it related to technology? One (local) measure of inequality is the return to skill,

$$\frac{\mathrm{d}\ln\omega(q)}{\mathrm{d}q} = \frac{\omega'(q)}{\omega(q)},$$

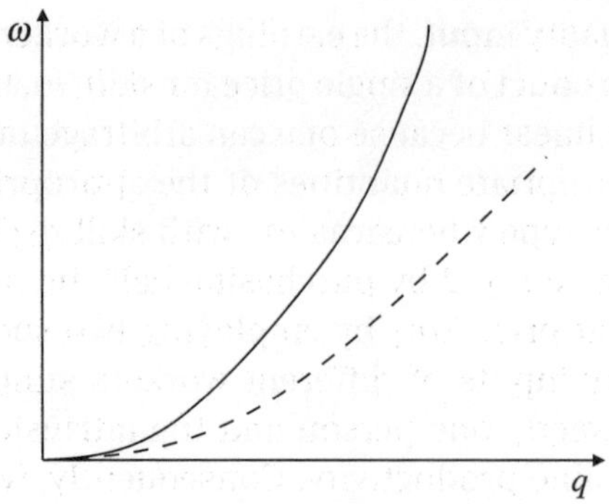


**Figure 7.1.** Impact of a reduction in $\gamma$ on the distribution of income.

which, using (7.3) and (7.1), is given by

$$\frac{\omega'(q)}{\omega(q)} = q^{-1}\left[\frac{y(q)c'(y(q))}{c(y(q))} - 1\right]^{-1}$$
$$= \left[q\frac{\int_0^{y(q)}(c'(y(q)) - c'(y))\,dy}{c(y(q))}\right]^{-1}. \tag{7.4}$$

We can see that the steeper the marginal cost curve, the greater the term in $\int_0^{y(q)}(c'(y(q)) - c'(y))\,dy$, and the lower the return to skill. In such a case, strong decreasing returns prevent output increasing by much in response to a marginal improvement in the worker's quality, which limits the rent accruing to that worker. Conversely, if the marginal cost curve is quite flat, an increase in worker quality will be matched by a large increase in the firm's output, which will increase the worker's rent substantially; this phenomenon generates a high return to skill.

An interesting special case is the one where costs are isoelastic:

$$c(y) = c_0\frac{y^\gamma}{\gamma}, \quad \gamma > 1. \tag{7.5}$$

In such a case, we get that

$$y(q) = \left(\frac{pq}{c_0}\right)^{1/(\gamma-1)}.$$

The elasticity of market size with respect to worker quality is therefore equal to $1/(\gamma - 1)$. The lower the value of $\gamma$, the lower the elasticity of costs with respect to output, and the greater the elasticity of market size with respect to worker quality. Turning now to the wage schedule, we get

$$\omega(q) = \frac{\gamma - 1}{\gamma}p^{\gamma/(\gamma-1)}q^{1/(\gamma-1)}c_0^{-1/(\gamma-1)}. \tag{7.6}$$

The lower the value of $\gamma$, the more convex the wage schedule and the greater the return to skill at any given $q$. Also, the wage gap between two worker qualities, $\omega(q_1)/\omega(q_2) = (q_1/q_2)^{1/(\gamma-1)}$, is always wider when $\gamma$ is smaller. Figure 7.1 shows the effect of a technological change which makes goods more easily replicable, in the sense that $\gamma$ falls. Clearly, inequality goes up.

If the cost function is not isoelastic, things are less simple. The formula (7.4) shows that the returns to skill are decreasing in the cost function's local elasticity around $y(q)$. But a shift in the cost function also changes $y(q)$, so it is not clear whether that elasticity goes up or down. One can indeed construct an example where relative inequality is invariant to a family of shifts in the cost function, despite the fact that these shifts make it less elastic. Consider the exponential cost function $c(y) = \mathrm{e}^{\phi y} - 1$. Then, by (7.1), the market size is given by $y(q) = (1/\phi)\ln(pq)$.[2] The local elasticity of $c(\cdot)$ around $y(q)$ is

$$\frac{y(q)c'(y(q))}{c(y(q))} = \frac{pq\ln(pq)}{pq-1}. \tag{7.7}$$

For $p$ constant, i.e., an infinite elasticity of the demand for the good, this quantity is independent of $\phi$. Therefore, a fall in $\phi$, which makes $c(\cdot)$ less elastic at any given $y$, leaves the local elasticity, and thus the return to skill, unchanged. This is because the elasticity is increasing in $y$ and the induced rise in $y(q)$ exactly offsets the direct negative effect of the fall in $\phi$ on the elasticity. Note, however, that if demand is not infinitely elastic, $p$ would fall to absorb the rise in $y(q)$, and that would raise the right-hand side of (7.7).[3] Inequality would thus again rise. But the point remains that the result that an increase in replicability increases inequality is not totally general. If the cost elasticity were falling with $y$ rather than rising, the effect of the rise in $y(q)$ would be to further increase inequality; but the fall in $p$ would then push in the other direction.

## 7.2 Occupational Choice and Displacement

So far, we have assumed that workers can only produce a single good. Let us now extend the model to allow for occupational choice, by assuming that they can also work in an alternative "commodity" sector.[4] Furthermore, let us assume that, in that sector, worker quality does not matter,

[2] We need $p > 1/q_{\min}$ for all firms to produce in positive quantities.

[3] The derivative

$$\frac{\mathrm{d}}{\mathrm{d}x}\frac{x\ln x}{x-1}$$

has the same sign as $x - 1 - \ln x > 0$.

[4] Alternatively, workers could work in the firms managed by the managers. This would introduce additional effects as managerial quality would then drive worker productivity and wages up. These effects are ignored here but reintroduced in section 7.4.

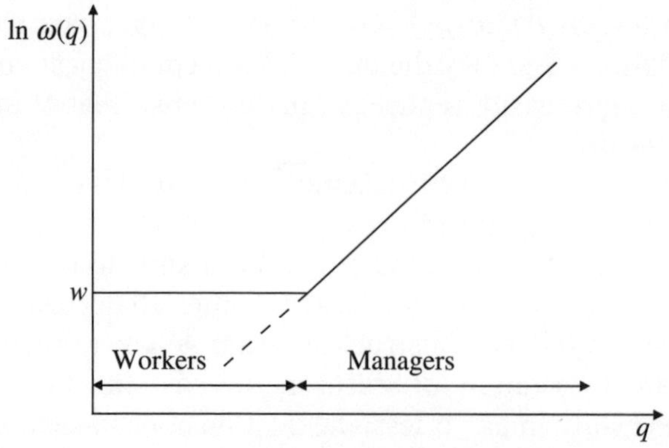


**Figure 7.2.** Income distribution and the allocation of talent.

and that all workers earn a wage $w$.[5] The price of the final good $p$ is now endogenous and determined by the equality of supply and demand. Finally, we assume that $q_{\min}$ is low enough so that low-quality workers are better-off working in the commodity sector.

Workers now allocate themselves optimally between the quality good sector and the commodity sector. That allocation is illustrated in figure 7.2. There exists a critical skill level $q^*$ such that workers specialize in the quality sector if and only if $q > q^*$. A worker with the critical skill level $q^*$ is indifferent between the two sectors, implying

$$\omega(q^*) = w.$$

Limiting ourselves to the isoelastic cost function (7.5), we get from (7.6) the first relationship between $q^*$ and $p$:

$$\frac{\gamma - 1}{\gamma} p^{\gamma/(\gamma-1)} q^{*1/(\gamma-1)} c_0^{-1/(\gamma-1)} = w.$$

This relationship is downward sloping; it is the supply curve of labor to the quality goods sector: the higher its price $p$, the lower the value of $q^*$, and the greater the fraction of the workforce which wants to specialize in the quality good.

To get another relationship, we need a formula for a demand curve. Assuming that $D(p)$, $D'(\cdot) < 0$, is the demand for the good, equilibrium in the goods market can be written as

$$D(p) = \int_{q^*}^{q_{\max}} y(q) g(q) \, \mathrm{d}q,$$

[5] One could be more general and consider instead a sector where earnings are less responsive to skills.

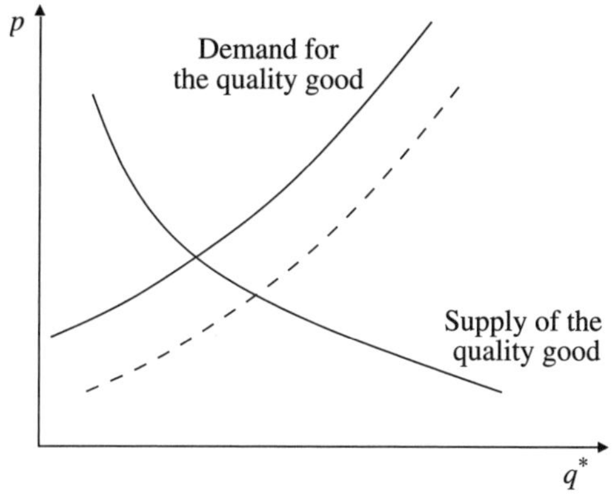


**Figure 7.3.** Impact of an increase in the demand for the quality good on the number of managers.

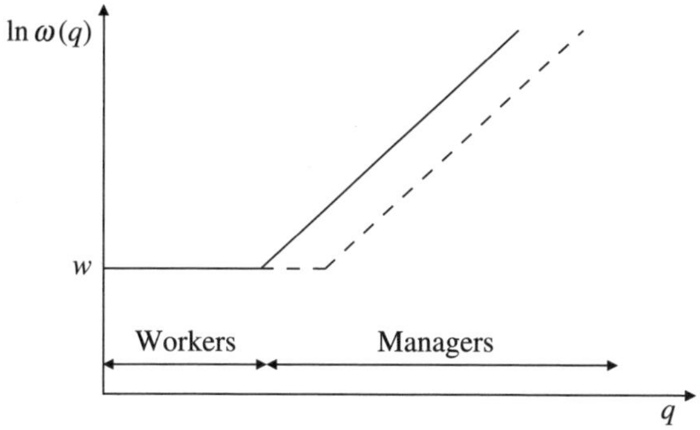


**Figure 7.4.** Impact of an increase in the demand for the quality good on the distribution of income.

or, equivalently,

$$D(p) = \left(\frac{p}{c_0}\right)^{1/(\gamma-1)} \int_{q^*}^{q_{\max}} q^{1/(\gamma-1)} g(q)\,\mathrm{d}q,$$

which determines an increasing relationship between $q^*$ and $p$. If $p$ is greater, the demand for the good falls and fewer people can work in that sector.

We are now in a position to study how various shifts affect inequality.

First, let us look at an increase in demand for the quality good $D(p)$. Such an increase in demand could come from economic growth, and non-homothetic utility. For example, people could want to spend a greater share of their income on DVDs, theater, and cable TV, relative to food, housing, and clothes, as they get richer. As figure 7.3 illustrates, this clearly triggers a rise in the equilibrium price $p$ as well as a fall in $q^*$.

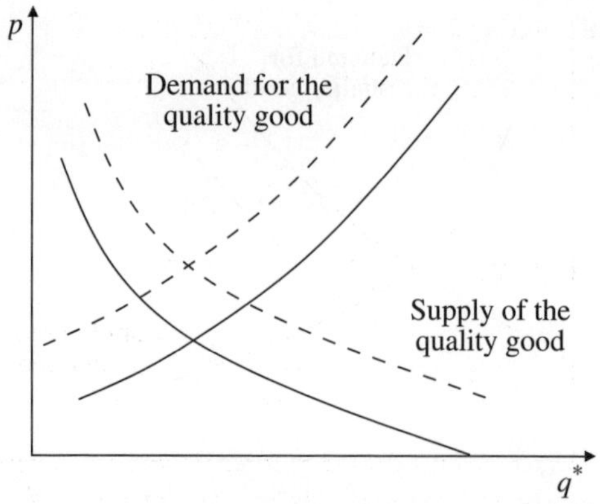


**Figure 7.5.** Impact of a greater replicability of the quality good.

Labor is being reallocated from the commodity sector to the quality sector. The effect on the distribution of income is illustrated in figure 7.4. While the return to skill does not change locally, the increase in $p$ is nevertheless skill biased because those who already work in the quality sector experience a wage increase, and are already earning more due to their greater skills. Relative inequality between two workers in that sector is unchanged—but it would change and could either go up or down were the cost function not isoelastic—while inequality between any two workers in different sectors goes up.

Now, let us look at a change in technology which makes the quality good more easily replicable. We assume that $y$ and possibly $c_0$ fall in such a way that the marginal cost $c'(y)$ falls over the relevant range. That clearly triggers an increase in the supply of quality workers. At any given $p$, they can produce more and thus make more money. If $p$ were unchanged, more people would want to move into the quality sector; thus, the supply curve shifts down in the $(q^*, p)$-plane. At the same time, the demand curve for quality labor also shifts down: since each worker can spread his talent over a larger market size, fewer workers are needed to produce a given quantity of output. For example, the labor input of actors that is needed to broadcast a given set of plays on TV is much lower than that which would be needed to reach the same audience in live theaters.

Thus, as illustrated in figure 7.5, both the supply and the demand curves shift down. While $p$ unambiguously falls, $q^*$ may go either up or down. These two cases have different implications for inequality.

If the demand curve $D(p)$ is sufficiently elastic, then $p$ will not fall much, and the distribution of income shifts as in figure 7.6: the return to skill goes up in the zone where workers supply the quality good, and

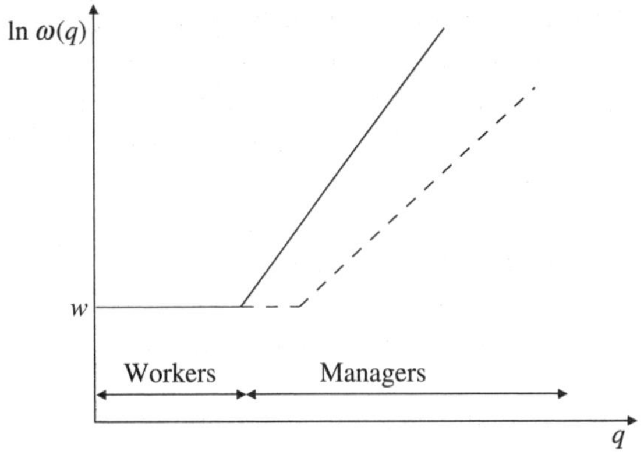


**Figure 7.6.** Impact of replicability on the distribution of income without displacement.

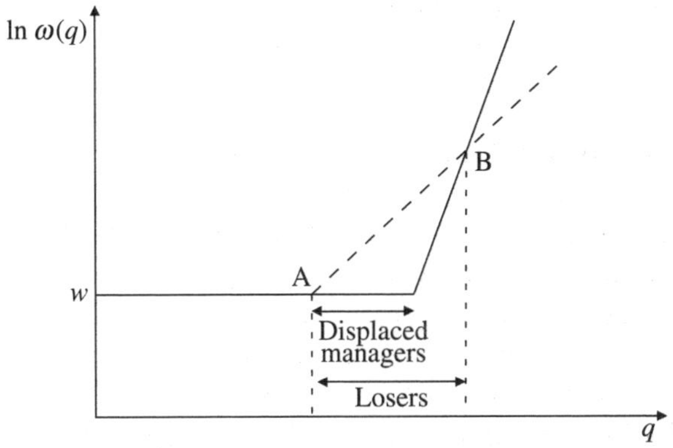


**Figure 7.7.** Impact of replicability on the distribution of income under displacement.

inequality between commodity workers and quality workers also goes up. However, all workers are better-off since commodity workers have an unchanged wage in terms of the numéraire and benefit from the fall in $p$ as consumers.

If $D(p)$ is inelastic, one may be in the configuration of figure 7.7, where $q^*$ goes up. Technical progress induces a displacement of workers out of the quality sector into the commodity sector. The less skilled managers, actors, and journalists are now less able to compete with the superstars in their fields. The latter take advantage of technical progress to increase the scale of their activity, and they trigger a fall in prices which makes it no longer profitable for the less talented to remain in that business.

In nominal terms, workers are worse-off if they are close enough to the new margin. These workers (interval AB of figure 7.7) either are displaced out of the quality sector or remain there but competition from the superstars drives their wages down, through its negative effect on $p$. These workers do not necessarily lose, however, because as consumers they benefit from the fall in $p$. But it is possible to construct examples where a number of them lose. Workers to the right of point B are sufficiently talented for the increase in their market size to offset the fall in prices, and they do gain, despite the fact that their wages fall relative to those of more talented workers. Workers to the left of point A remain in the commodity sector. Their nominal wage is unchanged but they benefit from the fall in $p$.

To conclude, in the inelastic case, those who are most likely to suffer from better replicability are workers with intermediate skills, who are at the lower end of the skill distribution among producers of the quality good; they suffer from competition from more talented workers, while workers in the commodity sector are immune to it as producers and gain from the technical change as consumers.

## 7.3 Growth and the Allocation of Talent

Murphy et al. (1991) make the point that the logic of the economics of superstars applies not only when the returns to skills are determined by technology and market competition, but also when they are determined by noncompetitive mechanisms such as bureaucracy and rent-seeking. Their main point is that if the "superstar" effect is stronger in the noncompetitive sector, then it will offer a steeper wage schedule, thus attracting the best workers. This allocation of talent need or need not be efficient, depending on the social value of the noncompetitive activity. If this activity is redistributive in nature, it does not create wealth and having the best people specialized in it is harmful for growth. However, it is conceivable that it be socially efficient to attract the best people in the noncompetitive activity. That would be the case if, for example, it consisted in producing a public infrastructure, or enforcement of the rule of law and of property rights, that increases the productivity of the private sector.

The return to work in the noncompetitive activity is determined by similar market size considerations. For example, a centralized government offers politicians opportunities to control large sectors of the economy. To the extent that private rents from political activity are commensurate with the size of the sector one controls, we expect centralized governments to offer large rewards to talented individuals and to attract the best people. On the other hand, under decentralized governments,

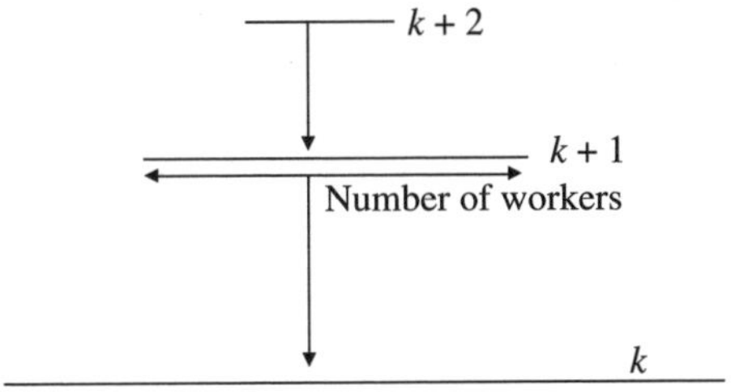


**Figure 7.8.** The flow of productivity between hierarchical levels.

the most talented people are more likely to shy away from politics and to become entrepreneurs instead. Globalization may also affect the arbitrage between the two activities. It allows the best people to become managers of large multinational corporations instead of smaller national firms, thus making the wage schedule for managers steeper and possibly triggering a move of the best people out of politics into business. At the same time though, talented workers at home compete with foreigners, making it less likely that one passes the threshold for becoming a manager.

## 7.4 Hierarchy and Span of Control

An interesting application of the superstars model is to hierarchies in the labor market. The actions of a worker affect more people, and therefore more output, the higher that person's rank is in the hierarchy. The preceding analysis suggests that this should have a number of consequences:

- People should typically earn more if their hierarchical position is higher.
- More highly skilled workers should work in higher ranking occupations.
- The returns to skill should be higher when one moves up the hierarchy, because a unit improvement in worker quality has a larger impact on total output.

In order to understand if and when these predictions are true, we need to extend the preceding model to represent such hierarchies. To do so, one must deal with the *assignment* problem: how do workers match with each other in firms, and at what hierarchical levels? For example, do workers with intermediate skills work under the supervision of workers with higher skills, or supervise workers with lower skills, or both? This is a tricky question whose answer depends on the shape of complementarities between workers at different hierarchical levels. Here, however, we want to focus on the effect of hierarchy on span of control, leaving aside such assignment problems. To do so, we adapt Rosen (1982) formalization, and assume that workers at a given hierarchical level produce a good, which we call "productivity," and that this good is used as an intermediate input at the next lower hierarchical level. Thus, the production process consists of $N + 1$ stages, or hierarchical levels, as shown in figure 7.8. These levels are indexed in ascending order by $m = 0, \ldots, N$. Each worker "controls," i.e., provides productivity to, $n$ workers at the lower level. The productivity $y_m$ of a worker $i$ at hierarchical level $m$ is given by

$$y_m(i) = f(s(i), y_{m+1}(\hat{\imath})),$$

where $s(i)$ is the *skill* of the worker, which is exogenous, and $y_{m+1}(\hat{\imath})$ is the productivity of the relevant worker $\hat{\imath}$ at the next superior level (the "supervisor"). It is important to note that $y_{m+1}$ is a nonrival, quality input, shared by all $n$ workers under the supervisor. Thus, the "supervising activity" has the same properties as the quality labor markets analyzed in section 7.1. $n$ is a worker's span of control, and an increase in $n$ is similar to a fall in $\gamma$ (in the analysis of section 7.1), in that it makes the input provided by the supervisor more easily replicable. An increase in $n$ may be interpreted as the consequence of an improvement in information technology. For example, an advisor can affect more people by embodying his knowledge in software, an overseer can make use of digital cameras, and so forth.

At the bottom of the hierarchy ($m = 0$) there are production workers. They produce a single, homogeneous final good output, whose price is normalized to 1. A worker with productivity $y_0(i)$ produces exactly $y_0(i)$ units of that good. At the top of the hierarchy, a worker's productivity is a function $f_T(s)$ of his skill $s$.[6]

The number of levels is endogenous, and is determined by the choices of firms. For a given lower hierarchical structure, they can either close it by appointing a "CEO" of skill $s$, who provides productivity $f_T(s)$ to the $n$ workers at the lower level, or decide to have a more integrated structure and have a "supervisor" with productivity $f(s, \hat{y})$, where $\hat{y}$ is provided from a higher-ranking worker (obviously, since that worker supplies inputs to $n$ supervisors, as compared with the first strategy,

[6] This assumption is made just to close the model and allow for hierarchies with a finite number of levels, but it plays no role in the model below. In the overlapping-generations version used by Saint-Paul (2007) and described at the end of this chapter, one can have an infinite number of hierarchical levels, since employment at each level falls geometrically with its rank in the hierarchy.

that involves replicating the original structure $n$ times). In principle, one can have $N = 0$ if a worker sells directly $f_{\mathrm{T}}(s)$ units of the final good. The worker is then self-employed and the hierarchical structure has a single layer.

The above problem remains complex. In particular, it involves analyzing the matching of workers of different skills within the same firm, within and between hierarchical levels. We will deal with this kind of issue in the next chapter. Here we want to focus on the effect of hierarchies and span of control on the distribution of income, ignoring sorting problems. To do so, we transform the problem into a slightly different one, building on Rosen (1982) and Saint-Paul (2007). Assume that there is a *market* to allocate productivity between different hierarchical levels and that workers allocate themselves in the appropriate workplace on the basis of the *prices* of productivity. More precisely, we denote by $p(y)$ the price, in terms of the final good, of $y$ units of productivity. Note that this price is nonlinear since productivity must be purchased from a single supplier, the worker at the upper hierarchical level. However, for production workers, one unit of productivity yields one unit of the final good. Therefore, $p(y) = y$ in the zone where workers with productivity $y$ elect to be production workers. Furthermore, workers at a higher level in the hierarchy can always elect to use their productivity to sell the final good. Therefore, it must be that $p(y) \geqslant y$ throughout. Then, the problem of a worker with skill $s$ boils down to maximizing

$$\omega(s) = \max\left(p(f_{\mathrm{T}}(s)), \max_{\hat{y}} p(f(s,\hat{y})) - \frac{1}{n}p(\hat{y})\right).$$

Thus, the allocation of workers to firms is entirely mediated by the price schedule $p(y)$ and we can ignore the complex problem of optimizing the composition of the workforce for a given hierarchical structure.[7] The term in $1/n$ in the preceding equation appears because the worker with productivity $\hat{y}$, at the upper level, sells productivity to $n$ different workers, each of them paying a fraction $n$ of the cost.[8] This formula captures the determination of the productivity input used by that worker, $\hat{y}$, as well as the choice between being at the top of the hierarchy (where I earn $p(f_{\mathrm{T}}(s))$), in the middle (where I earn $p(f(s,\hat{y})) - (1/n)p(\hat{y})$), or at the bottom, if my optimal choice is such that $p(f(s,\hat{y})) = f(s,\hat{y})$.

[7] Here workers can choose the productivity level of their supervisor among the whole set, by just paying $p(\hat{y})/n$, and they get a price $p(f(s,\hat{y}))$ for their own productivity, independently of the rest of the hierarchical structure. In the more complex problem, the equilibrium earnings of a worker depend on the whole hierarchical structure, and cannot a priori be reduced to a single price for each productivity level.

[8] The difficult public good problem of how $y$ would be priced to $n$ different users with different characteristics is then avoided.

Consider a worker who is not at the top of a hierarchy, i.e., $p(f_T(s)) < \max_{\hat{y}} p(f(s,\hat{y})) - (1/n)p(\hat{y})$. Then the first-order condition for the optimal choice of $\hat{y}$ is

$$p'(f(s,\hat{y}))f'_{\hat{y}}(s,\hat{y}) = \frac{1}{n}p'(\hat{y}). \tag{7.8}$$

For a given price schedule $p(\cdot)$, this condition determines a worker's optimal choice for the productivity input he uses, $\hat{y}(s)$, as well as his own optimal productivity, $y(s) = f(s,\hat{y}(s))$. Using the envelope theorem, we can also compute the marginal wage around that skill category:

$$\omega'(s) = p'(y(s))f'_s(s,\hat{y}). \tag{7.9}$$

Assuming the higher-level worker is also not at the top of the hierarchy, substituting (7.9) into (7.8), and denoting by $\hat{s}$ the skill of the higher-level worker, we get

$$\omega'(\hat{s}) = n\frac{f'_s(\hat{s},\hat{y}(\hat{s}))}{f'_s(s,\hat{y}(s))}f'_{\hat{y}}(s,\hat{y}(s))\omega'(s). \tag{7.10}$$

This formula relates the return to skill for a worker at one level of the hierarchy to the return to skill for workers at the level immediately below. Consider a marginal increase in the skill of agent $\hat{s}$ at level $m$. At the optimum, its favorable impact on the productivity of workers at the lower level must be offset by the increment in the wage that must be paid to $\hat{s}$. One measure of this impact is the amount of money that I could save by having less skilled workers at level $m-1$ while holding their productivity constant. This quantity is equal to the number of such workers, $n$, times the required reduction in $s$ per unit of productivity increase at level $m-1$, $f'_{\hat{y}}(s,\hat{y}(s))/f'_s(s,\hat{y}(s))$, times the productivity effect on $\hat{y}(s)$ of the increase in the skill of worker $\hat{s}$, $f'_s(\hat{s},\hat{y}(\hat{s}))$, which must finally be multiplied by the marginal wage at level $m-1$, $\omega'(s)$. Equation (7.10) tells us that these savings must equal the marginal wage at level $m$, otherwise a positive surplus would appear if one were to change $\hat{s}$.

The effect of span of control is apparent from the multiplicative effect of $n$ on the right-hand side of (7.10). The greater the number of workers controlled by the worker at level $m$, the greater the gains from increasing his skills—and the greater the marginal willingness to pay by lower-level workers for such an increase. Thus, the greater the span of control, the greater the increment in the return to skill when one moves up the hierarchical ladder. Span of control is in that sense "inegalitarian." Intuitively, when one moves up the hierarchy, the return to skill $\omega'(\cdot)$ is multiplied by a factor

$$\varsigma = n\frac{f'_s(\hat{s},\hat{y}(\hat{s}))}{f'_s(s,\hat{y}(s))}f'_{\hat{y}}(s,\hat{y}(s));$$

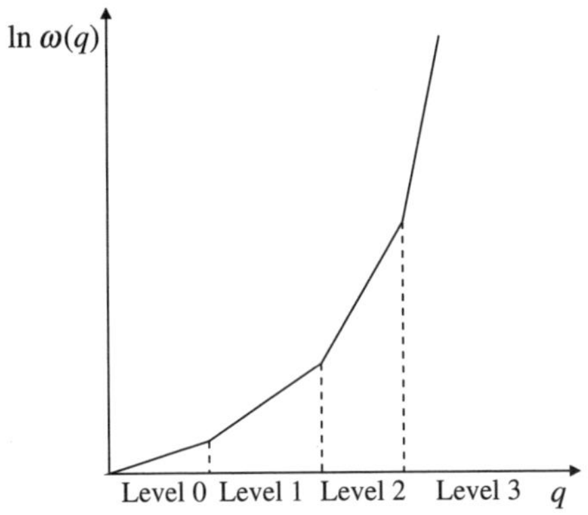


**Figure 7.9.** The distribution of wages across hierarchical levels.

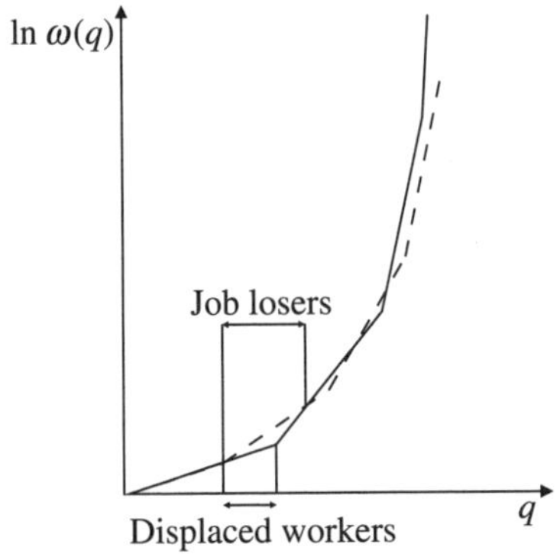


**Figure 7.10.** Increase in the span of control: displacement and wage losses.

this quantity is likely to be larger, and more likely to be above 1, when $n$ is larger. At the top of the hierarchy, the return to skill reflects the cumulative effect of an increment in $s$ on all the lower levels.

If the multiplier $\varsigma$ is greater than 1, then the marginal return to skill goes up as one climbs the hierarchical ladder. Consequently, we expect that there will be sorting, in that the skill space will be partitioned in a sequence of skill intervals such that each interval specializes in one ladder only; the logic is the same as that of the Roy model seen in chapter 1: people specialize in the occupation that yields the largest income to them.[9] The sorting of people by skill intervals as well as the wage schedule is depicted in figure 7.9. Since each worker can provide an input to $n$ workers in the lower interval, the total mass of workers in a given interval must be equal to $1/n$ times the mass in the preceding interval.

[9] There is more discussion of this in chapter 8, which deals with intra-firm segregation by skills.

Figure 7.10 illustrates the effect of an increase in span of control $n$. Each interval must widen, so that the least efficient producers are displaced to the lower level. Furthermore, the multiplier $\varsigma$ typically goes up, which tends to increase inequality between ladders. Workers tend to lose from being displaced to a lower level in the hierarchy (the *displacement effect*), because their input now benefits a (much) smaller number of people. This is the case depicted in figure 7.10: displaced workers end up on a lower portion of the new wage schedule. On the other hand, the increase in $n$ allows workers to purchase the input from more highly skilled workers, which tends to benefit everybody (the *productivity effect*). In particular, since production workers cannot be displaced, they necessary gain from the increase in span of control. Consequently, span of control is inegalitarian at the top of the distribution of wages but egalitarian at the bottom.

An attractive specification, used by Saint-Paul (2007), is the following. There is an overlapping-generations structure where people live for two periods. Knowledge, which is the equivalent of what we call "productivity," is transmitted between generations as follows. In the first period people purchase knowledge from the preceding generation. In the second period they work and consume and may decide to be a production worker or to sell their knowledge to the next generation. The distribution of intrinsic skills in each cohort is assumed to be exponential with density $g(s) = \upsilon e^{-\upsilon s}$. This specification is handy because a segregated partition of the workforce by hierarchical levels has intervals with constant length. In a segregated equilibrium, a worker with skill $s$ buys knowledge from a worker of the previous generation with skill

$$\hat{s}(s) = s + \sigma, \tag{7.11}$$

where

$$\sigma = \frac{\ln n}{\upsilon}. \tag{7.12}$$

Workers such that $s \in [0, \sigma]$ are production workers and buy knowledge from workers of the preceding generation in the skill interval $[\sigma, 2\sigma]$. Workers such that $s \in [m\sigma, (m+1)\sigma]$ buy knowledge from workers in the interval $[(m+1)\sigma, (m+2)\sigma]$ in the preceding generation and sell knowledge to workers in the interval $[(m-1)\sigma, m\sigma]$ in the subsequent generation. We further assume that

$$f(s, \hat{y}) = Ae^{\varepsilon s}\hat{y}^{\varphi}, \tag{7.13}$$

where $\varphi \in [0, 1)$.

Over time, the economy converges to a steady-state distribution of productivity, which we can represent by a function $y(s)$ that gives us the equilibrium productivity (or knowledge) of an agent with skill $s$. Such a distribution must clearly satisfy the following equation:

$$\begin{aligned} y(s) &= f(s, \hat{y}(s)) \\ &= f(s, y(\hat{s}(s))) \\ &= f(s, y(s+\sigma)). \end{aligned} \tag{7.14}$$

It is natural to look for a solution in the form of $y(s) = y_0 e^{\gamma s}$. Substituting into (7.14) and using (7.13) we simply get

$$y(s) = A^{1/(1-\varphi)} n^{\varphi\varepsilon/(\upsilon(1-\varphi)^2)} e^{\varepsilon s/(1-\varphi)}. \tag{7.15}$$

We note that an increase in span of control raises the productivity level of the whole population by the same shift factor: the productivity effect. We can also compute how wages vary through the hierarchical structure by using (7.10). Using (7.11), (7.12), (7.13), and (7.15), we get

$$\frac{\omega'(\hat{s})}{\omega'(s)} = \varphi n^{1-\varepsilon/\upsilon} = \varsigma.$$

If this quantity is less than 1, the return to skill would fall in the segregated equilibrium when one moves up the hierarchy. But one can then show that in this case a segregated equilibrium does not exist. Instead, the equilibrium is such that all workers are indifferent between being a production worker or supplying knowledge (see Saint-Paul 2007). The reason is simple: if the equilibrium were hierarchical, workers in the interval $[\sigma, 2\sigma]$ would be better-off becoming production workers than selling knowledge to the production workers of the next generation. Therefore, we need $\varphi n^{1-\varepsilon/\upsilon} > 1$ for our segregated equilibrium to arise. That implies, in particular, that $\varepsilon < \upsilon$. Consequently, an increase in $n$ unambiguously increases $\varsigma$. Inequality between intervals increases, and the above analysis of the displacement and productivity effects applies. In that paper, I also show that the productivity effect dominates the displacement effect if $n$ is not too large—in such a case all skill categories benefit from an improvement in information technology. On the other hand, the displacement effect dominates when $n$ gets large, and some displaced skill categories lose. One should also point out that, in this overlapping-generations model, upon an increase in $n$, displaced workers in the initial older generation lose. The reason is that they cannot benefit from the productivity effect since the additional human capital is acquired during the first period of life.

Another interesting application of the span-of-control model is the knowledge hierarchy model of Garicano (2000). There, a hierarchy arises because workers of different skills specialize in solving different types of problems. Workers with a greater skill level can solve problems that are more difficult. Furthermore, the difficulty of a problem is not known by the worker who encounters it. For this reason, the worker must climb the hierarchy until he encounters somebody sufficiently skilled to solve his problem. As discussed by Garicano and Rossi-Hansberg (2006), the predictions of such a model for displacement and the return to skill are similar to those discussed here.

## 7.5 Conclusion

It is easy to obtain large effects of technical change on inequality in superstar models. This will be the case when technical change allows the superstars to increase the size of the market they cover, as with inventions such as printing, television, and the Internet. On the other hand, such shifts tend to have large effects on the productivity of all workers, which makes it less likely that some workers lose. As workers, people can get higher quality complementary inputs from the "superstars," as seen in section 7.4. Their productivity therefore improves. As consumers, they can get access to higher quality performers, and/or consume more of the good produced by quality labor. When some workers lose, they are unlikely to be the workers at the bottom of the distribution of income. This is because the productivity of these workers increases, while they cannot be displaced to lower-level occupations. Hence, production workers gain if they end up working in a better-managed firm, due to the fact that better managers can now manage larger firms because of some organizational innovation. If some workers lose, it is because they are displaced to a lower-level occupation because of increased competition from the superstars. Low-quality managers, accountants, engineers, consultants, and so on may be displaced to a lower level or become production workers and experience an absolute fall in wages. Overall, the analysis suggests that organizational change and advances in information technology are likely to favor both ends of the distribution of earnings at the potential expense of the middle.

# 8
# Complementarities and Segregation by Skills

A determinant of the distribution of income which we have ignored so far is the assignment of workers to firms. It is known that firms within the same sector are quite heterogeneous with respect to their skill composition and the wages they pay. Casual intuition suggests that one is more productive if one's coworkers are also more productive; furthermore, in a number of sectors (for example, academia, sport), the assignment is segregated by skills: good workers team with good workers and bad workers team with bad workers.

We want to know which kind of technologies lead to such segregation, and how the assignment affects the distribution of income. This chapter focuses on the role of segregation by skills, which is probably the dimension in which technology matters most in creating a link between assignment and inequality. For more general surveys about assignment models of the distribution of income, the reader is referred to Sattinger (1993) and Neal and Rosen (2000).

## 8.1 A Simple Model

The first point to be noted is that the whole issue only arises if skills are a quality input. If workers are interchangeable, then assignment is irrelevant. The only thing that matters for the firm is how much of each homogeneous characteristic it buys from workers; the way these characteristics are embodied in workers does not matter.

In the preceding chapter, we avoided the issue of interactions between quality workers either by assuming there was a single one working in a firm (in the managerial model used to discuss the economics of superstars), or by assuming that interactions between them were mediated by a market with well-defined prices (in the models of hierarchies and span of control). We now need to go beyond these simplifications to be able to make predictions about how the structure of interactions at the firm level affects worker assignment, segregation, and the distribution of earnings.

A simple start is to consider a technology such that firms are teams of two workers, who jointly produce a quantity of output

$$y = f(q_1, q_2),$$

where $q_i$ is the quality of worker $i$. This production function is increasing in its arguments. We also assume that $f(\cdot, \cdot)$ is symmetrical: $f(q_1, q_2) = f(q_2, q_1)$. This means that a worker performs the same tasks as his coworkers, which is true in some settings but not all. Asymmetries may arise from hierarchical structures as well as from the division of labor. We do not then expect $f$ to be symmetrical, and a number of additional issues arise; these were partly tackled in the preceding chapter, but we will now ignore them.

We assume that there are only two skill levels in the population, $q_A$ and $q_B$. There is a mass $\theta$ of workers of type A and a mass $1 - \theta$ of workers of type B. To solve for a competitive equilibrium, we need to characterize how workers are assigned to firms. At most three types of firms may coexist in equilibrium: AA, AB, and BB, such that $q_1 = q_2 = q_A$, $q_1 = q_A$ and $q_2 = q_B$ or vice versa, and $q_1 = q_2 = q_B$, respectively. As usual, we assume that there is free entry of firms. The equilibrium wages of each worker type, $w_A$ and $w_B$, must then be such that profits are nonpositive for all firm types:

$$\begin{aligned} 2w_A &\geqslant f(q_A, q_A), \\ w_A + w_B &\geqslant f(q_A, q_B), \\ 2w_B &\geqslant f(q_B, q_B). \end{aligned}$$

We may have strict inequality for firm types that do not exist in equilibrium (no firm of that type can then be profitably formed), and must have equality for firms that exist in equilibrium, since these must have nonnegative profits.

The other set of equilibrium conditions tells us that supply equals demand for each worker type. Denoting by $v_j$ the mass of firms of type $j$, these are equivalent to

$$\begin{aligned} 2v_{AA} + v_{AB} &= \theta, \\ v_{AB} + 2v_{BB} &= 1 - \theta. \end{aligned}$$

### 8.1.1 Segregated Equilibria

First we try to construct a *segregated* equilibrium, where only firms, AA or BB, employing a single worker type exist. In such an equilibrium, wages are readily determined by

$$w_A = \tfrac{1}{2} f(q_A, q_A), \tag{8.1}$$

$$w_B = \tfrac{1}{2} f(q_B, q_B). \tag{8.2}$$

The third condition, for a mixed firm not to be strictly profitable, is thus

$$f(q_A, q_B) \leqslant \tfrac{1}{2}[f(q_A, q_A) + f(q_B, q_B)]. \tag{8.3}$$

If this inequality holds, then a segregated equilibrium exists, with

$$v_{AA} = \tfrac{1}{2}\theta,$$
$$v_{AB} = 0,$$
$$v_{BB} = \tfrac{1}{2}(1 - \theta),$$

and wages are given by (8.1) and (8.2).

Can we get a simple interpretation of formula (8.3)? We can show that it holds if skills are complementary, in the sense that the marginal product of increasing a worker's quality increases with the other worker's quality. Mathematically, this is equivalent to

$$f''_{12} \geqslant 0. \tag{8.4}$$

If (8.4) holds, then so does (8.3). To prove this, assume, without loss of generality, that $q_A < q_B$, and note that (8.3) is equivalent to

$$f(q_B, q_B) - f(q_A, q_B) \geqslant f(q_A, q_B) - f(q_A, q_A).$$

By symmetry, we can rewrite this as

$$f(q_B, q_B) - f(q_A, q_B) \geqslant f(q_B, q_A) - f(q_A, q_A), \tag{8.5}$$

or, equivalently,

$$\int_{q_A}^{q_B} f'_1(z, q_B)\,\mathrm{d}z \geqslant \int_{q_A}^{q_B} f'_1(z, q_A)\,\mathrm{d}z.$$

The latter condition clearly holds, as (8.4) implies that $f'_1(z, y)$ is weakly increasing with $y$.

Conversely, we can show that $f''_{12} \geqslant 0$ is necessary for a segregated equilibrium to exist for *any* value of $q_1$ and $q_2$. To see this, just apply (8.5) to $q_B = q_A + \mathrm{d}q$, and check that, with a second-order Taylor expansion, (8.5) is equivalent to (8.4).

Condition (8.4) is easily interpreted as a typical sorting condition. Firms that employ a high-skill worker in one position are willing to pay more to increase the quality of the worker in the other position, because such an increase is more profitable in these firms. Thus, a mixed firm cannot survive in equilibrium because it would be outbid for its more productive workers by segregated firms.

Note that the notion of complementarity highlighted here is quite different from that discussed in the context of the neoclassical models of chapters 2–5. In those models, there was complementarity between two different kinds of homogeneous labor inputs. Here, the two workers may well be identical (so they would bring two bits of the same input to the firm in a neoclassical model, and be substitutes by definition), but it is the *tasks* to which they are assigned that are highly complementary; for this reason, we cannot simply add the input vectors they provide to the firm.

### 8.1.2 Mixed Equilibria

Let us now characterize mixed equilibria where AB firms exist. The zero-profit condition for these firms is equivalent to

$$w_A + w_B = f(q_A, q_B).$$

Furthermore, we must also have $w_A \geqslant \frac{1}{2}f(q_A, q_A)$ and $w_B \geqslant \frac{1}{2}f(q_B, q_B)$. Adding these, we find that one must have

$$f(q_A, q_B) \geqslant \tfrac{1}{2}[f(q_A, q_A) + f(q_B, q_B)], \tag{8.6}$$

which is merely the opposite of (8.3) and will hold if $f''_{12} \leqslant 0$.

For the labor market to clear, segregated firms must exist, unless the number of skilled workers exactly balances the number of unskilled workers. Thus, if $\theta > \frac{1}{2}$, there must also be firms of type AA. The wages of A-type workers are determined by what they get in an AA firm:

$$w_A = \tfrac{1}{2}f(q_A, q_A).$$

Consequently, the remainder of the output in an AB firm goes to the B-type worker:

$$\begin{aligned} w_B &= f(q_A, q_B) - w_A \\ &= f(q_A, q_B) - \tfrac{1}{2}f(q_A, q_A). \end{aligned}$$

If (8.6) strictly holds, these two relations imply that $w_B > \frac{1}{2}f(q_B, q_B)$. Therefore, BB firms cannot exist in equilibrium. It must then be the case that $v_{AB} = 1 - \theta$ and $v_{AA} = \theta - \frac{1}{2}$.

If $\theta < \frac{1}{2}$, we get the reverse:

$$w_A = f(q_A, q_B) - \tfrac{1}{2}f(q_B, q_B), \quad w_B = \tfrac{1}{2}f(q_B, q_B),$$
$$v_{AB} = \theta, \quad v_{AA} = 0, \quad v_{BB} = \tfrac{1}{2} - \theta.$$

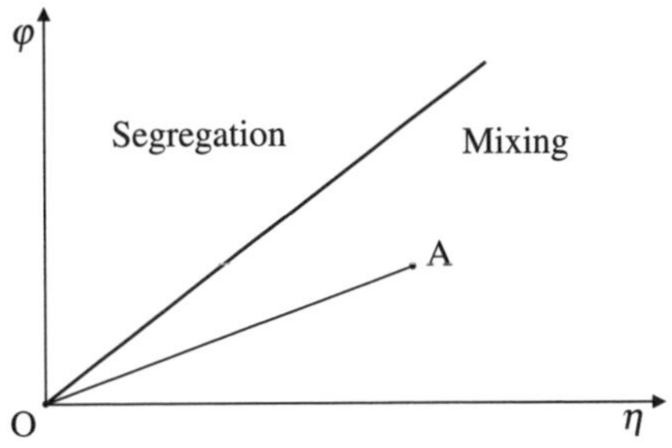


**Figure 8.1.** Mixing versus segregation.

### 8.1.3 Efficiency

Note that, in the two types of equilibria we have constructed, the assignment of workers to firms is efficient. Condition (8.3) states that the total output of two pairs of workers of each type is larger if workers are matched with the same type than it is if firms are mixed. Condition (8.6) states the opposite. While it is not straightforward to apply standard welfare theorems in this setting, as there is no homogeneous labor input and no a priori restriction on the $f(\cdot)$ function, efficiency comes from the fact that productive interactions between workers are entirely internalized by the firms.

### 8.1.4 Is Segregation Worrisome?

One is tempted to argue that segregation by skills "reinforces inequality," since high-productivity workers have highly productive coworkers who further increase their productivity relative to the low-skilled workers. However, segregation is itself endogenous to technology, so it is difficult to address such a claim without reformulating it, since two different segregation patterns must arise from two different technologies.

In particular, one should note that

- there is no discontinuity in the distribution of income when a technology smoothly changes from one that generates mixing to one that creates segregation,
- starting from a given technology that does not lead to segregation, one can construct a shift in the production function that does not lead to segregation and another that does lead to segregation, yet the former increases inequality more than the latter, and
- policies that block segregation run against productive efficiency and are likely to be inefficient.

To see this, it is useful to consider a simple example. Assume the production function is CES in the skills of the two workers:

$$f(q_1, q_2) = (q_1^\gamma + q_2^\gamma)^{\varphi/\gamma}, \quad \varphi > 0,\ \gamma \in (-\infty, +\infty).$$

The cross-derivative is

$$f''_{12}(q_1, q_2) = \varphi(\varphi - \gamma)(q_1^\gamma + q_2^\gamma)^{\varphi/\gamma - 2}(q_1 q_2)^{\gamma - 1}.$$

Therefore, we know that if $\varphi > \gamma$, the equilibrium is segregated, and it is mixed otherwise. The state of the economy as a function of the technological parameters is depicted in the phase diagram of figure 8.1. More complementarity between the two workers, as captured by a lower value of $\gamma$, makes segregation more likely, and so does a greater return to the overall quality of workers in the firm, as measured by $\varphi$.

It is then straightforward to compute the wages, as follows.

- If $\varphi > \gamma$, then

$$w_{\mathrm{A}} = 2^{\varphi/\gamma - 1} q_{\mathrm{A}}^{\varphi},$$
$$w_{\mathrm{B}} = 2^{\varphi/\gamma - 1} q_{\mathrm{B}}^{\varphi}.$$

- If $\varphi < \gamma$, then
  - if $\theta > \frac{1}{2}$,

$$w_{\mathrm{A}} = 2^{\varphi/\gamma - 1} q_{\mathrm{A}}^{\varphi},$$
$$w_{\mathrm{B}} = (q_{\mathrm{A}}^\gamma + q_{\mathrm{B}}^\gamma)^{\varphi/\gamma} - 2^{\varphi/\gamma - 1} q_{\mathrm{A}}^{\varphi},$$

  - if $\theta < \frac{1}{2}$,

$$w_{\mathrm{B}} = 2^{\varphi/\gamma - 1} q_{\mathrm{B}}^{\varphi},$$
$$w_{\mathrm{A}} = (q_{\mathrm{A}}^\gamma + q_{\mathrm{B}}^\gamma)^{\varphi/\gamma} - 2^{\varphi/\gamma - 1} q_{\mathrm{B}}^{\varphi}.$$

Clearly, when $\varphi = \gamma$, one has $w_{\mathrm{A}} = q_{\mathrm{A}}^\gamma$ and $w_{\mathrm{B}} = q_{\mathrm{B}}^\gamma$ in all cases. In this knife-edge case all types of firms can coexist, and the distribution of wages is a continuous function of the technological parameters $\varphi$ and $\gamma$.

Furthermore, one can get technical shifts that increase the inequality by an arbitrary amount, while segregation never arises. To see this, start from the mixing zone ($0 < \varphi < \gamma$) and increase $\varphi$ and $\gamma$ proportionally. The economy moves along a ray through the origin OA in figure 8.1 and remains in the mixing zone. The relative wage is given by

$$\frac{w_{\mathrm{B}}}{w_{\mathrm{A}}} = \left(1 + \left(\frac{q_{\mathrm{B}}}{q_{\mathrm{A}}}\right)^{\gamma}\right)^{\tau} - 2^{\tau - 1},$$

where $\tau < 1$ is the constant $\varphi/\gamma$ ratio. Clearly, since $q_B > q_A$ and $\tau > 0$, the ratio $w_B/w_A$ tends to infinity.

It is not even true that inequality is more "sensitive" to technical change in the segregated zone. In this zone, one has

$$\frac{w_B}{w_A} = \left(\frac{q_B}{q_A}\right)^{\gamma\tau}.$$

Consider the effect of an increase in $\tau$. Such a technological change means that the workers' skills at the two tasks are more complementary to each other ($\gamma$ falls) or that output is more elastic with respect to the overall skill level in the firm ($\varphi$ increases), in a way similar to the reduction in cost elasticity analyzed in the superstars model in the preceding chapter. In the mixed zone, the increase in inequality is given by

$$\frac{\partial}{\partial\tau}\frac{w_B}{w_A} = \left(1 + \left(\frac{q_B}{q_A}\right)^{\gamma}\right)^{\tau} \ln\left(1 + \left(\frac{q_B}{q_A}\right)^{\gamma}\right) - 2^{\tau-1}\ln 2.$$

In the segregated zone, we get

$$\frac{\partial}{\partial\tau}\frac{w_B}{w_A} = \left(\left(\frac{q_B}{q_A}\right)^{\gamma}\right)^{\tau} \ln\left(\frac{q_B}{q_A}\right)^{\gamma}.$$

To compare this effect with its counterpart in the mixed zone, let us consider it locally around the frontier between the two zones, i.e., compute both expressions for $\tau = 1$. Let $x = (q_B/q_A)^{\gamma} > 1$. We get

$$\frac{\partial}{\partial\tau}\frac{w_B}{w_A} = x\ln x$$

in the segregated zone and

$$\frac{\partial}{\partial\tau}\frac{w_B}{w_A} = (1+x)\ln(1+x) - \ln 2$$

in the mixed zone. The latter expression is actually the *larger*.[1] Thus, the inequality becomes *less* responsive to this type of skill-biased technical progress as one passes the frontier from mixing to segregation. In fact, starting from a segregated situation *protects* the unskilled from the increase in the outside option of the skilled brought about by an increase in $\tau$. In the mixed equilibrium the unskilled are forced to give a higher share of the output to the skilled, otherwise they would exit the mixed firms and team up with other skilled workers.

What would happen if the government attempted to block segregation?

[1] One has $(1+x)\ln(1+x) - \ln 2 > \ln(1+x) - \ln 2 + x\ln x > x\ln x$.

Assume $\theta > \frac{1}{2}$. Assume the government bans matches between two workers of type B. Then there will be only AA firms and AB firms in equilibrium. The wage of A-type workers would still be pinned down by what they get in AA firms. The wage of B-type workers would be equal to $\frac{1}{2}f(q_A, q_B) - f(q_A, q_A)$, which is lower than what they used to get, $\frac{1}{2}f(q_B, q_B)$. Thus, we have indeed reduced inequality, but by reducing the income of the rich rather than by increasing that of the poor. If, in addition, one were to block matches between two A-type workers, not all of them could match B-type workers. A mass $2\theta - 1$ of them would be unemployed and they would drive the wage of A-type workers to zero.

Consider now the less plausible case in which $\theta < \frac{1}{2}$. If one blocks matches between two B-type workers, *they* become underemployed and their wage falls to zero; while we have reversed inequality, it nevertheless increases: the ratio between the highest and lowest paid workers actually becomes infinite. If one blocks matches between two A-type workers, the reservation wage of B-type workers remains equal to that which they would get in a segregated firm, $\frac{1}{2}f(q_B, q_B)$. Type A workers are forced into mixed firms, where they get

$$f(q_A, q_B) - \tfrac{1}{2}f(q_B, q_B) < \tfrac{1}{2}f(q_A, q_A).$$

Thus, their wage falls and inequality increases again. The "bussing" of low-skilled workers to mixed firms does increase their productivity, all else being equal. But they now have to pay their skilled coworkers enough to convince them to participate, and the amount is determined by what these workers get in segregated firms. Because the output of workers in mixed firms is lower than that in segregated firms, participation of high-skilled workers in mixed firms can only be bought by lower wages for unskilled workers relative to what they get by teaming together. Finally, if one blocks both types of segregated firms, the skilled are again unemployed and inequality is again reversed but increases.

To conclude, segregation by skills in the workplace is an interesting outcome, which may be induced by changes in the production technology and can be tested in the data. But there is no sense in which it contributes per se to inequality; nor should a social planner pay special attention to it. That conclusion may be qualified, however, if one takes into account interactions that take place outside the labor market. For example, one may argue that segregation in the productive sector may reinforce residential and educational segregation, which may increase inequality through the channel of human-capital accumulation (see Bénabou 1993).

## 8.2 Application: Household Income Inequality and Assortative Mating

The model just described is useful in a variety of contexts in addition to the problem of assigning workers to firms. It can be applied to segregation in urban neighborhoods, schools, or households (see Bénabou 1993; Epple and Romano 1998). An interesting application of the framework is to marriage markets, because segregation in marriage markets has an impact on household income inequality. In particular, in recent years one has seen an increase in assortative mating: high-skill men tend to marry high-skill women. Even if earnings inequality is unchanged, a move to assortative matching will automatically tend to widen the distribution of household income. In this section we show (i) how the model can be reformulated to analyze segregation by skills in households and (ii) how it can be used to analyze the effect of technical change in the production of household goods on the pattern of assortative mating. Becker (1981) has shown that gains from specialization lead to mixed marriages, while gains from increasing returns in producing household public goods favor assortative mating. We show how a variant of the simple model discussed here validates these insights.

Assume that households produce a composite good, which they consume. This composite good is produced using two inputs: "money" and a "household quality." This latter good is a quality input which has to be produced by one of the two members of the household (traditionally, the wife). The amount of composite good produced by the household is then

$$y = m^{\alpha} h^{\beta}.$$

A household member of quality $q$ can specialize by working either in the market (where he or she earns $m = q$ units of money) or in the household (where she or he produces $h = q$ units of household quality). We assume that the household activity is less elastic with respect to skills than the market one, that is,

$$\alpha > \beta.$$

A household with two agents of quality $q_1$ and $q_2$ will allocate its labor effort so as to maximize

$$\max(q_1^{\alpha} q_2^{\beta}, q_2^{\alpha} q_1^{\beta}).$$

Since $\alpha > \beta$, it is efficient to allocate the more skilled person to the market and the other to the household, and the resulting household consumption level is

$$y = f(q_1, q_2) = \max(q_1, q_2)^{\alpha} \min(q_1, q_2)^{\beta}. \tag{8.7}$$

While we do not specify how the consumption good is allocated between the two members of the household, we assume that matches are formed efficiently, so that total output cannot increase by rearranging them. We again assume a population with only two types, $q_A$ and $q_B$, with $q_A < q_B$. The above analysis has shown that mixing is efficient if (8.6) holds. In this context, this is equivalent to

$$2\left(\frac{q_B}{q_A}\right)^{\alpha} \geqslant \left(\frac{q_B}{q_A}\right)^{\alpha+\beta} + 1. \tag{8.8}$$

The difference between the left-hand side and the right-hand side is a hump-shaped function of $q_B/q_A$, which is equal to zero at $q_B = 0$ and eventually becomes negative. Therefore, this formula will hold provided $q_B/q_A$ is not too large. What is the logic behind this result? If $\theta > \frac{1}{2}$, mixing arises because highly skilled workers are more productive working in the market and "hiring" a low-skilled worker to do their household work than they are mating with a high-skilled worker and specializing in the household activity. This is because household activity rewards improvement in skills less than the market does. The process has limits, however, because if $q_A$ is much lower than $q_B$, unskilled workers reduce output significantly in mixed marriages, despite their specialization in the household activity. Another way to put it is to observe that the marginal product of increasing the quality of the household worker can get very large if his or her productivity is small and that of the market worker is large. Consequently, for $q_B/q_A$ large enough, segregation arises: if a skilled worker moves out of a mixed marriage to "hire" another skilled worker to perform the domestic work, enough surplus is generated to compensate that worker for the forgone money he or she would have made on the market.

Thus, we predict that assortative mating becomes more likely with increasing degree of skill inequality. Furthermore, the lower $\beta$, the higher the degree of skill inequality $q_B/q_A$ beyond which segregation arises.[2] The likelihood of mixing thus increases when the sensitivity of the household activity with respect to skills increases. In the limit case when $\beta = 0$, (8.8) holds regardless of the value of $q_B/q_A$.

---

[2] Let us check this formally. The critical value of $x = q_B/q_A$, $x^*$, is the largest root of $x^{(\alpha+\beta)} + 1 - 2x^{\alpha} = 0$. Consider a perturbation of $\beta$. By differentiating, we get

$$[(\alpha+\beta)x^{*(\alpha+\beta-1)} - 2\alpha x^{*(\alpha-1)}]\,\mathrm{d}x^* + x^{*(\alpha+\beta)} \ln x^* \,\mathrm{d}\beta = 0.$$

The term in parentheses must be positive (see the preceding footnote), as must $\ln x^*$, as $x^* > 1$. Consequently, $\mathrm{d}x^*/\mathrm{d}\beta < 0$.

## 8.3 Extension: Increasing Firm Size and the Number of Worker Types in Segregated Equilibria

Characterizing the equilibrium becomes quite complex when the production function involves more than two workers and there are more than two worker types in the economy. In this section we explore one route, which consists in limiting oneself to segregated equilibria, while spelling out the properties of the production function which support such equilibria.

Let us thus assume that a firm consists of $n$ workers instead of 2, and that its output is

$$y = f(q_1, \dots, q_n),$$

where $q_i$ is the quality of worker $i$. As above, $f(\cdot)$ is increasing in each argument and symmetrical. We will refer to the vector $(q_1, \dots, q_n)$ as the "type" of the firm.

There is now a continuum of skill levels, distributed over $\Omega = [q_{\min}, q_{\max}]$ with density $g(q)$, such that $\int_0^{+\infty} g(q)\,\mathrm{d}q = 1$. We normalize the total labor force to 1.

What is a competitive equilibrium in such a context? It is an assignment of workers to firms, along with a wage schedule. The assignment of workers to firms tell us which worker types work in which firms, and it can be represented by an endogenous density measure over the firm type space, $\mu : \Omega^n \to [0, +\infty)$, which tells us the density of firms employing an $n$-tuple of workers with skills $(q_1, \dots, q_n)$. The endogenous wage schedule $\omega(q)$ tells us how much a worker of quality $q$ is being paid. The economy is in equilibrium if the following three properties are satisfied.

(1) Existing firms make zero profits:

$$\mu(q_1, \dots, q_n) > 0 \Longrightarrow f(q_1, \dots, q_n) = \sum_{i=1}^{n} \omega(q_i).$$

(2) An entrant cannot make positive profits:

$$\forall (q_1, \dots, q_n), \quad f(q_1, \dots, q_n) \leqslant \sum_{i=1}^{n} \omega(q_i). \tag{8.9}$$

(3) The supply of each labor type $q$ is equal to its demand. Formally, this means that the distribution of worker types, as implied by the distribution of firm types $\mu(\cdot)$, matches the distribution of worker types in the population $g(\cdot)$. To state this precisely, we introduce the following notation. Let $\boldsymbol{x} = (x_1, \dots, x_n)$ be any $n$-vector and let $\phi$ be any function of an $n$-vector. Then $\boldsymbol{x}_{-i} =$

$(x_1, \dots, x_{i-1}, x_{i+1}, \dots, x_n)$, $\mathrm{d}\boldsymbol{x} = \mathrm{d}x_1 \cdots \mathrm{d}x_n$, $\mathrm{d}\boldsymbol{x}_{-i} = \mathrm{d}\boldsymbol{x}/\mathrm{d}x_i$, $\phi(y; \boldsymbol{x}_{-i}) = \phi(x_1, \dots, x_{i-1}, y, x_{i+1}, \dots, x_n)$.

Equilibrium in the labor market can then be written as follows:

$$\forall q, \quad \sum_j \int_{\Omega^{n-1}} \mu(q, \boldsymbol{y}_{-j}) \, \mathrm{d}\boldsymbol{y}_{-j} = g(q),$$

which simply states (in density terms) that the demand for a given type of worker coming from all types of firms must be equal to the number of such workers in the population.

With these properties, it is easy to prove that an equilibrium necessarily maximizes total output. Consider such an equilibrium $(\mu(\cdot), \omega(\cdot))$ and consider an alternative assignment $\hat{\mu}(\cdot)$. To be feasible, such an assignment must not employ more workers than are available, that is,

$$\forall q, \quad \sum_j \int_{\Omega^{n-1}} \hat{\mu}(q, \boldsymbol{y}_{-j}) \, \mathrm{d}\boldsymbol{y}_{-j} \leqslant g(q).$$

It yields a total output level given by

$$\hat{Y} = \int_{\Omega^n} f(\boldsymbol{y}) \hat{\mu}(\boldsymbol{y}) \, \mathrm{d}\boldsymbol{y}.$$

Using (8.9), we see that

$$\begin{aligned}
\hat{Y} &\leqslant \int_{\Omega^n} \sum_{j=1}^{n} \omega(y_j) \hat{\mu}(\boldsymbol{y}) \, \mathrm{d}\boldsymbol{y} \\
&= \sum_{j=1}^{n} \int_0^{+\infty} \omega(q) \Big( \int_{\Omega^{n-1}} \hat{\mu}(q, \boldsymbol{y}_{-j}) \, \mathrm{d}\boldsymbol{y}_{-j} \Big) \, \mathrm{d}q \\
&= \int_0^{+\infty} \omega(q) \Big( \sum_{j=1}^{n} \int_{\Omega^{n-1}} \hat{\mu}(q, \boldsymbol{y}_{-j}) \, \mathrm{d}\boldsymbol{y}_{-j} \Big) \, \mathrm{d}q \\
&\leqslant \int_0^{+\infty} \omega(q) g(q) \, \mathrm{d}q \\
&= Y.
\end{aligned}$$

This is a standard proof, which states that, because of the no-entry condition, total output in an alternative assignment cannot exceed the total wages, computed with the equilibrium wage schedule; the total wages themselves are equal to the total output in the equilibrium assignment, because of the zero-profit condition.

When is the equilibrium segregated? In a segregated equilibrium, the wage of type $q$ is easy to compute:

$$\omega(q) = \frac{1}{n} f(q, \dots, q). \tag{8.10}$$

If this holds, then condition (1) above is clearly satisfied. Furthermore, condition (3) is met, provided the density of firms employing type-$q$ workers is equal to $f(q)/n$.

Therefore, to show that such an equilibrium exists, we need only to prove condition (2), i.e., to show that the following inequality holds:

$$\forall q_1, \dots, q_n, \quad f(q_1, \dots, q_n) \leqslant \frac{1}{n} \sum_{i=1}^{n} f(q_i, \dots, q_i). \tag{8.11}$$

Furthermore, if this inequality holds strictly, the only equilibrium is segregated. Otherwise, one could take a mass $\mathrm{d}m$ of firms of type $(q_1, \dots, q_n)$, replace it by $n$ masses $\mathrm{d}m/n$ of firms of type $(q_i, \dots, q_i)$, for $i = 1, \dots, n$, and total output would unambiguously increase, which contradicts the fact that it must be maximum at equilibrium.

Can we extend the preceding result and show that (8.11) holds if skill levels are complementary to each other, i.e., if

$$\frac{\partial^2 f}{\partial x_i \partial x_j} \geqslant 0$$

for any pair of worker types? The answer is yes. To prove this, we first establish the following preliminary result.

Consider two firm types $(q_1, \dots, q_n)$ and $(q'_1, \dots, q'_n)$, such that the distribution of skills in the first type dominates that in the second type. That is, there is an ordering of the two types such that $q'_i \leqslant q_i$ for all $i$. Consider a swap of workers between the two firms, such that worker $q_i$ switches with worker $q'_j$. Then, if $q_i \leqslant q'_j$, the total output for the two firms cannot fall.

This lemma, stated formally and proved in the appendix, says that if firm 1 employs better workers than firm 2 (in the above sense), then swapping workers in firm 1 for better workers in firm 2, if feasible, increases overall output. The essence of the proof is similar to the construction of a segregated equilibrium in section 8.1.1. Because of the cross-derivative condition

$$\frac{\partial^2 f}{\partial x_i \partial x_j} \geqslant 0,$$

the arrival of the better worker in firm 1, which has more highly skilled workers, increases output by a greater amount than the reduction of output this causes in firm 2.

Clearly, such a swap, while typically increasing output, increases segregation, as the more productive worker moves to the firm where other workers are more productive. This preliminary result therefore takes us a long way toward proving that (8.11) holds.

To conclude the proof, we construct an iteration procedure. Consider a set of $n^2$ workers, with $n$ workers of each type $q_1, \dots, q_n$. These workers can be matched in arbitrary combinations to create $n$ firms. The left-hand side of (8.11) is equal to the output per firm when all these firms are identical and of type $(q_1, \dots, q_n)$. The right-hand side is equal to the output per firm when the $n$ firms are all segregated and there is one firm of each type $(q_i, \dots, q_i)$. To prove that output is higher in this case, we start from the situation of identical firms, and reach the segregated case incrementally by iterating swaps that satisfy the lemma. At each step, output cannot decrease; hence, output must be higher at the end of the procedure than at its beginning, which implies that (8.11) holds. The procedure that we just outlined is described in detail in the appendix.

To conclude: if the cross-derivatives of the production function are positive, the equilibrium is segregated, and wages are simply given by (8.10).

### 8.3.1 Example: The O-Ring Production Function

An interesting application, proposed by Kremer (1993), is the so-called O-ring production function, where output is the product of the human capital of all workers:

$$f(q_1, \dots, q_n) = \prod_{i=1}^{n} q_i.$$

One interpretation is that, to produce one unit of output, one has to implement a "batch" of activity and perform $n$ tasks. Worker $i$ performs task $i$. There is a probability that one of the tasks fails, in which case no output is produced. Workers with more human capital perform better and have a lower probability of failure. We can always pick measurement units so that the probability of success in performing task $i$ is equal to the corresponding worker's quality, $q_i$. A unit of output is produced successfully if no worker fails, i.e., with productivity $\prod_{i=1}^{n} q_i$. Averaging over batches, this is also equal to the mean output level per batch.

The cross-derivatives of $f(\cdot)$ are all strictly positive. Therefore, the equilibrium is segregated and the wage schedule is

$$\omega(q) = \frac{q^n}{n}.$$

The value of increasing a worker's quality at one task is greater when their quality is higher at other tasks, because a low quality worker in a given post acts as a bottleneck by generating a high defect rate, irrespective of how well other workers perform (this can be seen most clearly in the case when $q_i = 0$). For this reason, firms with more human capital are willing to pay more to increase quality at task $i$, which triggers a segregated assignment pattern.

The elasticity of wages with respect to worker quality is equal to $n$. This means that the greater the number of tasks into which the production process is decomposed, the more inequality there is. The model therefore predicts that advances in the division of labor are intrinsically unequal. This effect is somewhat similar to the span of control effects studied in the preceding chapter: when $n$ is larger, a failure at one post destroys the contribution of more workers; an improvement at that post has a positive effect on a larger number of coworkers, and hence the willingness to pay for quality improvements is larger.

The O-ring production function is an example of "serial processing" of tasks. One can think of another extreme, where tasks are processed in parallel. Suppose, for example, that each worker in a firm is working in parallel at solving a problem, and that this is the same problem for all workers within the firm. All the firm cares about is that the problem is solved, in which case output is produced. It just requires that one of its $n$ workers finds the solution. Assume that a worker of quality $q$ finds the solution with probability $q\varepsilon$. Then, for a firm with $n$ workers of quality $q_1, \dots, q_n$, the expected output is given by

$$\begin{aligned} y &= f(q_1, \dots, q_n) \\ &= 1 - \prod_{i=1}^{n} (1 - q_i \varepsilon). \end{aligned} \tag{8.12}$$

Computing the cross-derivative, we obtain

$$f''_{ij}(q_1, \dots, q_n) = - \prod_{k \neq i,j} (1 - q_k \varepsilon) < 0.$$

Hence, the condition for segregation to arise is now not satisfied. In this example, an improvement in worker quality at post $i$ is only valuable when no other worker finds the solution to the problem. The likelihood of this being true decreases with increasing quality of the other workers. Therefore, the marginal value of improving the quality of worker $i$ is lower, the higher the quality of other workers.

## 8.4 Aggregating Individual Interactions

Another case where one can solve for the wage schedule is when the workers' skills contribute to the production function through a simple aggregate. For example, suppose, following Saint-Paul (2001), that

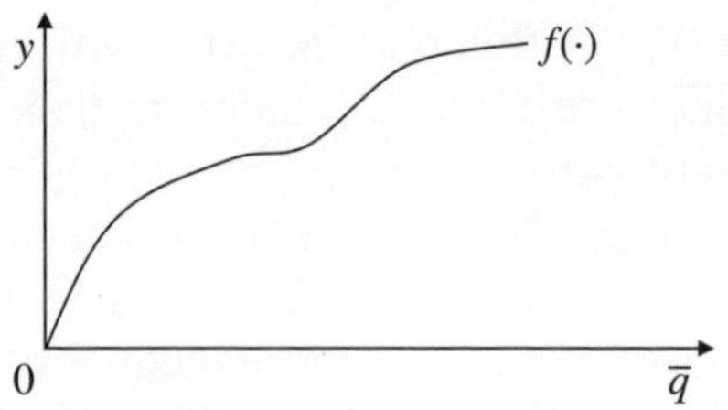


**Figure 8.2.** The output schedule.

each firm hires $n$ workers and that the firm's output is a function of the *average* quality of the workers:

$$y = f\left(\frac{\sum q_i}{n}\right). \tag{8.13}$$

Note that, by changing the way $q_i$ is measured, the above specification encompasses a number of ways the individual skills can enter the production function. For example, if the $q_i$s enter through some aggregate CES index,

$$y = f\left(\left(\frac{\sum q_i^{\gamma}}{n}\right)^{1/\gamma}\right),$$

one can just replace $q_i$ by $q_i^{\gamma}$ and $f(x)$ by $f(x^{1/\gamma})$. Similarly, the O-ring case mentioned above is a special case with an exponential $f$ and skills redefined as the logarithm of the probability of successfully performing the task.

The cross-derivative of $f$ is

$$\frac{\partial^2 f}{\partial q_i \partial q_j} = \frac{1}{n^2} f''\left(\frac{\sum q_i}{n}\right).$$

Therefore, if $f$ is convex throughout, the equilibrium is segregated and wages are simply given by

$$\omega(q) = \frac{f(q)}{n}.$$

Can we say more if $f$ has an arbitrary shape, as in figure 8.2? It turns out that the analysis is simpler and more revealing if we assume that, instead of employing $n$ workers, the firm employs a continuum of workers of mass $n$. Thus, indexing these workers by $\sigma \in [0, n]$, we can rewrite (8.13) as $y = f(\bar{q})$, with

$$\bar{q} = \frac{1}{n} \int_0^n q(\sigma)\, \mathrm{d}\sigma.$$

We can also use an alternative notation and assume that the firm employs a measure $\mathrm{d}\psi(\cdot)$ over the space $\Omega$ of possible worker types. Such a measure must satisfy

$$\int_{\Omega} \mathrm{d}\psi = n, \tag{8.14}$$

and one has

$$\bar{q} = \frac{1}{n} \int_{\Omega} q \, \mathrm{d}\psi.$$

The firm's profits are given by

$$\pi = f\left(\frac{1}{n} \int_{\Omega} q \, \mathrm{d}\psi\right) - \int_{\Omega} \omega(q) \, \mathrm{d}\psi. \tag{8.15}$$

Firms pick the measure $\psi(\cdot)$ so as to maximize (8.15) subject to (8.14). Denoting the Lagrange multiplier by $\lambda$, the FOC is

$$\frac{1}{n} f'(\bar{q})q = \omega(q) + \lambda. \tag{8.16}$$

This condition applies to any worker type such that $\mathrm{d}\psi > 0$, i.e., any type of worker actually employed by the firm. The FOC states that, at the margin, increasing the proportion of type $q$ at the expense of other worker types (whose effect on profits is summarized by the Lagrange multiplier $\lambda$) leaves the firm indifferent. If workers of type $q$ are not employed by the firm, then employing them cannot make the firm better-off at the optimum, and one then has

$$\frac{1}{n} f'(\bar{q})q \leqslant \omega(q) + \lambda. \tag{8.17}$$

Note that, in such a setting, the firm's optimal behavior is a sole function of its average skill level $\bar{q}$ and does not depend on the actual distribution $\psi(\cdot)$, provided it is compatible with the equilibrium conditions. Thus, we define $\bar{q}$ to be the type of firm. The preceding derivations tell us that, for any firm of type $\bar{q}$ that exists in equilibrium, (8.17) must hold. This equation is conveniently interpreted as the firm's marginal willingness to pay (MWP) to hire type-$q$ workers (as defined by $(f'(\bar{q})q - \lambda)/n$) not exceeding their wage $\omega(q)$; otherwise, it would pay the firm to increase the proportion of type $q$ in its staff. Furthermore, (8.17) must hold with equality if workers of type $q$ are employed in a positive number by the firm; otherwise it would pay to reduce the proportion of type-$q$ workers in the firm's staff.

The Lagrange multiplier $\lambda$ can be interpreted as the shadow price of a position in the firm, whose total mass of positions is fixed at $n$. The firm's willingness to pay for type $q$ is therefore equal to the additional worker's marginal effect on the firm's output (if he could simply be added to the existing workforce), $(f'(\bar{q})q)/n$, minus the shadow cost of an extra position, $\lambda$. It is enlightening to use the firm's zero-profit condition to

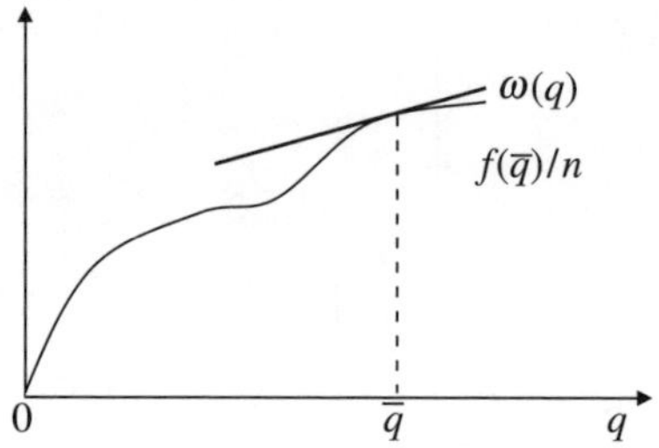


**Figure 8.3.** The wages offered by a given firm.

compute the value of $\lambda$ in equilibrium. Integrating both sides of (8.16) over the firm's workforce, we obtain

$$\begin{aligned}\lambda n &= f'(\bar{q})\bar{q} - \int_{\Omega} \omega(q)\,\mathrm{d}\psi \\ &= f'(\bar{q})\bar{q} - f(\bar{q}),\end{aligned}$$

where we have used the fact that the profits, defined by (8.15), must be equal to zero. Therefore, the marginal willingness to pay for worker type $q$ by any firm of type $\bar{q}$ is given by

$$\hat{\omega}(q,\bar{q}) = \frac{f(\bar{q})}{n} + \frac{f'(\bar{q})}{n}(q - \bar{q}). \tag{8.18}$$

This formula defines a linear schedule over the whole skill space. As shown above (equations (8.16) and (8.17)), the wage schedule must be above all the MWP schedules for existing firms and coincide with them for all types of worker employed by these firms.

The firm's willingness to pay is linear in $q$ because it employs a continuum of infinitesimal workers. Consider replacing an infinitesimal worker (of measure $\mathrm{d}q$) of skill $q$ with one of skill $q'$; the effect on the firm's average skill level is $((q' - q)/n)\,\mathrm{d}q$, so that the firm's output changes by $(f'(\bar{q})/n)(q' - q)\,\mathrm{d}q$. This defines the difference in the firm's willingness to pay between the two workers, which is proportional to the difference in their skill levels. Therefore, the MWP for a worker of type $q$ must be equal to $(f'(\bar{q})q)/n$ plus a constant. Furthermore, the zero-profit condition implies that the marginal willingness to pay for the "average" worker (of type $\bar{q}$) is equal to the average output $f(\bar{q})/n$. If the firm were to employ only workers of the same skill, they would be of skill $\bar{q}$ and each would contribute $f(\bar{q})/n$ to the firm's total output. Relative to that benchmark, the firm is willing to pay a premium to workers with skill higher than $\bar{q}$ and a discount to workers with skill lower than $\bar{q}$. This skill compensates (or taxes) these workers for the spillovers to other workers, i.e., for their effect on the firm's productivity. The "price" of this effect is given by the marginal effect on the average output of an improvement

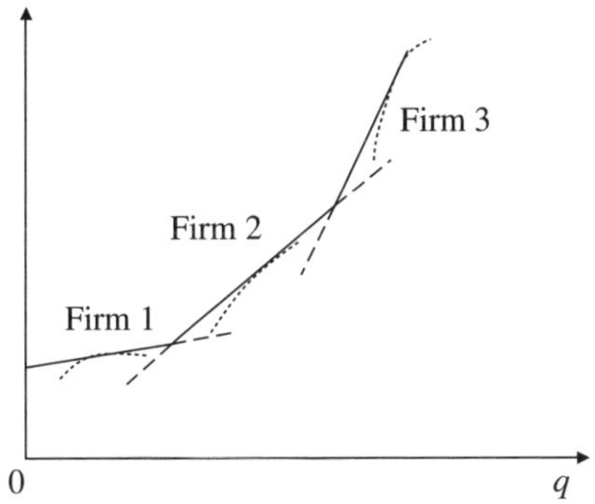


**Figure 8.4.** The wage schedule is convex.

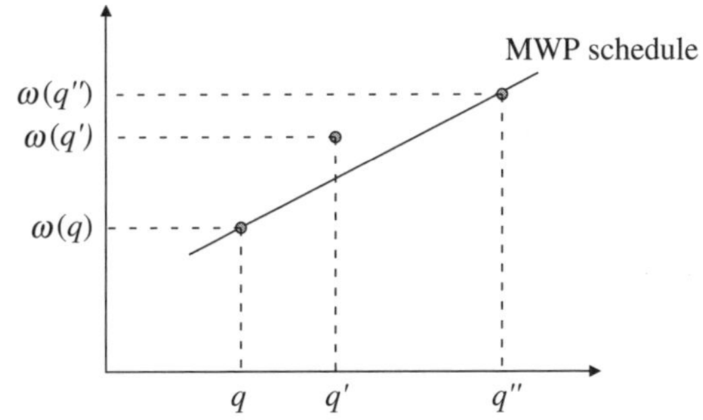


**Figure 8.5.** The wage schedule cannot be convex if the firm is not hiring from a connected set of workers.

in worker quality, $f'(\bar{q})/n$. Workers whose skill level is exactly equal to the average in the firm get no premium and are paid at the firm's average output. These considerations imply, as (8.18) makes clear, that the MWP schedule for a firm of type $\bar{q}$ is the *tangent* to the average output schedule at point $(\bar{q}, g(\bar{q})/n)$ (see figure 8.3).

Since a worker's wage is equal to the employer's marginal willingness to pay for him, and cannot be lower than other employers' MWP, the wage schedule must be the upper envelope of all the linear MWP schedules of existing firms. This property has a number of important implications.

First, as illustrated in figure 8.4, the wage schedule is necessarily *convex* in $q$; the marginal return to skill goes up as one advances up the skill space; this is because more highly skilled workers sort themselves into firms with steeper MWP schedules, i.e., with a greater return from increasing their average skill level.

Second, this leads to a *clustering* of the assignment of workers to firms. The skill space can be partitioned into intervals, and each firm type recruits in one of these intervals only. This property is illustrated in figure 8.5, which shows what happens to the wage schedule if it does not hold. Suppose a firm hires a worker of type $q''$ but does not want to hire a worker of type $q' < q''$. Then $\omega(q')$ must be strictly greater than the firm's willingness to pay for worker $q'$, while the wage of worker $q''$ must lie on the firm's linear MWP schedule. Clearly, if the firm were willing to hire any worker of quality $q < q'$, $\omega(q)$ would also lie on the MWP schedule, which would violate the convexity of the wage schedule. Therefore, if a firm is not willing to hire a worker of lower quality than one of its employees, it will not employ workers of even lower quality. The same reasoning can be applied for workers of higher quality than the firm's employees. Finally, assume that the firm is willing to employ two workers of quality $q$ and $q''$. Then both $\omega(q)$ and $\omega(q'')$ lie on its linear MWP schedule. Clearly, it is also willing to hire any worker $q'$ such that $q < q' < q''$. Otherwise, $\omega(q')$ would be above the MWP line and the convexity of the wage schedule would again be violated.

As figure 8.4 shows, the interval within which a firm of type $\bar{q}$ is willing to hire matches the linear portion of the wage schedule which coincides with its MWP schedule; beyond this interval the wage schedule is strictly above its MWP schedule, which means that it does not hire these workers. Within the interval, the firm is indifferent with respect to which particular workers it hires, but the distribution of its employees' skill levels, $\mathrm{d}\psi$, must be such that the firm is indeed of type $\bar{q}$, i.e., $\int q \,\mathrm{d}\psi = \bar{q}$.

Finally, the convexity of the wage schedule allows us to formulate another condition needed for equilibrium: that no entrant make positive profits. Because of the convex wage schedule, a firm of type $\bar{q}$ cannot have a wage bill lower than that it obtains by hiring only workers of quality $\bar{q}$. Therefore, the no-entry condition holds if and only if

$$\omega(\bar{q}) \geqslant \frac{f(\bar{q})}{n}, \quad \forall q.$$

Therefore, the wage schedule must always be above the average output schedule, and the tangency points between the two schedules define the firm types that can exist in equilibrium.

### 8.4.1 Equilibrium

Finally, for the labor market to be in equilibrium, the assignment of workers to firms, and the set of existing firms, must be such that the supply of any type of labor must be equal to the demand for it. One may state this formally as follows, using our density $g(\cdot)$ of workers. Given that the total population is equal to 1, in equilibrium there must be a mass of firms equal to $1/n$. Let these firms be indexed by $j \in [0, 1/n]$ and let

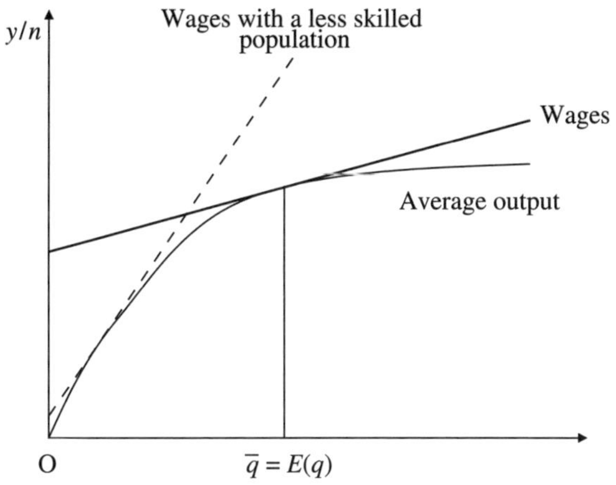


**Figure 8.6.** A single unitary zone.

$d\psi_j(q)$ be the distribution of workers hired by firm $j$. Then one must have

$$\int_0^{1/n} d\psi_j(q) = g(q)\,dq. \tag{8.19}$$

The left-hand side is the demand for workers around skill $q$, the right-hand side is the supply.

### 8.4.2 Examples

To illustrate equilibrium determination, we use some simple examples. We start by considering the case where the average output schedule is concave throughout. As shown in figure 8.6, there is a single firm type in equilibrium. Suppose there were more than one type of firm, and consider two firms of different types, A and B. Assume that firm A has a higher average skill than firm B. Then its MWP schedule must be flatter than that of firm B, since it is tangent to the concave average output schedule. Consequently, firm A's MWP schedule is below firm B's schedule on the right of their crossing point, and it is above it on the left. If we denote by $q^*$ the skill level at the crossing point, this implies that firm A only hires below skill level $q^*$, while firm B only hires above it. That clearly contradicts the assumption that firm A has a higher skill level.

The unique equilibrium firm type must hire from a single cluster of skills, which is the entire skill space $\Omega$. For (8.19) to hold, it must be that the average skill level in the single firm type is equal to that in the population, $\bar{q} = E(q) = \int_\Omega q g(q)\,dq$.

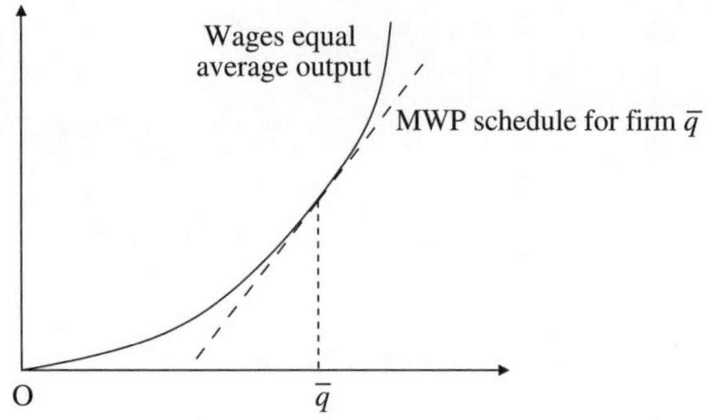


**Figure 8.7.** Hypersegregation.

Concavity implies that a high-skill firm is willing to pay less to improve the average quality of its workforce than a low-skill firm. This creates a force that induces low-skill firms to improve their type by buying high-quality workers from high-skill firms. This process leads to a single firm type in equilibrium.

Any increase in the average skill in the population triggers an equal increase in $\bar{q}$. As a result, the economy moves to the right in figure 8.6; the slope of the wage schedule falls, and there is less inequality.

At the other extreme, if the average output is convex throughout, we are back to the perfectly segregated case from the previous section. The MWP of any firm type is now strictly below the average output schedule except at $q = \bar{q}$ (figure 8.7); therefore, that is the only point at which it can coincide with the wage schedule, since it must lie above the average output schedule. Consequently, in equilibrium a firm of type $\bar{q}$ can only hire workers of quality $\bar{q}$. The clusters collapse to a single point, and wages are equal to average output: $\omega(q) = f(q)/n$.

Figure 8.8 illustrates the case of an S-shaped average output schedule. For the same reasons as given above, there is at most one firm type whose average skill level is in the concave portion of the average output schedule. The cluster (called the *unitary zone*) within which these firms recruit is the interval of values of $q$ such that their MWP schedule is above the average output schedule. This includes the entire concave portion plus a part of the convex portion. When the interval is smaller than the entire skill space, workers with quality $q$ below the frontier level $q^*$ work in perfectly segregated firms, which only employ workers of quality $q$. In the unitary zone, the average skill level of the employer must be equal to the average population skill level in that zone; otherwise, the labor market cannot clear, since all workers with these skills must be employed by firms of this single type.

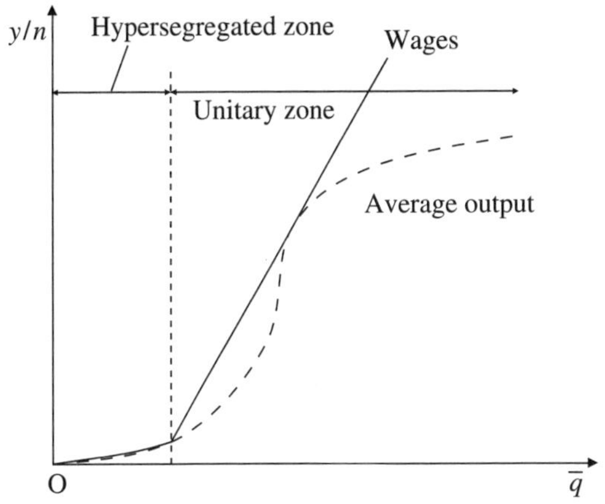


**Figure 8.8.** The S-shaped case with two zones.

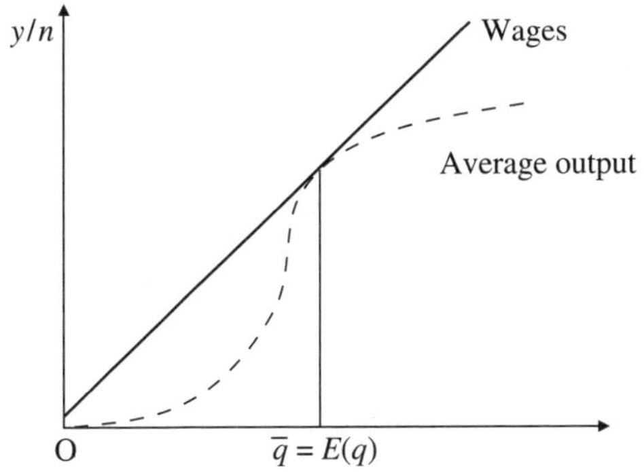


**Figure 8.9.** The S-shaped case with a single unitary zone.

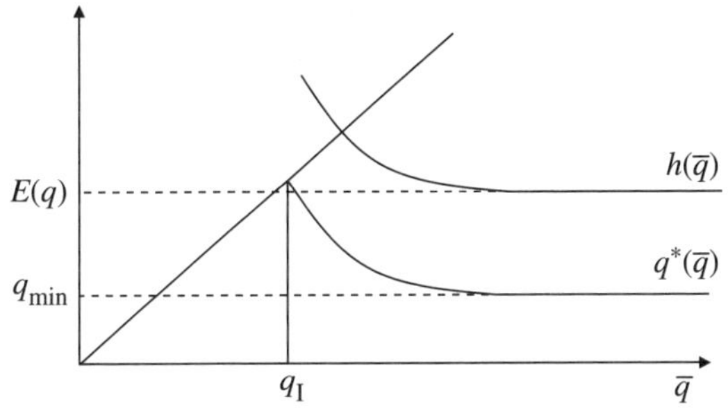


**Figure 8.10.** Existence and uniqueness of equilibrium.

It is easy to see that this requirement implies that the equilibrium is unique. Given a firm type $\bar{q}$, the unitary zone is $[q^*, q_{max}]$, where $q^*$ is the intersection (in the convex zone) between the MWP schedule at $\bar{q}$ and

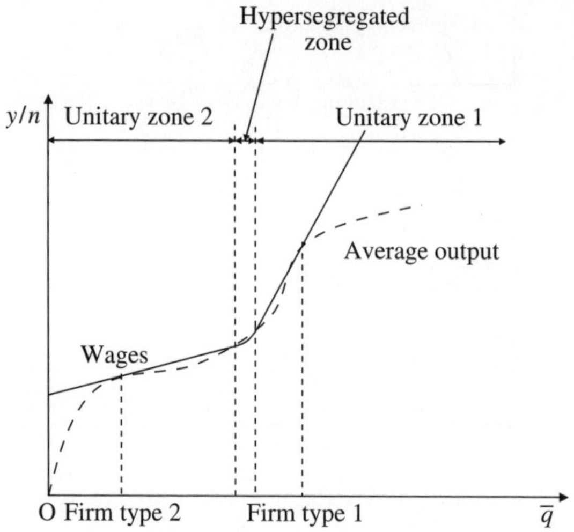


**Figure 8.11.** The two-humps case, A.

the average output schedule. It satisfies the following condition:

$$\frac{f(q^*) - f(\bar{q})}{n} = \frac{f'(\bar{q})}{n}(q^* - \bar{q}). \tag{8.20}$$

$q^*$ falls as $\bar{q}$ increases; hence, $q^*$ is a decreasing function of $\bar{q}$, $q^*(\bar{q})$. It may be that the tangent line is above the average output schedule throughout, in which case we extend the definition by setting $q^*(\bar{q}) = q_{\min}$. In such a case there is a critical value of $\bar{q}$ beyond which $q^*(\bar{q}) = q_{\min}$ and the whole labor market is in the unitary zone, as is the case with a concave $f(\cdot)$ (figure 8.9). The equilibrium value of $\bar{q}$ must lie between $q_{\mathrm{I}}$, the inflection point of $f(\cdot)$, and $q_{\max}$. We define $h(\bar{q}) = E(q \mid q \in [q^*(\bar{q}), q_{\max}])$. This is the conditional expectation of $q$ in the relevant candidate interval for the unitary zone, for a given candidate value of the tangency point $\bar{q}$. Labor-market clearing is then clearly equivalent to $\bar{q} = h(\bar{q})$, i.e., $\bar{q}$ is a fixed point of $h(\cdot)$. Furthermore, $h(\cdot)$ is decreasing so long as $q^*(\bar{q}) > q_{\min}$. If there is a zone where $q^*(\bar{q}) = q_{\min}$, $h(\cdot)$ is constant over this zone and equals the population mean of $q$, $E(q)$. Finally, $h(q_{\mathrm{I}}) > q_{\mathrm{I}}$, because $q^*(q_{\mathrm{I}}) = q_{\mathrm{I}}$, while $h(q_{\max}) < q_{\max}$. Consequently, $h(\cdot)$ intersects the 45° line exactly once; therefore, the equilibrium is unique. This is illustrated in figure 8.10. If the intersection is on a downward-sloping portion (as in figure 8.10), then the equilibrium is as in figure 8.8. If it is on a flat portion such that $h(q) = E(q)$, then all workers are in a single cluster, as in figure 8.9.

More complex shapes for the average output schedule generate a more complex pattern of segregation. Figures 8.11–8.14 illustrate various configurations that may arise when the average output schedule has two

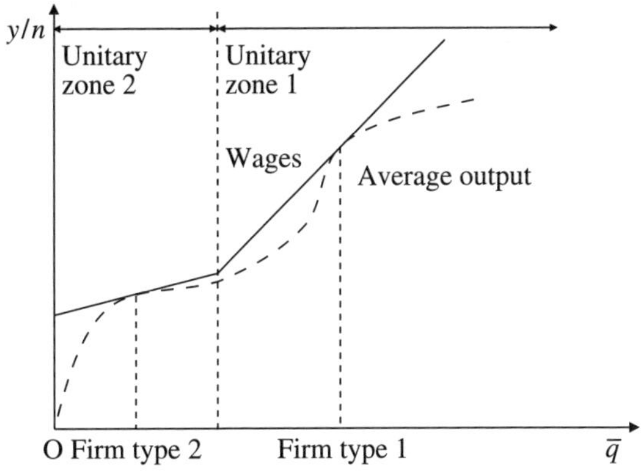


**Figure 8.12.** The two-humps case, B.

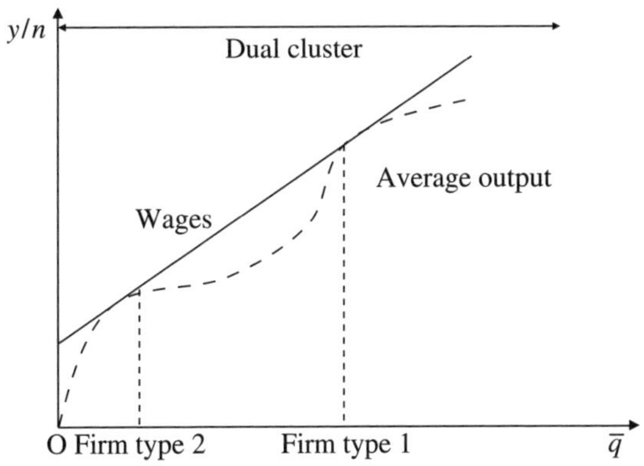


**Figure 8.13.** The two-humps case, C.

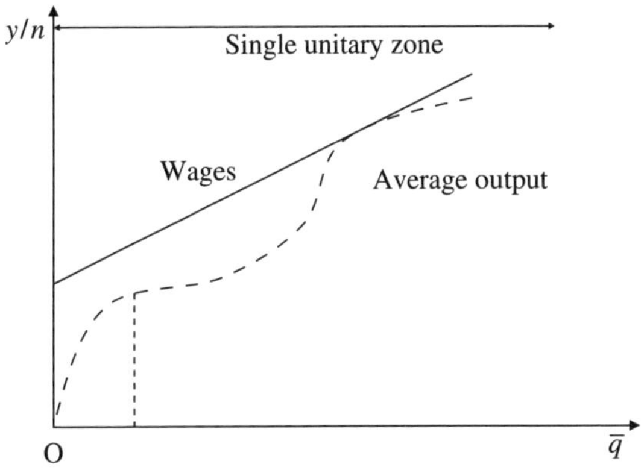


**Figure 8.14.** The two-humps case, D.

humps: two unitary zones separated by a hypersegregated zone; two consecutive unitary zones; a dual cluster where two types of firms, each with a different average skill level,[3] recruit in the same skill interval; and a single unitary zone. The general message remains that convex portions of the average output schedule tend to create segregated zones where all coworkers have the same skill levels, while concave portions tend to create unitary zones or dual clusters where firms recruit from a nontrivial interval of skill levels.

### 8.4.3 Applications

#### *8.4.3.1 Parallel Processing*

With our new knowledge in hand, we can return to the case of parallel processing introduced above. Remember that the production function was

$$f(q_1,\dots,q_n) = 1 - \prod_{i=1}^{n}(1 - q_i\varepsilon).$$

While this is not a sole function of the mean of the $q_i$s, we can change the units of measurement and redefine worker quality as $\hat{q} = -\ln(1 - q\varepsilon)$ instead of $q$. Then the production function can be rewritten as

$$f(\hat{q}_1,\dots,\hat{q}_n) = 1 - \mathrm{e}^{-\varepsilon n\bar{q}}, \tag{8.21}$$

where

$$\bar{q} = \frac{1}{n}\sum \hat{q}_i$$

is the worker average quality, using the new metric. Finally, we converge to the case where the firm employs a continuum of workers by just letting $n$ tend to infinity while $\varepsilon$ tends to zero, remaining proportional to $1/n$.

Equation (8.21) clearly defines a concave function of $\bar{q}$; therefore, we can readily apply the analysis of the previous section. We are in the case in figure 8.6: there is a single unitary zone, and the unique firm type is such that $\bar{q} = E(q)$. The wage schedule is the tangent to the average output schedule at $E(q)$. Hence,

$$\omega(q) = \frac{1 - \mathrm{e}^{-\varepsilon n\bar{q}}}{n} + \varepsilon\mathrm{e}^{-\varepsilon n\bar{q}}(q - \bar{q}). \tag{8.22}$$

---

[3] In a dual cluster, the two firm types are defined endogenously by the requirement that the linear wage schedule is tangent to both humps. There is only one straight line satisfying this requirement. The proportions of type-1 and type-2 firms are then determined by the requirement that all skill levels are fully employed. If we denote by $\bar{q}_i$ the average skill level in firm type $i$ and by $\theta_1$ the proportion of firms of type 1, it must be that $E(q) = \theta_1\bar{q}_1 + (1 - \theta_1)\bar{q}_2$.

Thus, under parallel processing, firms will typically not be segregated, but hire a variety of workers. The mix of workers in each firm will be such that their average skill level is the same as in the population at large. This is because the sorting condition does not hold. Firms are willing to pay less for increasing the skill of a given worker if other workers are more skilled, because that makes it more likely that the other workers will solve the problem anyway, thus reducing the probability that the greater skills of that worker are actually useful. Therefore, high-skill firms prefer to hire low-skill workers at the margin, and vice versa.

Furthermore, while, under serial processing, inequality increases with the number of workers involved in the production process, the contrary is true for parallel processing. We can show that the marginal returns to skill $\omega'(q)/\omega(q)$ fall at any level $q$ when $n$ increases.[4] When more people work in parallel to solve the same problem, this increases the likelihood that the problem is solved, all else being equal, which reduces the firms' marginal willingness to pay for better workers.

### 8.4.3.2 Parallel Processing with Total Factor Productivity Effects

A more complex situation arises if, in a firm, workers solve problems in parallel and at the same time produce a variable amount of output. Suppose that workers who are better at solving problems are also better at producing output or, in other words, that there is a positive correlation between intelligence and productivity. The firm's total output is now the product of its employees' total productivity and of the fraction of the time it is successful in solving its problems, which is the right-hand side of (8.21). Assuming that each employee contributes proportionally to his skill level $q$, we can write

$$y = An\bar{q}(1 - \mathrm{e}^{-\varepsilon n\bar{q}}). \tag{8.23}$$

With this specification, output is typically S-shaped, as illustrated in figures 8.8 and 8.9. In the configuration of figure 8.9, there is still a single unitary zone. In that of figure 8.8, workers above a critical skill level work in a unitary zone, while workers below it are segregated into firms that only hire a single worker type. In both cases, the wage schedule in the unitary zone can be computed by applying (8.18), which yields

$$\omega(q) = A\bar{q}_{\mathrm{u}}(1 - \mathrm{e}^{-\varepsilon n\bar{q}_{\mathrm{u}}}) + (q_u - \bar{q}_{\mathrm{u}})A[(1 - \mathrm{e}^{-\varepsilon n\bar{q}_{\mathrm{u}}}) + \bar{q}_{\mathrm{u}}\varepsilon n\mathrm{e}^{-\varepsilon n\bar{q}_{\mathrm{u}}}], \tag{8.24}$$

[4] Differentiating (8.22) with respect to $q$, we can write $\omega'(q)/\omega(q) = b(n)/(a(n) + b(n)q)$, with $a(n) = ((1 - \mathrm{e}^{-\varepsilon\bar{n}q})/n) - \varepsilon\bar{q}\mathrm{e}^{-\varepsilon\bar{n}q}$ and $b(n) = \varepsilon\mathrm{e}^{-\varepsilon\bar{n}q}$. The ratio $b(n)/(a(n)+b(n)q)$ decreases with decreasing $n$ if and only if $b'(n)a(n) < b(n)a'(n)$. Differentiating $a$ and $b$ with respect to $n$, substituting into this inequality, and simplifying, we find that this is true if and only if $\varepsilon\bar{q}n > 1 - \mathrm{e}^{-\varepsilon\bar{n}q}$, which always holds.

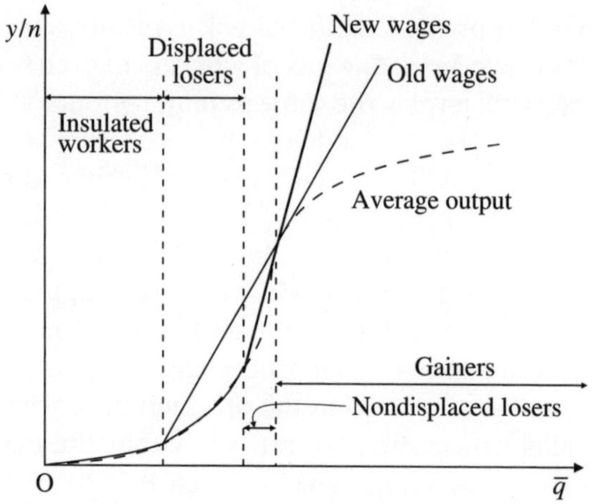


**Figure 8.15.** The effect of a deterioration in the skill distribution on wages.

where $\bar{q}_u$ is the equilibrium average skill level in the single firm type that recruits in the unitary zone, as determined by figure 8.10.

What is going on? At low levels of the firm's average skill, the cumulative effect of skills on productivity and problem solving is strong, and the sorting condition holds. Firms with low average skill levels do not want to pay a lot for highly skilled workers. These firms' high failure rate reduces the value of increasing their average productivity, and their low average productivity does not make it worth reducing their high failure rate. At high skill levels, however, the decreasing-returns logic kicks in again: the firm successfully produces output most of the time and the problem-solving value of hiring a highly skilled worker falls sharply with the firm's average skill.

It is interesting to perform some comparative statics experiments in this case. Consider first a downward shift in the distributions of skills. The firm type in the unitary zone, $\bar{q}_1$, must be equal to the average skill level in that zone. When skills fall, this average falls, and so must the firm type. Because of the local concavity of the average output schedule in a unitary zone, this is only possible if, as shown in figure 8.15, the unitary zone shrinks by getting rid of the least skilled workers and the wage schedule's linear portion gets steeper. The usual result of a greater return to skills when skills are scarcer applies. But we also get richer results due to the pattern of segregation. Workers who work in hypersegregated firms work only with workers of the same type, and are therefore insulated by the shift in the distribution of skills. If, say, the supply of workers of a given skill level in the hypersegregated zone increases, then the number of firms employing only that skill type increases proportionally, as if they were in a world where all workers had the same skill level. In the unitary zone, the relatively unskilled become more abundant. They compete to get into the "club," which pushes up the entry fee $\lambda$, as they have to compensate the "club" for their negative effect on its average quality. This depresses their wages. At the same time, the reduction in the firm's average skill level necessary to keep the labor market in equilibrium boosts the firm's willingness to pay for skills, $f'(\bar{q})$. As a result, the wages of sufficiently skilled workers go up despite the increase in the entry fee. Finally, the fall in the wages of the least skilled workers in the unitary zone makes it profitable, at the margin, for entrants to hire these workers in hypersegregated firms that were not profitable before the shift in $F(\cdot)$. Thus, these workers end up leaving the unitary zone and working in homogeneous firms.

As we have seen in the introduction to this book, globalization is often invoked in the debate over the rise in inequality. The bottom line is that, through trade, workers are immersed in a world economy where factor prices are determined by global, rather than local, relative supplies. Hence, skilled Western workers gain and unskilled Western workers lose, because the relative supply of unskilled workers worldwide is larger than its counterpart in the West.

Interestingly, advances in information technology create new channels of globalization: people can exchange information through electronic means in real time despite being remote from one another. Hence, a single work team can be scattered across several locations. Archetypal examples include the outsourcing of accounting departments or call centers to less developed countries. In terms of the above model, this means that the relevant distribution of skills $g(\cdot)$ from which a firm can draw its workers is the global one, rather than the skill distribution in the country where the firm is located. The effect of information technology is thus similar to that of trade, except that this is now due to factor content being embodied in the information exchanged within the firm rather than material goods shipped across national boundaries. This argument suggests that globalization should have the effect depicted in figure 8.15: an insulation of the least skilled, a displacement of the medium skilled from the unitary zone to hypersegregated firms, a reduction in the average skill level of the unitary firms (if properly measured by taking into account their overseas employees), and an increase in the return to skill within the unitary zone.

Another interesting phenomenon is, again, that of a rise in $n$, the size of the firm. One possible interpretation of such a shift is an improvement in "information technology," which makes it possible for somebody to solve problems that affect a larger number of workers than before (this is

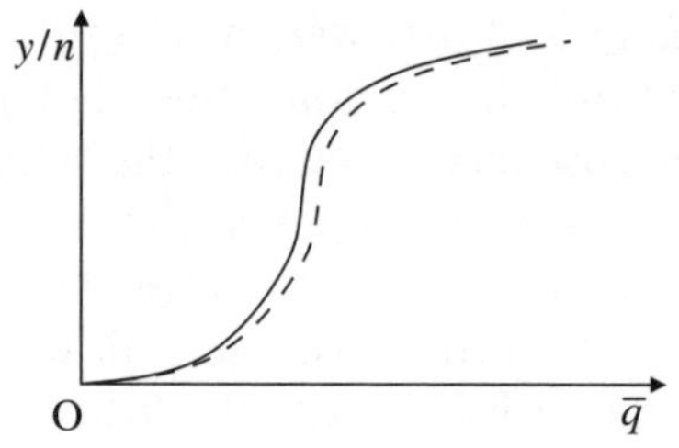


**Figure 8.16.** Impact of an increase in $n$ on average output.

similar to our discussion of span of control effects in chapter 7). Its effect on the average output schedule is shown in figure 8.16. Because of parallel processing, the average output schedule shifts upward: with more workers in the firm, problems are solved more often. Furthermore, its S-shape is attenuated; it becomes steeper below the inflection point, and flatter above it, while retaining the same slope at the inflection point.[5] This average output schedule is equal to the wage schedule in the hypersegregated zone. In this zone it is also convex, and thus becomes steeper. Consequently, *absolute* wage inequality increases with $n$ in this zone. This increase in absolute inequality is due to the fact that solving additional problems generates greater output gains in firms with a higher average skill level: an effect which would not be present in the pure parallel processing model with no total factor productivity effects. However, one can also show that *relative* inequality actually falls.[6] This is due to another effect: Firms with a lower average skill level benefit more from the increase in problem-solving abilities brought about by a higher value for $n$. As (8.12) suggests, the marginal value of an extra worker of a given skill level in terms of solving problems falls with the skills of his coworkers, because they are more likely to solve the problem anyway. (This effect becomes so strong as $\bar{q}$ becomes large that the increase in $n$ makes the average output effect flatter past the inflection point.)

What happens to the unitary zone? We can show algebraically (see the appendix) that it necessarily expands. The most skilled workers in the hypersegregated firms now become the least skilled workers employed

[5] To see this, compute the derivative of $y/n$ with respect to $\bar{q}$, $D_1 = 1 - e^{-\varepsilon n\bar{q}} + \bar{q}\varepsilon n e^{-\varepsilon n\bar{q}}$. Then note that $\partial D_1/\partial n = \varepsilon\bar{q}e^{-\varepsilon n\bar{q}}(2 - \varepsilon n\bar{q})$, which is proportional to $D_2 = \mathrm{d}D_1/\mathrm{d}n = \varepsilon n e^{-\varepsilon n\bar{q}}(2 - \varepsilon n\bar{q})$.

[6] The marginal relative return to skill is given by

$$\omega'(q)/\omega(q) = \frac{\varepsilon n e^{-\varepsilon n\bar{q}}}{1 - e^{-\varepsilon n\bar{q}}}.$$

Computing the derivative of this expression with respect to $n$, we see that it has the same sign as $1 - e^{-\varepsilon n\bar{q}} - \varepsilon\bar{q}n$, which is decreasing in $\bar{q}$ and zero at $\bar{q} = 0$, and hence negative throughout.

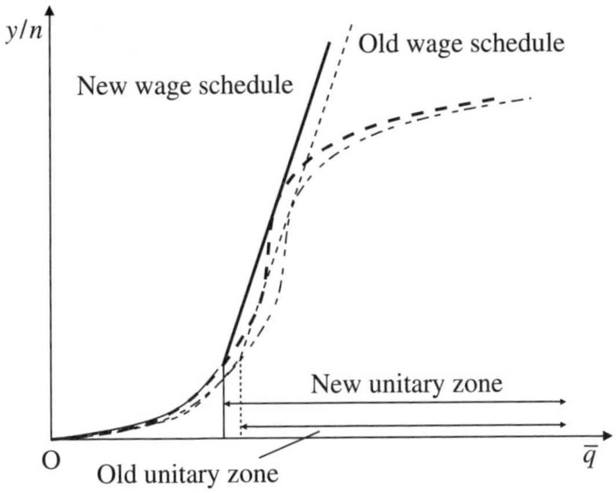


**Figure 8.17.** Impact of an increase in $n$ on segregation and wages.

in unitary firms. A unitary firm of any given skill level $\bar{q}$ is willing to pay a lower premium for skills, because having more workers allows more problems to be solved, which makes skills less valuable. Therefore, starting from a situation where the unitary firm hires from the same interval of skills as before the rise in $n$, the wage schedule shifts up and flattens, making the firm willing to pay more for the best hypersegregated workers than what they would have earned in their original homogeneous firm, i.e., its average output. Consequently, these are absorbed into the unitary zone, which widens.

What about the return to skill in the unitary zone? While the wage schedule would become flatter if the average skill in the unitary zone, $\bar{q}_{\mathrm{u}}$, remained unchanged, its widening reduces $\bar{q}_{\mathrm{u}}$, which tends to make the wage schedule steeper. Can we say anything about the net effect on inequality? In the appendix we show that the effect of a flatter average output schedule and that of the fall in $\bar{q}_{\mathrm{u}}$ cancel each other out so that the new wage schedule has the same slope as the old. On the other hand, the new wage schedule is above the old, since average output increases. Consequently, the relative return to skill—the ratio of the slope over the level of average output—also falls in the unitary zone. The only dimension in which inequality may increase is between workers who move from hypersegregated firms to the unitary zone: they may locally experience a steeper wage schedule.

The effect of the shift on the distribution of wages is summarized in figure 8.17. Overall, everybody benefits from the improvement in technology, and inequality falls. In the unitary zone, this is because the best workers compete more with each other, because they are more likely to be in the same firm, and because their contributions to problem solving increase the productivity of the less skilled workers. In the hypersegregated zone, this is because firms that employ less skilled workers benefit more from having an extra worker, as they have more unsolved problems that this worker may solve.

Thus, contrary to the displacement effects analyzed in the previous chapter, here we have the case of a technological improvement which benefits everybody.

## 8.5 Conclusion

In this chapter we have analyzed how segregation arises from technologies where complementarities between tasks are strong. We have highlighted how serial processing strengthens such complementarities, while parallel processing rather leads to substitutability. We have also seen the importance of increasing returns in the company's average skill level (as captured by the parameter $\varphi$ in section 8.1.4 and by a locally convex average output schedule in section 8.4). These increasing returns also tend to increase segregation. Segregation *per se* does not imply, though, that earnings inequality is larger or more sensitive to skill-biased technical change. We have given examples to the contrary and it appears that segregation may *insulate* the unskilled from skill-biased technical change, by suppressing their interactions with the skilled. However, some authors argue that segregation may have adverse effects of its own, for example, if externalities such as "peer effects" or "neighborhood effects" are important.

## 8.6 Appendix

### 8.6.1 Proof of the Preliminary Lemma

**Lemma 8.1.** *Consider two firm types* $(q_1, \dots, q_n)$ *and* $(q'_1, \dots, q'_n)$ *such that the distribution of skills in the first type dominates that in the second type, i.e., there is an ordering of the two types such that* $q'_i \leqslant q_i$ *for all* $i$. *Consider a swap of workers between the two firms, such that worker* $q_i$ *switches with worker* $q'_j$. *Then, if* $q_i \leqslant q'_j$, *the total output for the two firms cannot fall.*

*Proof.* The proof is the same as that in section 8.2. Because of symmetry, we can assume without loss of generality that $(q_1, \dots, q_n)$ and $(q'_1, \dots, q'_n)$ are ranked by increasing order. Consequently, one must have

$i \leqslant j$. Then we have

$$\begin{aligned} f(q'_j, \boldsymbol{q}_{-j}) - f(\boldsymbol{q}) &= f(q_1, \dots, q_{i-1}, q'_j, q_{i+1}, \dots, q_n) - f(q_1, \dots, q_n) \\ &= f(q_1, \dots, q_{i-1}, q_{i+1}, \dots, q_j, q'_j, q_{j+1}, \dots, q_n) \\ &\quad - f(q_1, \dots, q_{i-1}, q_{i+1}, \dots, q_j, q_i, q_{j+1}, \dots, q_n) \\ &= \int_{q_i}^{q'_j} f'_j(q_1, \dots, q_{i-1}, q_{i+1}, \dots, q_j, z, q_{j+1}, \dots, q_n)\,\mathrm{d}z, \\ f(\boldsymbol{q}') - f(q_i, \boldsymbol{q}'_{-j}) &= f(q'_1, \dots, q'_n) - f(q'_1, \dots, q'_{j-1}, q_i, q'_{j+1}, \dots, q'_n) \\ &= \int_{q_i}^{q'_j} f'_j(q'_1, \dots, q'_{j-1}, z, q'_{j+1}, \dots, q'_n)\,\mathrm{d}z. \end{aligned}$$

Since

$$\frac{\partial^2 f}{\partial x_i \partial x_j} \geqslant 0 \quad \text{and} \quad q'_\tau \leqslant q_\tau \leqslant q_{\tau+1},$$

we have that

$$\begin{aligned} &f'_j(q'_1, \dots, q'_{j-1}, z, q'_{j+1}, \dots, q'_n) \\ &\qquad \leqslant f'_j(q_1, \dots, q_{i-1}, q_{i+1}, \dots, q_j, z, q_{j+1}, \dots, q_n). \end{aligned}$$

Therefore, $f(q'_j, \boldsymbol{q}_{-j}) - f(\boldsymbol{q}) \geqslant f(\boldsymbol{q}') - f(q_i, \boldsymbol{q}'_{-j})$, or equivalently $f(q'_j, \boldsymbol{q}_{-j}) + f(q_i, \boldsymbol{q}'_{-j}) \geqslant f(\boldsymbol{q}) + f(\boldsymbol{q}')$, which proves that the swap cannot reduce output. □

### 8.6.2 The Iteration Procedure to Prove That (8.11) Holds

The procedure is as follows. At the beginning of each stage firms are ranked in such a way that the $k$th firm is of type $(q_1^{(k)}, \dots, q_n^{(k)})$. Without loss of generality, we assume that skill levels are ranked in ascending order: $q_i^{(k)} \leqslant q_{i+1}^{(k)}$ (the worker types in our population, $q_1, \dots, q_n$, are also ranked in increasing order). In order to be able to apply the lemma, we assume that the allocation of workers to firms is such that the distribution of skills improves with the firm's rank:

$$q_i^{(k)} \leqslant q_i^{(k+1)}, \quad \forall i, k. \tag{P}$$

This property certainly holds at the initial stage, $k = 0$, where all firms have the same type, $(q_1, \dots, q_n)$. We will construct our swaps so that this property is preserved.

Consider the highest rank, nonsegregated firm; let $k_s$ be its rank. Note that for $k > k_s$ all firms are segregated and it must be that $q_i^{(k)} = q_k$, otherwise (P) cannot hold. Let $j_s = \max\{j, q_j^{(k_s)} = q_1^{(k_s)}\}$. In other words, $j_s$ is the number of least skilled workers in firm $k_s$, also equal to the highest index of these workers in that firm. This worker type is equal to some $q_l$, with $l < k_s$. All types $q_m$ such that $m > k_s$ are in the segregated firms such that $k > k_s$. If the lowest type in firm $k_s$ were to equal $q_{k_s}$, all workers in that firm would have to be of this type, and it would be segregated. Therefore, the lowest type in firm $k_s$, $q_l$, must be such that $l < k_s$.

Let $k_m$ be the lowest ranking firm which employs workers of type $q_{l+1}$.[7] It must be that $k_m < k_s$, since firm $k_s$ can employ at most $n - 1$ workers of type $q_{l+1}$, and the higher ranking segregated firms do not employ that type. Let $j_m = \min\{j, q_j^{(k_m)} = q_{l+1}\}$. Consider a swap between worker $j_m$ in firm $k_m$, with type $q_{j_m}^{(k_m)} = q_{l+1}$, and worker $j_s$ in firm $k_s$, with type $q_{j_s}^{(k_s)} = q_l$. Since (P) holds and $q_{l+1} \geqslant q_l$, the lemma applies; this swap weakly increases output. Furthermore, in the new allocation of labor, property (P) still holds. To check this, note that $q_{j_{m-1}}^{(k_m)} < q_{l+1}$, and hence $q_{j_{m-1}}^{(k_m)} \leqslant q_l = \hat{q}_{j_m}^{(k_m)}$, where a hat denotes the new allocation, when it is different from the old one. Thus, the ordering in firm $k_m$ is preserved; one can also easily show that it is preserved in firm $k_s$. Similarly, since $k_m$ is minimal, $q_{j_m}^{(k_m-1)} < q_{l+1}$, and hence

$$q_{j_m}^{(k_m-1)} \leqslant q_l = \hat{q}_{j_m}^{(k_m)} < q_{l+1} = q_{j_m}^{(k_m)} \leqslant q_{j_m}^{(k_m+1)}.$$

Thus, (P) still holds around worker $j_m$. Finally, since $l + 1 \leqslant k_s$ and $q_j^{(k_s+1)} = q_{k_s+1}$ for all $j$, we have

$$q_{j_s}^{(k_s-1)} \leqslant q_{j_s}^{(k_s)} = q_l < q_{l+1} = \hat{q}_{j_s}^{(k_s)} < q_{j_s}^{(k_s+1)} = q_{k_{s+1}}.$$

Hence, (P) also holds around worker $j_s$. Therefore, the procedure can be iterated, until the stage where no nonsegregated firm exists, in which case the output per firm is equal to the right-hand side of (8.11). Since output cannot fall at any stage, the right-hand side is greater than the left-hand side, which gives output per firm at stage 0.

### 8.6.3 Showing That the Unitary Zone Widens When $n$ Increases

Let us return to the construction of figure 8.10. The unitary zone is defined by the interval $[q^*(\bar{q}), q_{\max}]$, where $\bar{q}$ must satisfy the equilibrium condition $\bar{q} = E(q \mid q > q^*(\bar{q})) = h(q^*)$. Recall from (8.20) that $q^*(\bar{q})$ is defined by

$$\frac{f(q^*) - f(\bar{q})}{n} = \frac{f'(\bar{q})}{n}(q^* - \bar{q}).$$

[7] If types $q_l$ and $q_{l+1}$ turn out to be identical, the swap is immaterial, and therefore output does not fall and (P) still holds. We can reallocate the (identical) workers of these two types so that type $q_{l+1}$ is in the highest ranking firms, and so on, until we have reached a stage where the relevant $l$ is such that $q_l < q_{l+1}$.

Substituting the right-hand side of (8.23) for $f(q)$, we get the following condition:

$$0 = q^*(\mathrm{e}^{-\varepsilon n\bar{q}} - \mathrm{e}^{-\varepsilon nq^*}) + \varepsilon n\bar{q}\mathrm{e}^{-\varepsilon n\bar{q}}(\bar{q} - q^*).$$

The key step is to perform a change in variables, defining $\bar{z} = n\bar{q}$ and $z^* = nq^*$. The preceding equation can then be rewritten in terms of these two variables, with $n$ not appearing:

$$0 = z^*(\mathrm{e}^{-\varepsilon\bar{z}} - \mathrm{e}^{-\varepsilon z^*}) + \varepsilon\bar{z}\mathrm{e}^{-\varepsilon\bar{z}}(\bar{z} - z^*).$$

This defines a function $z^*(z)$ which does not depend on $n$.

Furthermore, the equilibrium condition $\bar{q} = h(q^*)$ can also be written

$$\begin{aligned}\bar{z} = n\bar{q} &= nE(q \mid q > q^*(\bar{q})) \\ &= E(nq \mid nq > nq^*(q)) \\ &= E(z \mid z > z^*(z)).\end{aligned}$$

The variable change also eliminates $n$ from this condition. Consequently, the equilibrium values $\bar{z}_{\mathrm{u}}$ and $z^*$, which solve this system, are determined independently of $n$. Since $q^* = z^*/n$, an increase in $n$, which leaves $z^*$ unaffected, reduces $q^*$ proportionally. Therefore, the unitary zone widens. Also, since $\bar{q}_{\mathrm{u}} = \bar{z}_{\mathrm{u}}/n$, an increase in $n$ reduces $\bar{q}$. Turning now to the wage schedule, equation (8.24) implies that its slope, equal to $[(1 - \mathrm{e}^{-\varepsilon n\bar{q}_{\mathrm{u}}}) + \bar{q}_{\mathrm{u}}\varepsilon n\mathrm{e}^{-\varepsilon n\bar{q}_{\mathrm{u}}}]$, depends only on $\bar{z}_{\mathrm{u}}$. Since $\bar{z}_{\mathrm{u}}$ is unaffected, the absolute return to skills is unchanged in the unitary zone. The rise in $n$ therefore triggers a vertical translation of the wage schedule in the unitary zone, implying that the relative returns to skill, $\omega'(q)/\omega(q)$, also fall in this zone.

# 9
# Demand Effects

In the preceding chapters I have analyzed the many ways in which technical progress may be "skill-biased," in that its direct effect on the marginal product of different skill categories is not proportional. In this chapter, I analyze how technical progress can affect inequality through its general equilibrium effects on relative prices. That is, I assume that the direct effect of technical progress on relative marginal products is neutral but that relative incomes are eventually affected because the structure of demand is not invariant with technical change. This essentially arises because preferences are not homothetic.

We will analyze two different models. In model 1, based on Saint-Paul (2006a,b), there is a class of creative workers who invent goods and a class of production workers who make them. The creative workers are remunerated, indirectly, by the monopoly rents associated with the goods; consequently, the distribution of income between creative and production workers depends on the distribution between wages and profits. The shape of the utility function affects this distribution through the monopoly markup, which depends on the shape of the demand function for each good. By making people richer, technical progress affects markups and thus the distribution of income, if utility is not homothetic. We focus especially on the case of "limited needs," where cardinal utility is bounded, and show that this phenomenon of quasi-satiation generates higher markups when the economy as a whole gets richer, thus shifting the distribution of income in favor of the creative class.

In model 2, from Matsuyama (2002), nonhomotheticity arises from several sources. There is a range of industrial goods, and an individual can consume either 0 units or 1 unit of that good; thus, goods are indivisible and consumers are satiated. Furthermore, there is a hierarchy of needs, in that goods are ranked and a higher ranking good yields utility only if lower ranking goods are also consumed. An important consequence is that people with different income levels consume different goods and therefore benefit differently from technical progress, depending on the sectors in which it takes place. Furthermore, as in

Murphy et al. (1989), technical progress can be endogenized through learning-by-doing effects, in which case the progress itself depends on the distribution of income through the market size for each good.

## 9.1 The Isoelastic Benchmark

Our starting point is a simple model of the Dixit–Stiglitz family, as described in chapter 1. There is a continuum of consumers indexed by $i \in [0, 1]$. To highlight our main point, we assume a more general utility function than in chapter 1. Utility at a point in time is no longer given by (1.14); instead, we have the more general formulation

$$U = U(C_i) = U\left(u^{-1}\left(\left[\int_0^N u(x_{ij})\,\mathrm{d}j\right]\right)\right). \tag{9.1}$$

Each individual good (or "variety") $j$ is again produced by a monopoly, with a linear production function and production labor as the only input:

$$y_j = al_j,$$

where $a$ is the productivity level, assumed to be the same for all goods. Denoting by $p_j$ the price of good $j$, and by $w$ the wage of raw labor, the monopoly pricing formula can be written as

$$p_j = \mu\frac{w}{a}, \tag{9.2}$$

where $\mu$ is the monopoly markup.

The total labor force, in terms of raw labor, is given by $L$. Equilibrium in the labor market implies that

$$L = \int_0^N l_j\,\mathrm{d}j.$$

Given that the utility function is symmetrical in the set of goods, and that all goods have the same production function, it is convenient to characterize an equilibrium where all goods have the same price. Without loss of generality we can normalize this price to 1. Therefore, $p_j = 1$. Substituting into (9.2), we get the following expression for the equilibrium wage:

$$w = \frac{a}{\mu}. \tag{9.3}$$

This determines the wages expressed in terms of *physical* purchasing power. This differs from the real wage, expressed in terms of utility, because there is a taste for diversity: if the number of goods $N$ goes up, people may be happier even though $w$ as measured here might fall. However, so long as the number of varieties remains constant, an increase in the utility of production workers must be associated with a rise in $w$.

In such a symmetrical equilibrium, employment in any firm $j$ is given by $l_j = L/N$.

Under the Dixit–Stiglitz specification, the utility function is isoelastic: $u(x) = x^{\varepsilon}$. As seen in chapter 1, the monopoly markup is then a constant, $\mu = \sigma/(\sigma - 1) = 1/\varepsilon$. In particular, it does not depend on productivity $a$. Therefore, an increase in productivity increases wages proportionally.

Furthermore, the profit of any individual firm $j$ is given by

$$\begin{aligned}\pi_j &= p_j y_j - w l_j \\ &= (a - w) l_j \\ &= a \frac{\mu - 1}{\mu} \frac{L}{N}.\end{aligned}$$

For a constant labor force and number of varieties and an isoelastic utility, profits are also proportional to $a$. The relative factor income distribution, as measured, say, by the share of wages in value added, is unaffected by productivity growth.[1]

With isoelastic preferences, nonbiased technical progress has no effect on the distribution of income.

## 9.2 Nonhomothetic Utility

With a nonisoelastic utility, the markup is no longer constant. To compute it, we need to derive the demand curve for each individual good $j$. Let $R_i$ denote the total expenditure of consumer $i$. To allocate their expenditure optimally across the individual goods, people maximize their instantaneous utility function (9.1) subject to their budget constraint

$$\int_0^N p_j x_{ij} = R_i.$$

Assuming an interior solution for each good,[2] the resulting demand function is given by

$$x_{ij} = v(\lambda_i p_j), \tag{9.4}$$

[1] An increase in $N_t$ would not change total profits either; profits per firm fall proportionally, while the number of firms rises proportionally.

[2] Saint-Paul (2006a) deals with the technical problems associated with this issue.

where $v(\cdot) = u'^{-1}(\cdot)$ and $\lambda_i$ is the Lagrange multiplier, which is the solution to

$$\int_0^N p_j v(\lambda_i p_j)\,\mathrm{d}j = R_i.$$

Note that a change in any given price $p_j$ has only an infinitesimal effect on $\lambda_i$. The aggregate demand for good $j$ is then given by

$$X_j = \int_0^1 v(\lambda_i p_j)\,\mathrm{d}i. \tag{9.5}$$

The monopoly maximizes its profit $p_j X_j - wX_j/a$, subject to (9.5). As each monopoly is atomistic, we may neglect the effect of its price on wages and on other prices. Consequently, its optimal price must satisfy the following first-order condition:

$$\left(p_j - \frac{w}{a}\right)\int_0^1 \lambda_i v'(\lambda_i p_j)\,\mathrm{d}i + \int_0^1 v(\lambda_i p_j)\,\mathrm{d}j = 0. \tag{9.6}$$

Assume that there exists a symmetrical equilibrium where, again, all prices are equal and normalized to 1. Given the definition of $v$, in symmetrical equilibrium (9.6) is equivalent to

$$\left(1 - \frac{w}{a}\right)\int_0^1 \frac{u'(R_i/N)}{u''(R_i/N)}\,\mathrm{d}i + \frac{R}{N} = 0. \tag{9.7}$$

In the preceding equation, $R$ is aggregate expenditure, given by $R = \int_0^1 R_i\,\mathrm{d}i$.

Equation (9.7) can be rewritten as

$$\mu = \frac{\eta}{\eta - 1}, \tag{9.8}$$

where

$$\eta = -\int_0^1 \frac{u'(R_i/N)}{u''(R_i/N)R/N}\,\mathrm{d}i$$

is the price elasticity of demand.

The markup is no longer constant and depends on both the level of expenditure and its distribution across consumers.

## 9.3 The Limited Needs Property

The central property from which I will derive results is the "limited needs" property, i.e., the assumption that the utility function $u(x)$ is bounded. The inverse elasticity of marginal utility for a consumer who consumes $x$ units of an individual good, which is also the price elasticity of demand that would prevail if all consumers were consuming the same amount, is given by $\eta(x) = -u'(x)/xu''(x)$. One can show that, for any bounded utility, as $x$ increases, the elasticity $\eta(x)$ ends up being lower than any $\upsilon > 1$. The proof is as follows. Assume that $-u'/xu'' > \upsilon > 1$ for all $x \geqslant x_0$. Then, integrating the inequality $-u''/u' < 1/(\upsilon x)$ between $x$ and $x_0$ yields $\ln u'(x) > \ln u'(x_0) - (\ln x - \ln x_0)/\upsilon$, i.e., $u'(x) > u'(x_0)(x/x_0)^{-1/\upsilon}$. Integrating again, we get

$$u(x) > \frac{u'(x_0)}{x_0^{-1/\upsilon}} \frac{\upsilon}{\upsilon - 1}(x^{1-1/\upsilon} - x_0^{1-1/\upsilon}),$$

which is not bounded. This is a contradiction.

For most utility functions, $\eta(x)$ will be monotonic, and we then get the stronger prediction that it has to decline with $x$ and converge to a limit which is at most equal to 1.

The limited needs property implies that consumers with a bounded utility become less sensitive to the price of a good when their consumption of that good goes up. This is despite the fact that they are also willing to pay less for the good. Why? Essentially, marginal utility has to fall fast enough with the quantity consumed for utility to remain bounded. This is why people become less sensitive to prices when they consume more. At high consumption levels, a price fall is met with only a small increase in consumption, because a small increase is enough to reduce the marginal utility by enough to leave the consumer indifferent.

Next, note that the elasticity of aggregate demand $\eta$ is given by

$$\eta = -\int_0^1 \eta\left(\frac{R_i}{N}\right)\frac{R_i}{R}\,\mathrm{d}i.$$

This is merely the average of consumer-specific elasticities, weighted by the share of each consumer in the total expenditure. Assume that the economy gets richer, so that all expenditures grow. Hold the shares constant. Then if $\eta(x)$ is decreasing, $\eta$ will also decrease and the markup $\mu$ will increase.

Furthermore, since $\lim_{x\to+\infty}\eta(x) \leqslant 1$, the markup will become arbitrarily large as the economy becomes arbitrarily rich.

Returning to (9.3), we can conclude that wages must decrease over some range. To illustrate this, let us select a functional form for $u(\cdot)$ that has the limited needs property and can be handled conveniently:

$$u(x) = 1 - \mathrm{e}^{-\varphi x}. \tag{9.9}$$

In such a formulation, "needs are bounded," since $u(x)$ has an upper bound. This generates a strongly decreasing pattern of the elasticity $-u'/xu''$. We have $u'(x)/u''(x) = -1/\varphi$, so $\eta$ does not depend on the distribution of income:

$$\eta = \frac{N}{\varphi R}.$$

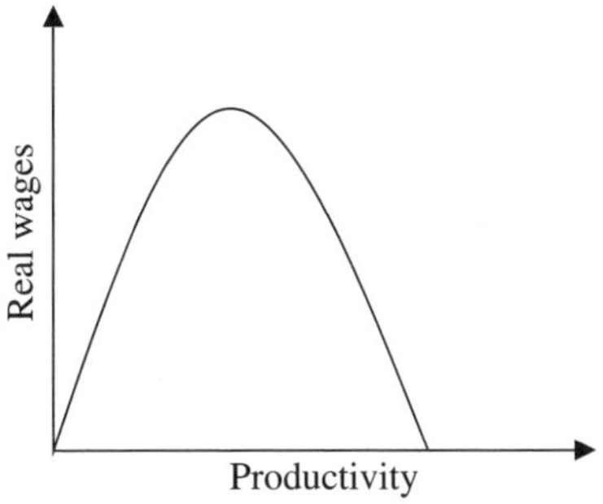


**Figure 9.1.** The effect of productivity on wages.

In symmetrical equilibrium, labor-market clearing implies that $R/N = y_i = aL/N$. Consequently, $\eta = N/\varphi aL$. Substituting into (9.8) and then (9.3), we obtain a formula linking wages with productivity:

$$w = a\left(1 - \frac{\varphi aL}{N}\right). \tag{9.10}$$

The most interesting property of (9.10) is that $w$ is not monotonous in $a$. Rather, it is hump-shaped, as illustrated in figure 9.1. As productivity increases, the economy gradually moves from a Solovian zone, where productivity improvements raise wages, to a Marxian zone, where productivity growth is more than entirely appropriated by profits and wages actually fall. There exists a critical level of productivity where wages are exactly equal to zero, given by $a = N/\varphi L$.

Thus, wages grow less than proportionally to productivity, and may even fall with it. Conversely, profits grow faster than productivity, as we can check algebraically:

$$\begin{aligned}\pi_j &= \left(p - \frac{w}{a}\right)X_j \\ &= \left(1 - \frac{w}{a}\right)\frac{aL}{N} \\ &= \varphi\left[\frac{aL}{N}\right]^2. \end{aligned} \tag{9.11}$$

This limited needs utility function has the property that its elasticity decreases, and converges to zero, as consumption increases. As productivity increases, each worker produces more goods, which tends to increase wages. But people also spend more, which brings them closer to satiation and reduces the elasticity of demand. The corresponding rise in the markup accelerates as consumers spend more, eventually offsetting the positive impact of productivity on wages and pushing the economy into a zone where wages fall on net with productivity. That is, more than

100% of the growth in GDP permitted by productivity growth is appropriated by profits, i.e., by those who own property rights over blueprints. The end point of the Marxian zone, where wages become equal to zero, corresponds to the point where markups are infinite, i.e., the elasticity of demand for each good is equal to 1.

If workers were consuming different goods from capitalists, by getting poorer they would consume less of each good, which would actually increase the demand elasticity for these goods and lower the markup; thus, workers could not become poorer. However, here it is the capitalists who are pushing markups up by being brought closer to satiation, and thus harming workers, who must pay more for the same goods.

## 9.4 Dynamics: Growth and the Introduction of New Varieties

An important property of the wage schedule (9.10) is that an increase in the number of varieties $N$ raises wages. This is because when $N$ goes up less of each good is being consumed in equilibrium. Therefore, the elasticity of demand is higher, and the markup is lower. When $a$ goes up, profits increase relative to wages (and the latter do fall in the Marxian zone); this would tend to induce innovators to increase the number of varieties, which in turn would dampen or offset the impact effect of productivity on wages. Thus, we have identified a mechanism which runs counter to the negative effects of productivity on wages that are analyzed above.

To embody this mechanism in the model and study its implications for the distribution of income, we assume that new varieties are introduced by "creative" workers who appropriate the corresponding monopoly profits. We also allow for the exogenous growth over time of physical productivity and of researchers' abilities to produce new blueprints.

Let us first discuss how talent is allocated between the physical production sector and the R&D activity. We go back to the Roy model discussed in chapter 1. There is a continuum of workers endowed with a skill level $s$. These skills are distributed with density $g(s)$. A worker with skill $s$ is endowed with $l(s)$ units of raw labor and $h(s)$ units of creativity. To fix ideas we will assume that both $l(\cdot)$ and $h(\cdot)$ are linear in $s$:

$$l(s) = \gamma_l + \delta_l s,$$
$$h(s) = \gamma_h + \delta_h s.$$

As in chapter 1, we will focus on the case where $h(\cdot)$ is more elastic with respect to skills than $l(\cdot)$. This is equivalent to

$$\frac{\delta_h}{\delta_l} > \frac{\gamma_h}{\gamma_l}.$$

Workers have to specialize and to decide whether they supply their creativity or their productivity to the market. Again, there is a critical skill level at date $t$,

$$s^*(\omega_t/w_t) = \frac{w_t y_l - \omega_t y_h}{\omega_t \delta_h - w_t \delta_l},$$

such that workers specialize in labor if and only if $s_t < s^*(\omega_t/w_t)$.

The supply of labor and creativity at $t$ are given by equations (1.6) and (1.7), which we rewrite here for convenience, using the linearity of $l(s)$ and $h(s)$ and normalizing total population to 1:

$$H_t = \int_{s^*(w_t/\omega_t)}^{+\infty} (y_h + \delta_h s) g(s)\,\mathrm{d}s = H\left(\frac{\omega_t}{w_t}\right), \quad H' > 0, \tag{9.12}$$

$$L_t = \int_0^{s^*(w_t/\omega_t)} (y_l + \delta_l s) g(s)\,\mathrm{d}s = L\left(\frac{\omega_t}{w_t}\right), \quad L' < 0. \tag{9.13}$$

Dividing (9.12) by (9.13), we get an upward-sloping relationship in the $(\omega/w, H/L)$-plane which is the *relative supply* of creativity.

Let us now describe the dynamics of the economy. The number of varieties grows endogenously as in the model described in chapter 1. One efficiency unit of creativity dedicated to innovation during a small time interval $\mathrm{d}t$ allows the introduction of $b_t\,\mathrm{d}t$ new varieties. Consequently, the number of varieties $N_t$ evolves according to

$$\dot{N}_t = b_t H_t. \tag{9.14}$$

The expenditure level at $t$, $R_t$, must maximize intertemporal utility:

$$\mathcal{U}_i = \int_0^{+\infty} U_{it} \mathrm{e}^{-\rho t}\,\mathrm{d}t. \tag{9.15}$$

Our price normalization is unchanged and consumption of each good is still determined by $x_{ijt} = x_{it} = R_{it}/N_t$.

Within each period, the labor market must clear, implying that $R_t/N_t = X_t = a_t L_t/N_t$. Therefore, expenditure at $t$ must be equal to $a_t L_t$, as in the static model of the preceding section. Pricing is still determined by (9.7). Consequently, the wage equation (9.10) still holds.

R&D firms compete to hire creative workers, and the value of their patents is dissipated in the wages of creative workers. They get a patent which gives them monopoly power over the production of the new variety for ever. The value of such a patent, $V_t$, evolves according to the Bellman equation (1.24),

$$rV_t = \pi_t + \dot{V}_t, \tag{9.16}$$

where $\pi_t$ is the profit of a monopoly at $t$, which remains determined by (9.11):

$$\pi_t = \varphi\left[\frac{a_t L_t}{N_t}\right]^2. \tag{9.17}$$

Competition in the R&D sector implies that the cost of producing a variety equals the value of a patent:

$$\omega_t = b_t V_t. \tag{9.18}$$

This equation, along with (9.16), determines the value of a patent $V$ and the wage of creativity $w$ for a given interest rate $r$. One can show that $r = \rho$ in the simple case where $U(\cdot) = u(\cdot)$ (see the appendix).

Let us now characterize a balanced-growth path. We assume that productivity grows at an exogenous rate $g$ both in the physical sector and in the R&D sector. That is,

$$a_t = a_0 e^{gt},$$
$$b_t = b_0 e^{gt}.$$

Along a balanced-growth path, we expect $H$ and $L$ to remain constant. Furthermore, we expect $N_t$ to grow at rate $g$, since (9.14) must hold. This property allows us to compute it as follows:

$$N_t = \frac{b_0 H}{g} e^{gt}. \tag{9.19}$$

As $\pi$ is constant, so is $V$, and the wage of creativity is equal to $\omega_t = b_t \pi / \rho$. Substituting this into (9.17), and using (9.19), we obtain

$$\omega_t = e^{gt} \frac{\varphi}{\rho} \frac{g^2}{b_0} \left[ \frac{a_0 L}{H} \right]^2. \tag{9.20}$$

We note that $\omega_t$ grows at rate $g$. Similarly, substituting (9.19) into (9.10), one can compute $w_t$, which also grows at rate $g$, and is given by

$$w_t = a_0 e^{gt} \left( 1 - \varphi g \frac{a_0 L}{b_0 H} \right). \tag{9.21}$$

Dividing (9.20) by (9.21), we get an equation for the *relative demand* for creativity:

$$\frac{\omega}{w} = \frac{g^2 a_0}{\rho (H/L)(b_0 H/L - \varphi a_0 g)}. \tag{9.22}$$

The downward-sloping aspect of this relation captures the fact that, when $H/L$ increases, each variety is consumed in lower amounts, which reduces markups.

The equilibrium values of $\omega/w$ and $H/L$ are determined by the intersection of the relative supply and relative demand curves for creativity: these two ratios are constant in steady state. Next, one can just use (9.12) and (9.13) to get the absolute values of $H$ and $L$, and the rest of the model is easily solved by using the equations above.

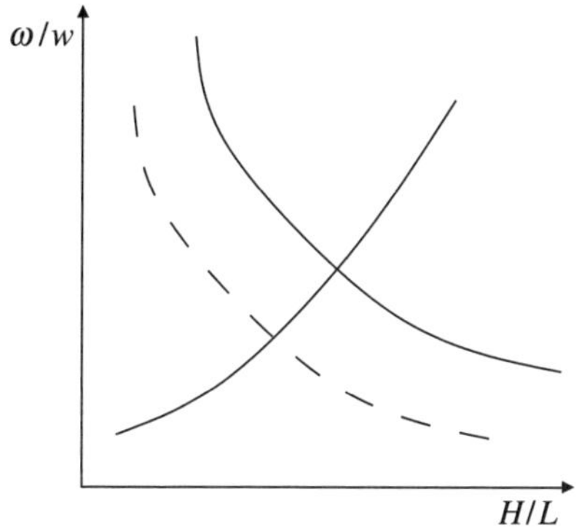


**Figure 9.2.** Impact of an increase in total factor productivity.

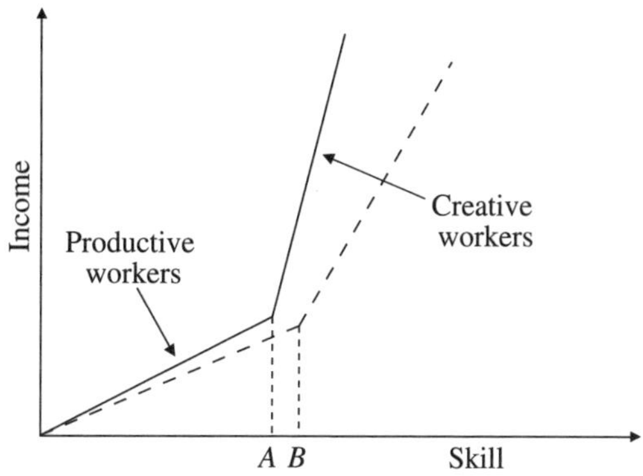


**Figure 9.3.** Impact of productivity growth on the distribution of wages in a Solovian zone.

Note that in this balanced-growth path, all wages grow at the same rate, which is the common growth rate of physical and R&D productivity. Thus, along this path, productivity growth increases the incomes of all workers homothetically, leaving relative inequality unchanged. However, a permanent change in the level of physical productivity, for a given path of creativity, will affect inequality in the new steady state compared with the original one.

As illustrated in figure 9.2, an increase in the level of total factor productivity, captured by a shift in $a_0$, shifts the "demand curve" upward. The relative wage $\omega/w$ goes up, implying that inequality increases. $H$ increases and $L$ falls: new goods are introduced that tend to reduce markups and to partly offset the increase in inequality. The corresponding shifts in the distribution of income are described in figures 9.3 and 9.4. Relative inequality increases for two reasons. First, the return to the high-paying creative activity goes up relative to the return to the

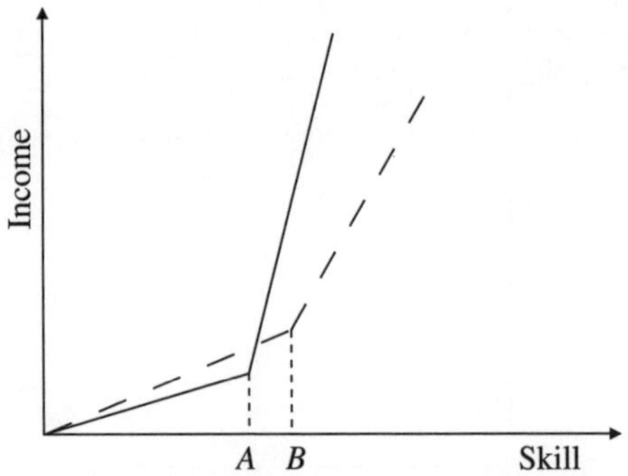


**Figure 9.4.** Impact of productivity growth on the distribution of wages in a Marxian zone.

low-paying productive activity. Second, more people specialize in the creative activity, where income is more sensitive to skills. In figure 9.3 the economy is in the Solovian zone and all workers gain. In figure 9.4 it is in the Marxian zone and productive workers lose, except for the upper tier of those who shift to the creative activity.

Conversely, an increase in R&D productivity, captured by a rise in $b_0$, has the opposite effect: the relative wage $\omega/w$ falls. Further inspection of the formulas reveals that if $b_0$ and $a_0$ both increase proportionally, the inequality is unaffected and both wages increase proportionally. It is because one has assumed such proportionality in the growth process that a balanced-growth path exists. One can check that if $b_t$ were to grow less than $a_t$, inequality would continue to widen and the economy would eventually enter a Marxian zone.

This discussion shows that it is not productivity growth per se which generates inequality (and a potential Marxian zone), but rather *imbalances* between productivity growth in the physical goods sector and in the R&D sector.

Returning to the comparative statics exercise where $a_0$ increases, we want to know the conditions under which the induced supply response of $H$ can be strong enough to prevent the increase in $a_0$ from having a negative effect on wages. The most favorable case is when the response is infinitely elastic, i.e., when $\omega/w$ is constant. In such a case, we can show (see the appendix) that the Marxian zone disappears; but, as $a_0$ goes to infinity, its effect on wages (in physical terms) remains bounded. This is because more and more people move to the R&D activity, so that the total physical quantity produced remains finite despite the fact that productivity becomes infinite. On the other hand, one can also show that if the supply elasticity of $H/L$ with respect to $\omega/w$ is bounded above, then a Marxian zone must arise as $a_0$ becomes arbitrarily large (Saint-Paul 2006b, proposition 1).

## 9.5 An Application to Globalization

In this section, we extend the model in order to study how foreign trade affects wages in the limited needs model.

I assume that there are two countries, "home" and "foreign." Variables relating to the latter are denoted by a star. Consumers' preferences are still defined by (9.9). There is a fixed endowment of labor in each country, $L, L^*$, which is immobile. There are initially $N_{\mathrm{A}}$ firms at home and $N_{\mathrm{A}}^*$ firms abroad, but firms can freely relocate. In equilibrium, there is an endogenous mass $N$ of firms producing at home, and $N^* = N_{\mathrm{A}} + N_{\mathrm{A}}^* - N$ firms producing abroad. Goods are traded in a worldwide integrated market. The two countries differ in their productivity $a$ and $a^*$.

The demand for any good $j$ (now indexed between 0 and $N + N^*$, with good $j$ produced at home if and only if $0 \leqslant j < N$) is now given by

$$\begin{aligned} X_j &= -\frac{1}{\varphi}\ln\frac{p_j}{\varphi} + \frac{\int_0^{N_{\mathrm{A}}+N_{\mathrm{A}}^*}(p_m/\varphi)\ln(p_m/\varphi)\,\mathrm{d}m}{\int_0^{N_{\mathrm{A}}+N_{\mathrm{A}}^*}p_m\,\mathrm{d}m} + \frac{Y+Y^*}{\int_0^{N_{\mathrm{A}}+N_{\mathrm{A}}^*}p_m\,\mathrm{d}m} \\ &= X(p_j), \end{aligned}$$

where $Y$ and $Y^*$ are the national incomes at home and abroad, respectively. The first-order condition for optimal pricing reads

$$\begin{aligned} -\frac{1}{\varphi}\ln\frac{p_j}{\varphi} &+ \frac{\int_0^{N_{\mathrm{A}}+N_{\mathrm{A}}^*}(p_m/\varphi)\ln(p_m/\varphi)\,\mathrm{d}m}{\int_0^{N_{\mathrm{A}}+N_{\mathrm{A}}^*}p_m\,\mathrm{d}m} \\ &+ \frac{Y}{\int_0^{N_{\mathrm{A}}+N_{\mathrm{A}}^*}p_m\,\mathrm{d}m} = \frac{p_j - w_j/a_j}{\varphi p_j}, \end{aligned} \tag{9.23}$$

where $w_j = w$, $a_j = a$ if the firm is located at home and $w_j = w^*$, $a_j = a^*$ if it is located abroad.

This defines the optimal $p_j$ as a function of local marginal cost: $p_j = p(w_j/a_j)$. Note that, except for the fact that its argument is deflated by the local productivity level $a_j$, the $p(\cdot)$ function does not depend on country-specific characteristics, because firms face the same world demand regardless of their location.

Mobility of firms between the two countries implies that profits must be equalized:

$$\left(p\left(\frac{w}{a}\right) - \frac{w}{a}\right)X\left(p\left(\frac{w}{a}\right)\right) = \left(p\left(\frac{w^*}{a^*}\right) - \frac{w^*}{a^*}\right)X\left(p\left(\frac{w^*}{a^*}\right)\right).$$

The model is closed by defining national incomes,

$$Y = \int_0^N p_m X_m \, dm, \qquad Y^* = \int_N^{N_A^* + N_A} p_m X_m, \tag{9.24}$$

and writing down the equilibrium conditions for the labor market:

$$aL = \int_0^N X_m \, dm, \qquad aL^* = \int_N^{N_A^* + N_A} X_m \, dm. \tag{9.25}$$

Clearly, one can construct a symmetrical equilibrium where

$$\frac{w}{a} = \frac{w^*}{a^*}, \qquad X_m = \frac{aL + a^*L^*}{N_A + N_A^*}, \quad \forall m, \qquad N = \frac{aL}{aL + a^*L^*},$$

and $p = p^* = 1$, where the latter equality is a normalization. Equations (9.23)–(9.25) allow us to compute equilibrium wages in both countries:

$$w = a\left(1 - \varphi \frac{aL + a^*L^*}{N_A + N_A^*}\right),$$

with a symmetrical formula for the foreign country. Under autarky, one simply applies the model of section 9.3 (with the prices of all goods again set to 1) to get

$$w_A = a\left(1 - \varphi \frac{aL}{N_A}\right),$$

$$w_B = a\left(1 - \varphi \frac{a^*L^*}{N_A^*}\right).$$

These three formulas imply that trade increases wages at home and reduces them abroad if

$$\frac{aL}{N_A} > \frac{a^*L^*}{N_A^*}.$$

The country in which wages fall is that where consumption of each good is initially lower, i.e., the country where the number of firms is higher relative to total productive capacity, or, equivalently, the country where markups are lower under autarky than under trade. By increasing the output of firms based in this country, globalization moves it closer to the Marxian zone, and its workers suffer from the higher markups applied by its firms to new customers, who care less about the good. From a factual point of view, this may well be the poorer country: one may think that it has a lower value of $a$ but also fewer varieties.[3] This result has a Stolper–Samuelson flavor: the country where wages go up when moving from autarky to trade is that where labor (as defined by $aL$, i.e., adjusted for

[3] Another interesting implication is that productivity growth in one country unambiguously reduces wages in the other.

productivity) is more abundant relative to the number of varieties, which is generated using human capital. However, the mechanism is totally different from that underlying the Stolper–Samuelson theorem, since it is due entirely to variable markups.

Note that these results hold if wages are expressed in physical terms, i.e., we ignore the fact that wages can purchase more utility under trade because they are spent on a greater variety of goods. If these effects are reintroduced, one can show that, in the country where wages fall, workers gain provided that their labor endowment is larger than a critical value.[4] Again, these results are all due to the evolution of markups. If markups were constant and equal to $\mu$, one could check that the solution would be the same, except for wages which would be given by $w_k = a_k/\mu$, and therefore would be equal to their level under autarky. Globalization would then not affect wages in physical terms and all workers would gain because it allows them to access a greater variety of goods.

## 9.6 Asymmetries between Goods

In the preceding analysis, all goods are symmetrical. Nonhomotheticity only comes from the fact that $u(\cdot)$ is not isoelastic. In this section, we study the implications of asymmetries between goods. These may arise, for example, if some goods are indivisible while others are not, or if there is some hierarchy of needs by which some goods are consumed before the others, as consumers get richer. We study a model, based on Matsuyama (2002), where growth is associated with technical progress in an industrial good which is indivisible, implying that the demand for it will depend on the distribution of income. We then briefly discuss the effect of hierarchical preferences in endogenous growth models. In these models, contrary to our earlier discussion, inequality in nominal income is, by assumption, exogenous. Thus, it is not affected by technical progress. However, there is another dimension in inequality, which comes from differences in the set of goods that people can consume. Technical progress affects this dimension by making some goods affordable to more people.

Let us assume that there are two goods: a generic good (good 0) and an industrial good (good 1). A key assumption is that utility is nonconvex in good 1. More specifically, one must purchase either one or zero

---

[4] It is easy to check that, if that country is "foreign," this critical level is the value of $l$ which satisfies

$$\frac{1 - \mathrm{e}^{-w^* l}}{1 - \mathrm{e}^{-w_\mathrm{A}^* l}} = \frac{N_\mathrm{A}^*}{N_\mathrm{A} + N_\mathrm{A}^*}.$$

units of good 1. Furthermore, I assume that the utility given by good 1 is sufficiently high that everybody wants to purchase it if they can.

There is a continuum of workers, each endowed with $z$ units of raw labor. $z$ is distributed according to the c.d.f. $G(z)$. Thus, the distribution of nominal income is exogenous. We take the wage as the numéraire, so that $z$ is also the income of the agent. Let $p_j$ be the price of good $j$. If $p_1 > z$, then the consumer can only consume good 0, and his indirect utility is $z/p_0$. If $p_1 < z$, then the consumer consumes good 1. His indirect utility is then $(z - p_1)/p_0 + \bar{u}$, where $\bar{u}$ is the utility obtained from consuming the industrial good. We will confine our analysis to cases where it is indeed worth purchasing the industrial good, i.e., $\bar{u} > p_1/p_0$.

Despite the fact that the distribution of wages is exogenous, uneven technical change affects the distribution of utility, as a result of the nonhomotheticity of preferences. While technical progress in the generic good (which reduces $p_0$) benefits everybody, technical progress in the industrial good (which reduces $p_1$) benefits only those who consume the good. At the same time, a new class of consumers who could not consume the industrial good before can now consume it.

Matsuyama (2002) builds on this basic insight and endogenizes technical progress by assuming learning by doing. Each good is produced with a constant-returns-to-scale technology, with labor as the only factor of production. Productivity in the generic good is given by $a_0$, and we assume it is fixed.[5] Thus, its price is also fixed and equal to $p_0 = 1/a_0$. Productivity in the industrial good is equal to $a_1$, and evolves over time as people learn better techniques to produce it. This learning is the outcome of production activity. The more one produces of good 1, the faster one learns about producing it. Formally, this is modeled as the following evolution for $a_1$:

$$\frac{da_1}{dt} = \phi(D(p_1) - a_1), \tag{9.26}$$

where $D(p_1)$ is the demand curve for good 1 and the term in $a_1$ captures some depreciation in the stock of knowledge.[6]

The central property of this class of models is that the demand for the industrial good depends on the distribution of income,

$$D(p_1) = P(1 - G(p_1)),$$

where $P$ denotes population size. Therefore, the ability of this economy to accumulate knowledge of the technology for producing the industrial

[5] A natural interpretation is that the generic good is "mature" and all the scope for productivity improvement has been exhausted.

[6] Technically, this assumption guarantees that $a_1$ will eventually settle to a constant level, rather than grow without bounds. This property is more convenient in the present context.

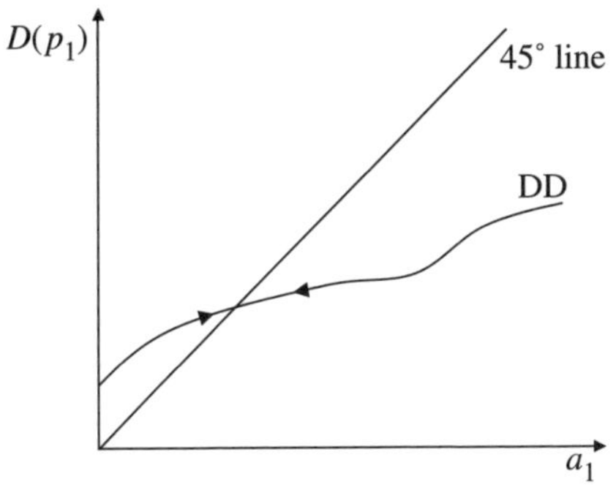


**Figure 9.5.** Convergence to steady-state in the Matsuyama model.

good crucially depends on how many people can afford that good. When more people buy the good (the "massification" of consumption), $\mathrm{d}a_1/\mathrm{d}t$ increases for a given initial value of $a_1$. Conversely, by reducing the price of the good, learning by doing exerts a feedback effect on the market size for the industrial good. If this feedback effect is strong enough, more people are then induced to consume the good. The joint process of learning by doing and of consumption massification then accelerates, as these new consumers allow for further technological improvements. On the other hand, the process dies out if not enough people join the pool of consumers of the industrial good.

Figure 9.5 describes how the equilibrium is determined. As one must have $p_1 = 1/a_1$, $D(p_1) = P(1 - G(1/a_1))$ is increasing in $a_1$. This is depicted by the DD curve in figure 9.5. By virtue of (9.26), a steady state occurs if DD crosses the 45° line.[7] In figure 9.5, we have assumed a single equilibrium.[8] The arrows indicate the economy's trajectory along DD: $a_1$ goes up if DD is above the 45° line and goes down if it is below the 45° line.

The shape of DD is derived directly from the distribution of income, and determines the number and location of equilibria. The market size for the industrial good is the fraction of the population whose income is greater than its price, $1/a_1$. To illustrate this, it is best to look at a few examples.

In a poor society, the market size for the industrial good is small. Only the richest people can buy it. An increase in inequality will then typically increase the demand for good 1, provided that it implies that there are

[7] This would be another ray through the origin if the specification of the learning-by-doing process did not have a unit coefficient in front of $a_1$, but the analysis would be unchanged.

[8] Sensu stricto, if $a_1 = 0$, then the price of the good is infinite, nobody buys it, and this is an equilibrium. We obtain interior equilibria by assuming that the origin in figures 9.5–9.10 is some minimum value of $a_1$ which one cannot go below.

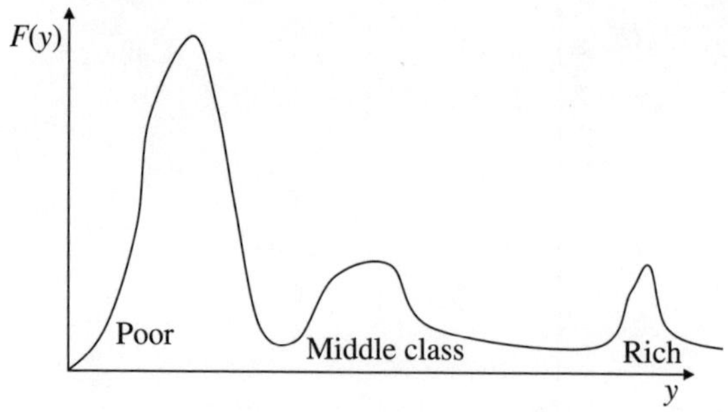


**Figure 9.6.** A distribution of income with three classes.

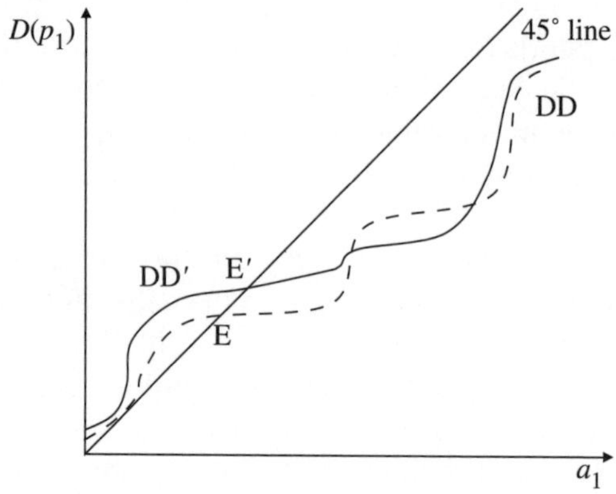


**Figure 9.7.** Inequality is good for growth in the poor society.

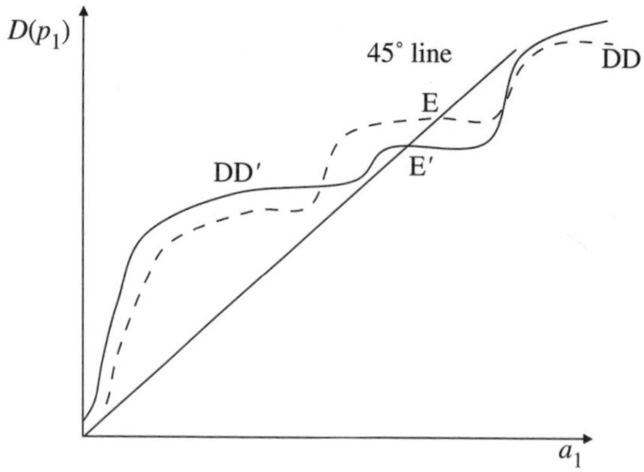


**Figure 9.8.** Inequality is bad for growth in a richer society.

more rich people. Figure 9.6 illustrates a distribution of income with three classes: there is a poor "underclass," the first hump in the distribution of income, which is assumed to be large in figure 9.6. Above them

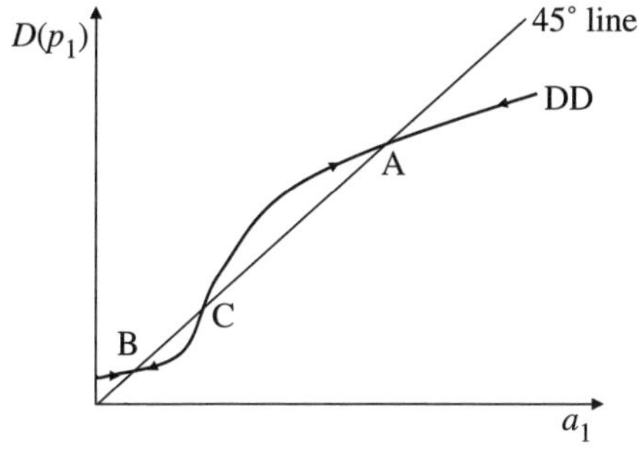


**Figure 9.9.** Multiple steady states in the Matsuyama model.

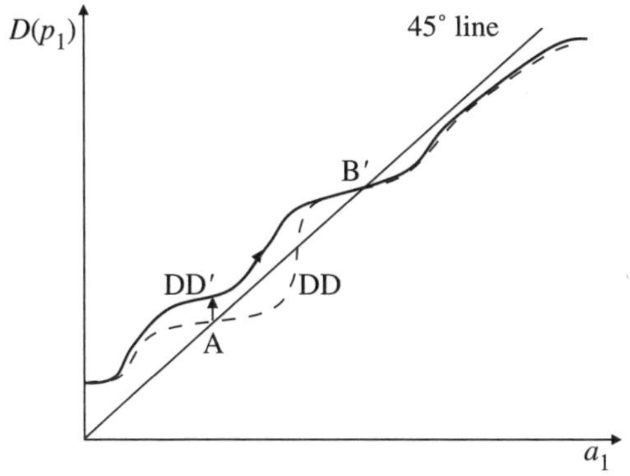


**Figure 9.10.** Trickle down: toward a mass consumption society.

there are two other humps: a small middle class and a rich upper class. Figure 9.7 shows how equilibrium is determined for this distribution of income, for a value of $P$ such that the demand for industrial goods is not too large. As one moves to the right, each steep increase in the DD curves corresponds to a hump in the distribution of income of figure 9.6, starting with the rich. The only stable equilibrium is at point E, just to the right of the first steep portion, i.e., where only the rich can afford to buy the good. The solid line describes an increase in inequality such that the middle class shrinks in favor of the rich and the poor. The extreme humps in figure 9.6 become wider and higher, while the central hump shrinks. As a result, the solid line ends up above the dotted line at its extreme, but not in the middle, where its intermediate steep portion is much shorter than that of the original DD curve. The shift increases the market size for the industrial good. The DD curve shifts up in the neighborhood of point E and the economy moves to point E′, where, because more rich people buy the good, the economy is more productive. More people consume the industrial good, as a result of both the direct effect of the change in the distribution of income and the induced reduction in the price $p_1$. But it is still essentially the "rich" who consume the good.

In a richer society, most of the middle class can afford the good (figure 9.8). The converse occurs: the rise in inequality reduces the market size for the industrial good, as a number of people who could afford it as members of the lower middle class are now poor and can no longer afford it. This lower market size in turn induces a reduction in $a_1$ and a rise in $p_1$. Therefore, more people stop consuming the good, and all the other consumers have to pay a higher price.

If DD has enough nonlinearities (figure 9.9), then there may be multiple steady states. The arrows on DD show the dynamics defined by (9.26). Point A is a steady state where $a_1$ is large, $p_1$ is small, and a large number of consumers buy the industrial good (a "mass consumption society"). Point B is a steady state where only the richest can afford the good (an "impoverished society"). Each steady state sustains itself because low costs and large market size mutually reinforce each other, due to learning by doing. In between, there in an unstable equilibrium, C. Whether a mass consumption society or an impoverished society arises depends on the initial conditions. If the economy starts to the right of C, it converges to the mass consumption society. If it starts to the left of C, it converges to the impoverished society.

When is such multiplicity likely to arise? The derivative of the demand curve with respect to $a_1$ is $g(a_1)/a_1^2$. The local density of consumers $g(a_1)$ appears in this expression: the greater the number of consumers who are close to affording the good, the greater the increase in market size in response to a price fall. Loosely speaking, the greater the variations in the density $g(\cdot)$, the more nonlinear the DD curve. Thus, a polarized society, where two (or more) income groups ("social classes") are separated by relatively empty income intervals, as in figure 9.6, is more likely to have multiple equilibria than a society with a diffuse distribution of income. The reason is that, in the case of figure 9.6, when the price is such that the indifferent consumers fall between the two humps of the distribution of income, very few additional buyers enter the market for a given reduction in the price. Hence, the learning process is slowed, or even reversed if knowledge attrition is strong enough. This stabilizing force tends to create an equilibrium somewhere between the "hole" and the thick part of the hump, where price reductions trigger a large increase in market size and the learning process is stronger than attrition. Roughly, each hump may generate an equilibrium, where the critical consumer who can just afford the good is part of the corresponding income class; higher classes consume the good and lower ones do not. Starting from such an equilibrium, the path toward a mass consumption society may resume if some shock initiates the transition to another equilibrium where the lower social class can afford the consumption good. Figure 9.10 illustrates such a transition. The economy is initially at point A, where only the rich consume the good. The distribution of income changes in such a way that some people move up the income ladder and can now afford the good: the DD curve shifts to DD′. They trigger a new virtuous circle of market size growth and learning by doing, which allows the economy to settle in a new equilibrium, point B′, where more income classes consume the good.

Foellmi and Zweimüller (2006) go beyond the analysis of Matsuyama by assuming that growth is horizontal, rather than vertical, i.e., it takes the form of the introduction of new goods by an R&D sector. As in the endogenous growth models described in chapter 1, inventors then earn monopoly rents on the good they have introduced. The new goods are ranked after the existing ones in the hierarchy of needs: they are less essential. The distribution of income now affects the *pricing* of goods by monopolies. The markup is affected by the marginal density of the distribution of income around the consumers whose income is such that they are just indifferent about consuming the good. The greater that density, the more elastic the demand and the smaller the price. Foellmi and Zweimüller focus on a case in which there are only two income classes: the poor and the rich. In equilibrium, the more essential goods are sold to both the poor and the rich, and the more sophisticated ones are sold to the rich only. The latter are sold at a higher price than the former. Consequently, each product has a life cycle. It is initially sold only to the rich; after a while, as the economy gets richer, it becomes optimal for the monopoly to lower its price and extend its market by selling the product to the poor as well as the rich. Typically, in this model, inequality is good for growth, because it allows firms to sell to the rich at a higher price in the initial phase of the product life cycle. The smaller profits made from selling it at a lower price to the poor in the subsequent phase do not compensate for this effect, because they come much later and are highly discounted when computing the value of a new patent.

## 9.7 Conclusion

Nonhomothetic preferences generate novel mechanisms through which technical change can affect inequality. A first channel is through noncompetitive price setting; technical progress makes people richer and affects markups and the structure of demand. A second channel is through the basket of goods being consumed. Technical progress in some goods does not benefit those who are too poor to consume them; inequality increases in this sense. In the two models that we have seen, the dynamic response of the economy tends to offset these inegalitarian effects. In the first model, the asymmetric effects of technology on factor income distribution increase profits and the wages of creative workers, thus boosting the incentives to introduce new goods. Introducing new goods in turn moves consumption of each individual good away from satiation, which reduces markups. In the second model, when new income groups can now afford the industrial goods, this generates another round of technical progress because of learning by doing. This cumulative process may lead to a mass consumption society (i.e., an egalitarian outcome) where everybody can consume the industrial good.

## 9.8 Appendix

### 9.8.1 Determination of the Interest Rate

Consumers maximize (9.15), setting their optimal expenditure level at $t$ as $R_{it}$, and allocating it optimally across the individual goods. In a symmetrical equilibrium with the price of each good normalized to 1 at each date, individual consumption of each good is simply equal to $x_{ijt} = R_{it}/N_t$. If $U(\cdot) = u(\cdot)$, the marginal utility from increasing $R_{it}$ at $t$ is then equal to $u'(R_{it}/N_t)$, since instantaneous utility is $N_t u(R_{it}/N_t)$. Call $r$ the interest rate in this economy, which is the interest rate in physical terms, rather than hedonic terms, given our price normalization. The continuous-time equivalent of the Euler equation in chapter 1 is that the marginal utility of expenditure must grow at rate $\rho - r$, that is,

$$\frac{\mathrm{d}}{\mathrm{d}t}\left[u'\left(\frac{R_{it}}{N_t}\right)\right] = \rho - r.$$

Or, equivalently,

$$\frac{u''(R_{it}/N_t)}{u'(R_{it}/N_t)}\left(\frac{\dot{R}_{it}}{N_t} - \frac{\dot{N}_t}{N_t}\frac{R_{it}}{N_t}\right) = \rho - r.$$

Under the specification $u(x) = 1 - \mathrm{e}^{-\varphi x}$, this equation becomes linear in $\dot{R}_{it}$ and $R_{it}$ and can be aggregated across consumers, yielding

$$\varphi\left(\frac{\dot{R}_t}{R_t} - \frac{\dot{N}_t}{N_t}\right) = (\rho - r)\frac{N_t}{R_t}.$$

In a balanced-growth path, $R_t = Y_t = a_t L$ and grows at the same rate $g$ as $N_t$. Consequently, we have $\rho = r$.

### 9.8.2 Effect of Productivity on Wages When the Response of Creativity Is Infinitely Elastic

This will be the case if creativity is exactly as concentrated as productivity, i.e., $d = \gamma_l/\gamma_h = \delta_l/\delta_h$. One must then have $\omega/w = d$.

The equilibrium value of $H/L$ can then be computed by plugging the equilibrium ratio $\omega/w = d$ into (9.22). Normalizing $\gamma_0 = \varphi = 1$ for simplicity, we get the following solution:

$$\frac{H}{L} = \frac{ga_0}{2}\left(1 + \sqrt{1 + \frac{4}{\rho a_0 d}}\right).$$

Plugging this into (9.21) allows us to compute the wages as follows:

$$w_t = a_0\left(1 - \frac{2}{1 + \sqrt{1 + (4/\rho a_0 d)}}\right)e^{gt}.$$

As $a_0$ tends to infinity, the expression here converges from below to $e^{gt}/(\rho d)$.

# 10

# Nonhomothetic Preferences and the Distributive Effects of Innovation and Intellectual Property

In this chapter, we build on the models analyzed in the previous chapter to discuss the distributive effects of innovation between rich and poor. While the previous chapter analyzed how, under nonhomothetic preferences, productivity growth and innovation affect the functional distribution of income, in particular through markups, here we focus on their effect on utility. We focus on how rich and poor may value the introduction of new goods differently, because, under nonhomothetic utility, they face a different trade-off between the physical quantity of goods consumed and the number of different goods. To understand this conflict of interest and insulate it from the effect of markups, which is a different issue, we compute the social optimum for a social welfare function which potentially gives different weights to different skill categories. We show that, under isoelastic preferences, there is unanimity over the rate of innovation, in that this rate does not depend on the distribution of weights. If preferences are not isoelastic, then the optimal rate of innovation depends on the distribution of weights. We characterize the conditions under which the utility function is such that a set of weights more biased in favor of the rich will lead to a larger desired rate of innovation, and show that these conditions are satisfied under our limited needs utility function. We then show that if society votes on a single instrument, the level of intellectual property, then the poor support a lower level of intellectual property than the rich, provided the feedback effects on monopoly pricing are not too strong.

This chapter differs from the preceding ones in that it considers the distributive effects of horizontal rather than vertical innovation. While vertical innovation matters to the distribution of income only through its asymmetric effects on factor prices, horizontal innovation also matters through preferences; if preferences are not homothetic, the taste for variety differs between agents with different incomes.

A related literature, not discussed in this book, addresses the problem of interest groups blocking innovation, and the effects of that phenomenon on growth. The general theme is that some groups own a fixed factor whose return falls when an innovation is introduced, say because that innovation uses substitute factors. The reader is referred to Krusell and Ríos-Rull (1996) and Parente and Prescott (1994, 1999) for more details. In this literature, there is no particular reason why those who object to innovation should be poor; there is no direct link between the fact of owning the fixed factor that is exposed to innovation and one's position in the distribution of income.

## 10.1 The Social Welfare Problem

Building on the model of chapter 9, we consider a more general framework and study the optimal determination of the number of goods for a social planner, who may potentially give different weight to different individuals.

As a starting point, we assume a single representative individual. This individual has a utility function given by (9.1). We again take $U(\cdot) = u(\cdot)$, and by symmetry we can assume that the individual consumes the same amount, $x$, of each good. His utility can then be written simply as a function of the number of goods and of the consumption level of each good:

$$\tilde{U}(N, x) = Nu(x).$$

The allocation of resources in the productive sphere yields a trade-off between $x$ and $N$. We assume that this trade-off is given by a decreasing function $f(\cdot)$:

$$x = f(N). \tag{10.1}$$

For example, in the context of the model of chapter 9, we had, in a balanced-growth path, $x = aL(s^*)/N$ and $N = bH(s^*)/g$. This corresponds to $f(N) = aL(H^{-1}(gN/b))/N$.[1]

In such a case, it is very easy to compute the optimal $N$. Differentiating $\tilde{U}$, we get

$$\frac{\mathrm{d}\tilde{U}}{\mathrm{d}N} = u(x)[1 - \eta_u \eta_f],$$

[1] It can be checked that our assumptions about the values of $\gamma$ and $\delta$ parameters in section 9.4 imply that it is efficient for production to allocate workers below a skill level $s^*$ to labor and those above it to introducing new blueprints. Therefore, a central planner would select some value of $s^*$, which may be different from the equilibrium one, and allocate workers in that fashion, as the market does in equilibrium.

where $\eta_u = xu'/u$ is the elasticity of the utility function and $\eta_f = -Nf'/f$ is, in absolute value, the elasticity of the quantity–variety trade-off. Consequently, the optimum value of $N$ must be such that

$$\eta_u = \frac{1}{\eta_f}. \tag{10.2}$$

To obtain a unique interior solution to this first-order condition, we assume that the product $\eta_u \eta_f$ grows with $N$. In particular, this would imply that $\eta_f$ is an increasing function of $N$ if $\eta_u$ were constant. Because of the concavity of $u(\cdot)$, we must have $\eta_u \leqslant 1$. The smaller the $\eta_u$, the greater the value of $\mathrm{d}\tilde{U}/\mathrm{d}N$. The smaller the elasticity of utility, that is, the more concave the utility is, the larger the gains from introducing new products. Introducing a new good must be financed by reducing consumption of existing goods. This implies a loss of marginal utility for each of the existing goods. This loss is equal to $Nu'(x)f'(N)$. The gain from the new goods is in terms of total utility, not marginal utility, and is given by $u(x)$. The smaller the $\eta_u$, the greater the curvature of the utility function, and the greater the gains from the inframarginal units of the new good compared with the losses from the forgone marginal units of the existing goods. Therefore, the willingness to pay to introduce new goods is greater.

Let us now assume that there are several consumers, indexed by $i \in [0, 1]$ and uniformly distributed over this interval, and that product variety is determined by a social planner who maximizes

$$\int_0^1 \tilde{U}(N, x_i)\theta(i)\,\mathrm{d}i,$$

where $\theta(i)$ is the weight given to consumer $i$. While a strict utilitarian would set $\theta(i) = 1$ for all $i$, we use these weights to highlight the conflicts of interest over the degree of innovation. People with a larger value of $\theta(i)$ can be interpreted as having more political influence than others. They will also receive a larger share of total consumption.

The production–innovation trade-off (10.1) is now formulated in terms of the average consumption of an individual good across consumers:

$$\int_0^1 x_i\,\mathrm{d}i = f(N). \tag{10.3}$$

The first-order conditions for this optimization problem are

$$Nu'(x_i)\theta(i) = \lambda, \tag{10.4}$$

$$\int_0^1 u(x_i)\theta(i)\,\mathrm{d}i = -\lambda f'(N), \tag{10.5}$$

where $\lambda$ denotes the Lagrange multiplier. These two equations, along with the resource constraint (10.3), determine the allocation of consumption $\{x_s\}$, the number of varieties $N$, and the multiplier $\lambda$.

### 10.1.1 The Isoelastic Case

Let us examine the isoelastic case. We can use (10.4) to obtain

$$\frac{\theta(i)}{\lambda} = \frac{1}{Nu'} = \frac{x_i}{N\eta_u u},$$

where $\eta_u$ is now *constant*. We can then substitute into (10.5) and we get exactly (10.2). Therefore, when utility is isoelastic, the optimality condition (10.2) can be aggregated across consumers. The optimal level of $N$ does not depend on the distribution of weights $\theta(i)$. Because $\eta_u$ is constant, each individual would pick the same level of $N$ if he were a dictator. Consequently, the social planner selects that level irrespective of the weights. People with a greater weight consume more but there is unanimity over the optimal level of innovation. In other words, if there were a complete set of taxes and transfers which allowed us to implement the first-best optimum, political resistance to technical change would never be observed.

Under isoelastic preferences, the costs and benefits of introducing new goods, expressed in consumption terms, are all proportional to the individual's consumption level, $x_i$.[2] This consumption level just acts as a scale effect and does not affect the point at which costs and benefits exactly balance each other.

### 10.1.2 The Limited Needs Case

Things may be different, however, if utility is not isoelastic. Let us write the elasticity of $u(\cdot)$ as a function $\eta_u(x)$ of the individual's consumption of a given good. In this case, we can just substitute $1/Nu'$ for $\theta(i)/\lambda$ in (10.5), and we get

$$\int_0^1 \frac{1}{\eta_u(x_i)}\hat{\theta}(i)\,\mathrm{d}i = \eta_f, \tag{10.6}$$

where $\hat{\theta}(i) = x_i/f(N)$ is now the consumption weight of agent $i$. Thus, we now see that the *consumption-weighted* inverse elasticity of utility must be equal to the elasticity of $f$. The optimal level of innovation now depends, in general, on the distribution of the weights $\hat{\theta}(i)$. How? The

[2] The cost of introducing a new good and consuming $x$ units of it is equal to $x$. The benefit, in consumption terms, is divided by the marginal utility of consumption $u'(x)$. The ratio $u(x)/u'(x)$ is proportional to $x$ if preferences are isoelastic.

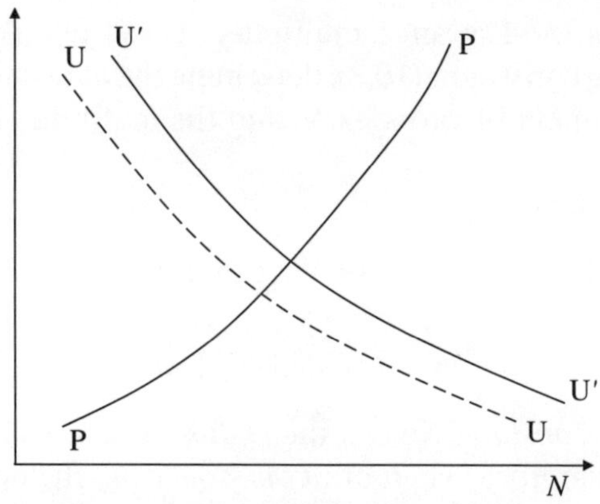


**Figure 10.1.** Optimum determination and impact of an increase in the rich's political influence.

determination of the optimum is depicted in figure 10.1, at the intersection of the PP schedule, which plots $\eta_f$ as a function of $N$, and UU, which plots the consumption-weighted average of $\eta_u$ as a function of $N$. For the stability property that $\eta_u \eta_f$ grows with $N$ to hold locally, UU must be flatter than PP at the equilibrium point. To fix ideas, we actually assume that PP is upward sloping and UU downward sloping. In the isoelastic case, UU would be horizontal and PP would indeed have to be upward sloping for the stability condition to hold.

To make our deviation from isoelasticity more specific, we again assume that $u(\cdot)$ has the limited needs property. It is easy to see that the elasticity $\eta_u(x)$ must fall to arbitrarily low levels as $x$ tends to infinity. The proof is along similar lines to the proof that the price elasticity in chapter 9 (then called $\eta(x)$) could not be bounded above 1. Assume that $\eta_u(x) > \upsilon$ for all $x > x_0$. This is equivalent to $u'/u > \upsilon/x$. Integrating between $x_0$ and $x$ and taking exponentials, we get $u(x) > u(x_0)(x/x_0)^{\upsilon}$. This tends to infinity unless $\upsilon = 0$. This is a contradiction if needs are bounded.

For convenience, then, let us assume that $u(\cdot)$ is sufficiently regular that $\eta_u(\cdot)$ decreases with $x$. This is true of our favorite specification, $u(x) = 1 - \mathrm{e}^{-\varphi x}$.[3] In such a case, UU will indeed be downward sloping; given the consumption weights, an increase in $N$ reduces all the $x_i$, thus increasing all the $\eta_u(x_i)$, so that the left-hand side of (10.6) decreases. What happens when richer people have more political influence over

[3] In this case we have

$$\eta_u(x) = \frac{\varphi x \mathrm{e}^{-\varphi x}}{1 - \mathrm{e}^{-\varphi x}}.$$

Therefore, $\eta_u'(x)$ has the same sign as $1 - \varphi x - \mathrm{e}^{-\varphi x} < 0$.

innovation? This amounts to a change in the weights $\hat{\theta}(i)$, with more weight on agents with a larger $x_i$.[4] This means a larger weight on the low values of $\eta_u$. Therefore, the UU schedule shifts up to U′U′ and $N$ increases (see figure 10.1). The greater the weight of the rich in collective decision making, the greater the level of innovation. The reason is simple: an increase in consumption brings an individual closer to satiation; therefore, this individual's willingness to pay for the introduction of new products increases more than proportionally to his consumption.

People disagree about the optimal level of innovation because they have different marginal rates of substitution between product variety and physical consumption. If innovation were vertical, rather than horizontal, and shifted productivity in all sectors proportionally, then this conflict would not arise. For example, (10.3) would now be replaced by an equation such as

$$\int_0^1 x_i \, di = A(1 - \phi(A)),$$

where $A$ is the total factor productivity and $\phi(A)$ is an increasing function that denotes the fraction of output which must be sacrificed to get a level of productivity equal to $A$. In such a situation, for a given set of consumption weights $\hat{\theta}(i)$, consumers would clearly agree that $A$ should be set so as to maximize $A(1 - \phi(A))$.

## 10.2 Second-Best Analysis: The Role of Intellectual Property

An important aspect of the preceding analysis is that it is a first-best one. In particular, when there is more weight on the poor, the social planner reduces the level of innovation while raising the consumption of the poor. This can only happen if there are sufficient policy instruments. If this is not the case, then the conflict of interest between rich and poor over the degree of innovation needs to be reconsidered. For example, in the preceding chapter, horizontal innovation reduces monopoly markups and that effect alone benefits workers.

Clearly, there are as many potential second-best results as there are restricted sets of instruments available to the policy-maker. Here we focus on one in particular: intellectual property. How does the level of intellectual property affect the welfare of different agents?

[4] Note that, by taking the $\hat{\theta}(i)$ rather than the $\theta(i)$ as the exogenous force, we can ignore the weights on the consumption levels $x(i)$. Given $N$, the $x(i)$ are entirely determined by the set of weights $\hat{\theta}(i)$. Therefore, the shift in UU is entirely driven by the direct effect of the change in the consumption weights.

Intellectual property refers to a complex set of rules and one has to make choices in order to formalize it in a tractable way. A natural route, in a dynamic model, is to assume that patents have a finite length; so long as the patent is valid, the owner receives the monopoly profits associated with the good. Once the patent has expired, the good is in the public domain and is priced at marginal cost. Note that, in addition to the usual effects of introducing a monopoly price distortion and increasing the profitability of innovation, intellectual property is also associated with a distortion in the relative prices of the goods: nonpatented goods are cheaper than patented ones. In the static models that we use here, we can formalize finite patent length in a simplified way by assuming that, when invented, a good gets its patent with probability $\sigma < 1$. The greater the value of $\sigma$, the more protected is intellectual property.[5]

In a steady state with $N$ goods, then, there will be $\sigma N$ patented goods and $(1 - \sigma)N$ nonpatented goods. A consumer $i$ with income $z_i$ will set his consumption[6] of a patented good $x_{\text{P}}$, and of a nonpatented good $x_{\text{NP}}$, so as to maximize his utility, which is given by

$$\hat{U}(x_{\text{P}}, x_{\text{NP}}) = N(\sigma u(x_{\text{P}}) + (1 - \sigma)u(x_{\text{NP}})).$$

Each individual good is produced with a linear production function, $y_j = al_j$. Therefore, the price of a nonpatented good is $p_{\text{NP}} = w/a$, where $w$ is the wage. The price of a patented good is $p_{\text{P}} = \mu w/a$, where $\mu$ is the markup. The consumer's budget constraint is

$$N\left(\sigma x_{\text{P}}\mu\frac{w}{a} + (1 - \sigma)x_{\text{NP}}\frac{w}{a}\right) = z_i. \tag{10.7}$$

The Lagrangian of this problem is

$$\begin{aligned}\mathcal{L}(x_{\text{P}}, x_{\text{NP}}, \lambda; N, \sigma, \mu) = {} & N(\sigma u(x_{\text{P}}) + (1 - \sigma)u(x_{\text{NP}})) \\ & + \lambda[az_i - N(\sigma x_{\text{P}}\mu w + (1 - \sigma)x_{\text{NP}}w)].\end{aligned}$$

The first-order conditions are

$$u'(x_{\text{P}}) = \lambda\mu, \tag{10.8}$$

$$u'(x_{\text{NP}}) = \lambda. \tag{10.9}$$

These two equations, together with (10.7), allow us to compute $x_{\text{P}}$ and $x_{\text{NP}}$ and the resulting level of utility. Suppose, now, that this economy faces a trade-off between $\sigma$ and $N$:

$$N = \psi(\sigma), \quad \psi'(\cdot) > 0.$$

---

[5] The following discussion is based on Saint-Paul (2004).

[6] We assume right away that, by symmetry, consumption of an individual good is the same across goods of the same patent status.

This trade-off tells us that when intellectual property is stronger we get more varieties. To get interior equilibria, we will also assume that $\psi'' < 0$. We can now ask the following question: which level of intellectual property will an individual support, given his income? Let us normalize the wage to 1 and assume that the individual is a worker with labor endowment $l_i$; hence, $z_i = l_i$. Let us assume that the markup $\mu$ is unaffected, an assumption to which we return later. To compute the effect of a change in $\sigma$ on the individual's welfare, we apply the envelope theorem. We know that

$$\frac{\partial \hat{U}}{\partial \sigma} = \frac{\partial \mathcal{L}}{\partial \sigma} \quad \text{and} \quad \frac{\partial \hat{U}}{\partial N} = \frac{\partial \mathcal{L}}{\partial N}.$$

Computing these expressions and making use of (10.8) and (10.9), we obtain

$$\frac{\partial \hat{U}}{\partial N} = \sigma v(x_{\mathrm{P}}) + (1 - \sigma) v(x_{\mathrm{NP}}) > 0$$

and

$$\frac{\partial \hat{U}}{\partial \sigma} = -N(v(x_{\mathrm{NP}}) - v(x_{\mathrm{P}})) < 0.$$

In the above formulas, $v(x) = u(x) - xu'(x)$ is the consumer's "rent" on his inframarginal consumption units. As discussed in section 10.1, this rent measures the net gain from introducing a new good, i.e., the difference between all the inframarginal utility gains from consuming a good that did not previously exist and the marginal utility losses from small reductions in the consumption of all existing goods. Concavity in $u$ implies that $v(x) > 0$ and $v'(x) = -xu'' > 0$.

The optimal level of intellectual property for this individual is such that the marginal rate of substitution between $\sigma$ and $N$ is equal to the marginal rate of transformation:

$$-\frac{\partial \hat{U} / \partial \sigma}{\partial \hat{U} / \partial N} = \psi'(\sigma). \tag{10.10}$$

### 10.2.1 The Isoelastic Case

We can now prove that if $v(\cdot)$ is isoelastic, the left-hand side of (10.10) does not depend on $z_i$. To see this, just note that if $u(x) = x^{\gamma}$, then $v(x) = (1 - \gamma)x^{\gamma}$, and the left-hand side can be expressed as a function of $N$, $\sigma$, and the ratio $x_{\mathrm{NP}}/x_{\mathrm{P}}$. But that ratio is pinned down by the condition $u'(x_{\mathrm{P}})/u'(x_{\mathrm{NP}}) = \mu$, which implies that $x_{\mathrm{NP}} = x_{\mathrm{P}}\mu^{1/(1-\gamma)}$. Thus, $z_i$ appears nowhere in (10.10). We again get the result that all agents agree on the same level of intellectual property.

### 10.2.2 The Limited Needs Case

Under what conditions would poorer people want less innovation? This would be the case provided that the left-hand side of (10.10), which is the inverse of the marginal willingness to pay for increasing $N$, decreases with $z_i$. Computations show that this condition is equivalent to

$$\eta_u(x_{\text{NP}}) < \eta_u(x_{\text{P}}). \tag{10.11}$$

This condition indeed holds if, as we have assumed above, $\eta_u(\cdot)$ is a decreasing function of $x$. If that condition is satisfied, the results of the preceding section still hold in the sense that poorer agents will support a lower level of intellectual property. The mechanism underlying this effect is fundamentally the same as that spelled out above.

### 10.2.3 Markup Effects

The preceding analysis holds $\mu$ constant. We know from chapter 9 that, under limited needs, when more varieties are introduced, $\mu$ falls. How is the analysis changed if we take this effect into account? The monopoly markup is now a function $\mu(N, \sigma)$. Intuitively, we should have that $\mu_1' < 0$ and $\mu_2' < 0$: more goods reduce the consumption of each good, and therefore increase the price elasticity of demand for each good; more proprietary goods have the same effect, since these goods are more expensive. We now have

$$\frac{\partial \hat{U}}{\partial N} = \frac{\partial \mathcal{L}}{\partial N} + \frac{\partial \mathcal{L}}{\partial \mu}\mu_1' \quad \text{and} \quad \frac{\partial \hat{U}}{\partial \sigma} = \frac{\partial \mathcal{L}}{\partial \sigma} + \frac{\partial \mathcal{L}}{\partial \mu}\mu_2'.$$

A positive term is added to both derivatives. The conclusion that the poor prefer less intellectual property is now no longer warranted. Based on the preceding subsection's results, we conclude that the conclusion is robust, provided that markup effects are not too strong.

## 10.3 Conclusion

In this chapter we have analyzed how, when utility is nonhomothetic, the rich and the poor have different preferences with respect to the optimal rate of innovation. We have shown that, under the limited needs assumption, the poor typically want less innovation than the rich. This is true both in a first-best situation, where a social optimum which reflects the relative influence of all agents can be reached by using taxes and transfers, and in a second-best situation, where the only instrument is the level of intellectual property rights. In the latter case, we have shown that, under limited needs, the poor want lower intellectual property protection than the rich, for a given markup. However, this result ignores the fact that monopoly prices would go up as the number of goods falls. When the price mechanisms identified in the preceding chapter are brought back into the picture, the conclusion becomes unclear.

## 10.4 Appendix: Derivation of (10.11)

Define $m = v(x_{\mathrm{NP}})/v(x_{\mathrm{P}})$. The left-hand side of (10.10) can be expressed as

$$\frac{N(m-1)}{\sigma + (1-\sigma)m}.$$

This expression is clearly increasing in $m$. For the left-hand side to fall with income, we therefore need $m$ to fall with income. Next, note that $\mathrm{d}m$ has the same sign as $v'(x_{\mathrm{NP}})v(x_{\mathrm{P}})\,\mathrm{d}x_{\mathrm{NP}} - v(x_{\mathrm{P}})v'(x_{\mathrm{NP}})\,\mathrm{d}x_{\mathrm{P}}$. Furthermore, the FOCs (10.8) and (10.9) for consumption imply that $u'(x_{\mathrm{P}})/u'(x_{\mathrm{NP}}) = \mu$, so that

$$\mathrm{d}x_{\mathrm{NP}} = \frac{u''(x_{\mathrm{P}})}{\mu u''(x_{\mathrm{NP}})}\,\mathrm{d}x_{\mathrm{P}}.$$

Substituting, and noting that $\mathrm{d}x_{\mathrm{P}}, \mathrm{d}x_{\mathrm{NP}} > 0$ if the individual becomes richer, we find that $\mathrm{d}m < 0$ if and only if

$$v'(x_{\mathrm{NP}})v(x_{\mathrm{P}})\frac{u''(x_{\mathrm{P}})}{\mu u''(x_{\mathrm{NP}})} - v(x_{\mathrm{NP}})v'(x_{\mathrm{P}}) < 0.$$

Given that $v'(x) = -xu''(x)$, this condition simplifies to $v(x_{\mathrm{P}})x_{\mathrm{NP}}/\mu - x_{\mathrm{P}}v(x_{\mathrm{NP}}) < 0$. Replacing $\mu$ with $u'(x_{\mathrm{P}})/u'(x_{\mathrm{NP}})$, we get

$$\frac{v(x_{\mathrm{P}})}{x_{\mathrm{P}}u'(x_{\mathrm{P}})} < \frac{v(x_{\mathrm{NP}})}{x_{\mathrm{NP}}u'(x_{\mathrm{NP}})},$$

which is equivalent to (10.11).

# Epilogue

We have analyzed the different channels through which technical change affects the distribution of income.

We started with models where labor is a homogeneous input, and the only distributive issue is between labor and capital. In these models, there are two basic effects. On the one hand, technical progress makes workers more productive: this tends to increase their income, as the physical number of goods that they can produce per unit of time goes up. On the other hand, technical progress may increase the total amount of labor, defined in efficiency units, available. That effect reduces the price of labor per efficiency unit. If complementarity between labor and capital is sufficiently strong, the fall in the price of labor may be larger, proportionally, than the rise in the number of efficiency units per worker. There is a "capital shortage" and technical progress reduces individual wages. In the long run, though, more capital is accumulated: due to the capital shortage, the marginal product of capital rises above the long-term required rate of return. As capital converges to its new value, wages go up, and we have shown that they must be higher in the long run than if technical progress had not taken place. The basic conclusion is that, because capital is accumulable, technical progress cannot, in the long run, be redistributed in favor of capitalists and at the expense of workers. This can only occur in the short run before capital has adjusted, and only if complementarities are strong enough.

We then asked the question, can technical progress redistribute between different categories of workers? To answer this, we discussed models of skill-biased technical progress. Several mechanisms have been highlighted. First, technical progress may be a substitute for unskilled labor and a complement to skilled labor. This provides a natural channel through which inequality would increase between these two categories of worker. One variant of this mechanism is when capital and skills are complementary, and technical progress takes place in the capital goods sectors. Another mechanism arises when skilled workers are assumed to be better at handling new technology, as in Nelson and Phelps (1966). This mechanism is captured in the Caselli (1999) model that we discussed, where skill can be defined as the inverse cost of learning the new technology. Inequality then arises as the consequence of a new technology being introduced. Two important predictions are that

- the unskilled may suffer from an absolute fall in wages, because the new technology outbids the old one for productive resources such as capital, and
- the rise in inequality is likely to be transitory, as the new technology becomes easier to learn once it has spread throughout the economy.

Finally, we have discussed how skill-biased technical change can be directed and induced by an increase in the relative supply of skills, which provides a multiplier mechanism which may potentially magnify the increase in inequality. This multiplier mechanism arises as the increase in the return to skill raises the number of skilled workers, which in turn induces skill-biased technical change and further increases in the return to skill.

We then moved to models where people, rather than owning different factors of production, own similar factors of production but differ in their talent. The superstars model predicts that people with greater talent spread their ability over a larger market. This provides a natural mechanism for one type of technical change to increase inequality, namely for improvements in information technologies that make it easier for the superstars to reach a larger market. We discussed in detail how such changes affect individuals at different positions in the distribution of income. The assignment models go one step beyond the superstars model by assuming that several workers, each with his own talent, cooperate in the workplace. They predict that workers will be matched with coworkers of similar or different talent, depending on the shape of the production function. Technical change which affects this shape, such as a move from parallel to serial processing of tasks, affects the structure of assignment and thus the pattern of inequality. Serial processing leads to assortative matching (hypersegregation) and typically delivers a less equal distribution of earnings than parallel processing.

To conclude, we have shown that technical progress may also affect inequality, even when it shifts the production function in an entirely proportional way. This may occur if demand is nonhomothetic. We have seen that the limited needs property leads to a positive relationship between the consumption of each good and the markup of prices over costs, so that vertical innovation benefits profits more than wages and may even reduce wages, while horizontal innovation has the opposite effect. We have also shown that the (near-satiated) rich tend to benefit more from the introduction of new goods than the poor.

The scope for further empirical and theoretical research remains large. On the empirical side, the skill-biased technical change hypothesis has been over-researched, compared with the other mechanisms described in chapters 6–10 and also compared with the nontechnological explanations discussed in the introduction to the book. On the theoretical side, we need more analysis of the interactions between the main driving forces of the distribution of earnings, which are typically studied separately: technology, trade, institutions, and the demography of skills.

# References


Acemoglu, D. 1998. Why do new technologies complement skills? Directed technical change and wage inequality. *Quarterly Journal of Economics* 113(4): 1055–89.

——. 2002a. Directed technical change. *Review of Economic Studies* 69(4):781–809.

——. 2002b. Technical change, inequality, and the labor market. *Journal of Economic Literature* 40(1):7–72.

Acemoglu, D., P. Aghion, and G. L. Violante. 2001. Deunionization, technical change, and inequality. *Carnegie-Rochester Conference Series on Public Policy* 55:229–64.

Aghion, P. 2002. Schumpeterian growth theory and the dynamics of income inequality. *Econometrica* 70(3):855–82.

Aghion, P., and P. Howitt. 1992. A model of growth through creative destruction. *Econometrica* 62(2):323–51.

——. 1997. *Endogenous Growth Theory*. Cambridge, MA: MIT Press.

Aghion, P., P. Howitt, and G. L. Violante. 2002. General purpose technology and wage inequality. *Journal of Economic Growth* 7(4):315–45.

Autor, D. H., L. F. Katz, and A. B. Krueger. 1998. Computing inequality: have computers changed the labor market? *Quarterly Journal of Economics* 113(4): 1169–214.

Autor, D., F. Levy, and R. Murnane. 2003. The skill content of recent technological change: an empirical exploration. *Quarterly Journal of Economics* 118: 4.

Barro, R., and X. Sala-i-Martin. 2003. *Economic Growth*. Cambridge, MA: MIT Press.

Bartel, A. P., and F. R. Lichtenberg. 1987. The comparative advantage of educated workers in implementing new technology. *Review of Economics and Statistics* 69(1):1–11.

Baumol, W. J. 1967. Macroeconomics of unbalanced growth: the anatomy of urban crisis. *American Economic Review* 57:415–26.

Beach, E. 1971. Hicks on Ricardo on machinery. *Economic Journal* 81:916–22.

Beaudry, P., and D. Green. 2003. Wages and employment in the U.S. and Germany: what explains the difference? *American Economic Review* 93(3): 573–602.

Becker, G. 1981. *A Treatise on the Family*. Cambridge, MA: Harvard University Press.

Bénabou, R. 1993. Workings of a city: location, education, and production. *Quarterly Journal of Economics* 108(3):619–52.

Bénassy, J.-P. 1996. Taste for variety and optimum production patterns in monopolistic competition. *Economics Letters* 52(1):41–47.

Bertola, G., R. Foellmi, and J. Zweimüller. 2005. *Income Distribution in Macroeconomics Models*. Princeton University Press.

Blanchard, O., and S. Fischer. 1989. *Lectures on Macroeconomics.* Cambridge, MA: MIT Press.

Blau, F., and L. M. Kahn. 1996. International differences in male wage inequality: institutions versus market forces. *Journal of Political Economy* 104(4):791–837.

Borjas, G., R. B. Freeman, and L. F. Katz. 1997. How much do immigration and trade affect labor market outcomes? *Brookings Papers on Economic Activity* 1997(1):1-67.

Caroli, E., and J. van Reenen. 2001. Skill-biased organizational change? Evidence from a panel of British and French establishments. *Quarterly Journal of Economics* 116(4):1449–92.

Caselli, F. 1999. Technological revolutions. *American Economic Review* 89(1): 78–102.

Chari, V. V., and H. Hopenhayn. 1991. Vintage human capital, growth, and the diffusion of new technology. *Journal of Political Economy* 99(6):1142–65.

Cohen, D., and G. Saint-Paul. 1994. Uneven technical progress and job destructions. CEPR Working Paper 979.

Diamond, P. 1965. National debt in a neoclassical growth model. *American Economic Review* 55:1126–50.

DiNardo, J., N. Fortin, and T. Lemieux. 1996. Labor market institutions and the distribution of wages, 1973–1992: a semiparametric analysis. *Econometrica* 64:1001–44.

Dixit, A. K., and J. E. Stiglitz. 1977. Monopolistic competition and optimal product diversity. *American Economic Review* 67(3):297–308.

Epple, D., and R. Romano. 1998. Competition between private and public schools, vouchers, and peer-group effects. *American Economic Review* 88(1): 33–62.

Foellmi, R., and J. Zweimüller. 2006. Income distribution and demand-induced innovations. *Review of Economic Studies* 73(4):941–60.

Galor, O., and D. Tsiddon. 1997. Technological progress, mobility, and economic growth. *American Economic Review* 87(3):363–82.

Garicano, L. 2000. Hierarchies and the organization of knowledge in production. *Journal of Political Economy* 108(5):874–904.

Garicano, L., and E. Rossi-Hansberg. 2006. Organization and inequality in a knowledge economy. *Quarterly Journal of Economics* 121(4):1383–435.

Goldin, C., and L. F. Katz. 1998. The origins of technology–skill complementarity. *Quarterly Journal of Economics* 113(3):693–732.

Greenwood, J., and M. Yorukoglu. 1997. 1974. *Carnegie–Rochester Conference Series on Public Policy* 46:49–95.

Greenwood, J., A. Seshadri, and M. Yorukoglu. 2005. Engines of liberation. *Review of Economic Studies* 72:109–33.

Grossman, G. M., and E. Helpman. 1991. *Innovation and Growth in the Global Economy.* Cambridge, MA: MIT Press.

Grossman, G. M., and G. Maggi. 2000. Diversity and trade. *American Economic Review* 90(5):1255–75.

Guesnerie, R. 2005. *Assessing Rational Expectations 2: "Eductive" Stability in Economics.* Cambridge, MA: MIT Press.

Hassler, J., and J. V. Rodriguez Mora. 2000. Intelligence, social mobility, and growth. *American Economic Review* 90(4):888–908.

Heckman, J., and J. A. Scheinkman. 1987. The importance of bundling in a Gorman-Lancaster model of earnings. *Review of Economic Studies* 54:243-55.

Hicks, J. 1932. *Theory of Wages.* London: Macmillan.

Hornstein, A., P. Krusell, and G. L. Violante. 2002. Vintage capital as an origin of inequalities. *Proceedings of the Federal Reserve Bank of San Francisco,* November 2002.

Juhn, C., K. M. Murphy, and B. Pierce. 1993. Wage inequality and the rise in the returns to skill. *Journal of Political Economy* 101(3):410-42.

Katz, L. F., and K. M. Murphy. 1992. Changes in relative wages, 1963-1987: supply and demand factors. *Quarterly Journal of Economics* 107:35-78.

Kremer, M. 1993. The O-ring theory of economic development. *Quarterly Journal of Economics* 108:551-75.

Krusell, P., and J.-V. Ríos-Rull. 1996. Vested interests in a positive theory of stagnation and growth. *Review of Economic Studies* 63(2):301-29.

Krusell, P., L. Ohanian, J.-V. Ríos-Rull, and G. L. Violante. 2000. Capital-skill complementarity and inequality. *Econometrica* 68(5):1029-53.

Lawrence, R. Z., and M. J. Slaughter. 1993. International trade and American wages in the 1980s: giant sucking sound or small hiccup? *Brookings Papers on Economic Activity. Microeconomics* 2:161-226.

Levy, F., and R. J. Murnane. 1992. U.S. earnings levels and earnings inequality: a review of recent trends and proposed explanations. *Journal of Economic Literature* 30(3):1333-81.

MacDonald, G. M. 1998. The economics of rising stars. *American Economic Review* 78(1):155-66.

Manasse, P., and A. Turrini. 2001. Trade, wages, and "superstars." *Journal of International Economics* 54(1):97-117.

Marx, K. 1867. *Das Kapital.* Hamburg: Otto Meissner.

Matsuyama, K. 2002. The rise of mass consumption societies. *Journal of Political Economy* 110:1035-70.

Murphy, K. M., A. Shleifer, and R. W. Vishny. 1989. Income distribution, market size, and industrialization. *Quarterly Journal of Economics* 104:533-64.

——. 1991. The allocation of talent: implications for growth. *Quarterly Journal of Economics* 106(2):503-30.

Neal, D., and S. Rosen. 2000. Theories of the distribution of earnings. In *Handbook of Income Distribution* (ed. A. B. Atkinson and F. Bourguignon), chapter 7, pp. 379-427. Elsevier.

Nelson, R., and E. S. Phelps. 1966. Investment in humans, technological diffusion and economic growth. *American Economic Review* 56(1):69-75.

Parente, S. L., and E. C. Prescott. 1994. Barriers to technology adoption and development. *Journal of Political Economy* 102(2):298-321.

——. 1999. Monopoly rights: a barrier to riches. *American Economic Review* 89(5):1216-33.

Romer, D. 2000. *Advanced Macroeconomics.* McGraw-Hill.

Romer, P. 1990. Endogenous technological change. *Journal of Political Economy* 98(5):71-102.

Rosen, S. 1981. The economics of superstars. *American Economic Review* 71(5): 845-58.

——. 1982. Authority, control and the distribution of earnings. *Bell Journal of Economics* 13(2):311-23.

Rosen, S. 1983. A note on the aggregation of skills and labor quality. *Journal of Human Resources* 18:425–31.

Roy, A. D. 1951. Some thoughts on the distribution of earnings. *Oxford Economic Papers* 3(2): 135–46.

Rubinstein, Y., and D. Tsiddon. 2004. Coping with technological change: the role of ability in making inequality so persistent. *Journal of Economic Growth* 9(3): 305–46.

Saint-Paul, G. 2001. On the distribution of income and worker assignment under intra firm spillovers, with an application to ideas and networks. *Journal of Political Economy* 109(1):1–37.

——. 2004. Are intellectual property rights unfair? *Labour Economics* 11:129–44.

——. 2006a. Distribution and growth in an economy with limited needs. *Economic Journal* 116:382–407.

——. 2006b. Will limited needs kill capitalism? *Capitalism and Society* 1(1): article 4. (Available at www.bepress.com/cas/vol1/iss1/art4.)

——. 2007. Knowledge hierarchies in the labor market. *Journal of Economic Theory* 137:104–26.

Sattinger, M. 1993. Assignment models of the distribution of earnings. *Journal of Economic Literature* 31(2):831–80.

Shepard, R. 1953. *Cost and Production Functions.* Princeton University Press.

Solow, R. 1956. A contribution to the theory of economic growth. *Quarterly Journal of Economics* 70(1):65–94.

Stokey, N. 1996. Free trade, factor returns, and factor accumulation. *Journal of Economic Growth* 1:421–47.

Stolper, W. F., and P. A. Samuelson. 1941. Protection and real wages. *Review of Economic Studies* 9:58–73.

Thesmar, D., and M. Thoenig. 2000. Creative destruction and firm organization choice. *Quarterly Journal of Economics* 115(4):1201–37.

Thoenig, M., and T. Verdier. 2003. A theory of defensive skill-biased innovation and globalization. *American Economic Review* 93(3):709–28.

Violante, G. L. 2002. Technological acceleration, skill transferability, and the rise in residual inequality. *Quarterly Journal of Economics* 117(1):297–338.

Zeira, J. 1998. Workers, machines and economic growth. *Quarterly Journal of Economics* 113(4):1091–117.